# The Private Life of Mr. Pepys

*Samuel Pepys, 1632-1703*

PORTRAIT BY JOHN HAYLS
PAINTED IN 1666

*By the kind permission of*
*National Portrait Gallery, London*

# THE
# PRIVATE LIFE OF
# Mr. Pepys

✳✳✳

John Harold Wilson

✳✳✳

*Farrar, Straus and Cudahy*

NEW YORK

FOR LOUISE

Published simultaneously in Canada by
Ambassador Books, Ltd., Toronto

Manufactured in the United States of America

# Contents

# I

# Mr. Pepys

On a warm September day in 1668, Bartholomew Fair was going full blast with rope-dancers, mountebanks, drolls, tumblers, music booths, cook-shops, and hordes of holiday-making Londoners. Near the center of the dust and confusion a circle of spectators surrounded an educated mare, applauding her tricks. When her master ordered her "to go him of the company that most loved a pretty wench in a corner," the wise mare ambled straight to Mr. Samuel Pepys. The company laughed, but Mr. Pepys was not abashed. Flinging a shilling to the showman, he proved the horse right by kissing a plainly dressed but very pretty girl who stood nearby. Late that night, on his way home in a hackney coach, Mr. Pepys further approved the mare's judgment by picking up "a wench that was naught." She urged him to go with her to her lodgings in Shoe Lane, but Mr. Pepys gave her a shilling and employed as much of her professional service as the straitness of the coach permitted. In public or private, in coach or corner, in tavern, office, or bedroom, Mr. Pepys truly loved a pretty wench.

Most of his friends and neighbors would have laughed at the notion that Pepys was a wencher. They believed him to be a moral, decent citizen, a good Protestant of upright and unblemished life. Certainly he looked respectable. He was a well-dressed, rather plain man of only average height (for the seventeenth century), some five feet six inches tall—not a "little" man. Under the heavy brown periwig which fell in curls to his shoulders, his face was alert and animated. His brown-blue eyes were large, prominent, and, because he suffered from eye-strain, somewhat watery. He had strongly marked eyebrows with a distinct pleat between them, a long, low-bridged nose, and a sensuous mouth with a heavy lower lip. There was nothing dashing or romantic about him. He looked to be exactly what he was: a clever, middle-class citizen, thirty-five years old, married, childless, and prosperous. As Commissioner of the Navy and Clerk of the Acts, and as Treasurer of the Tangier Commission, he was an important cog in the state machinery, a man known among bureaucrats for his integrity and application to business. He was good-natured and fond of fun and pleasure, but not given to drinking, gambling, or—so far as his public world knew—to wenching. Yet quite a few women had yielded in some measure to Mr. Pepys' advances, and some outwardly respectable wives had committed adultery with him, not just once but often.[1]

Pepys was no Casanova; he kept his affairs secret within his own private world, and confided only to his diary. Unlike more famous libertines who wrote their memoirs to prove their virility (conveniently forgetting their defeats), Pepys wrote only to himself and told almost everything. When we read his diary we take him unfairly in the purging of his soul or the zestful recollection of carnal pleasure. It is unkind to dismiss his rogueries as "surreptitious and rather sordid." He committed them by stealth, of course; he could not afford to have his pleasures spied upon by his superiors (who might think him idle) or reported to his jealous and hot-tempered wife. But to say that they were sordid is to make a value judgment which tells as much about the judge as about the culprit. Only the fastidious consider his amours ignoble. To the prudish they are wicked; to the true libertine, petty; to the historian, only human. Pepys was not unique in his time; many Restoration gentlemen were as promiscuous as he, and some far more so. Wisely they kept no diaries.[2]

Pepys kept his diary faithfully for almost ten years—from January, 1660, through May, 1669—recording in Thomas Shelton's shorthand (for convenience, not secrecy) the events of each day. (He kept his diary locked in his desk; during his lifetime no one else ever saw it.) At first his accounts were so impersonal that they could have been read by the most tender-eyed, but as the procession of days went on he came to make his journal his confidant, setting down his most private thoughts and describing all his erotic adventures, usually in a jargon of French, Spanish, Portuguese, Latin, and English. Because of the frequency and the intimate nature of these entries (often made to seem worse by his editor's use of dots to indicate prudish omissions) we tend to think of merry Mr. Pepys as beyond all measure lustful. We find it hard to understand how a man of intelligence, education, and well developed sensibility—a man of "a liberal genius," as he called himself—could be so promiscuous. Pepys was married to a woman so beautiful that other men envied him, and some tried "many and great temptations" to seduce her from her loyalty. Yet, although she retained his affection, she could not keep him from straying to other beds. He went to church regularly, and often spent his time gazing at beauties, neglecting the sermon and his soul. He would dawdle over his morning draught of ale at a tavern (taken in lieu of breakfast) to flirt with a pretty barmaid, stealing a kiss or a naked caress, and then plunge headlong into the Navy's most important business, conducting it admirably. He could play with his maid's breasts as she helped him dress of a morning, slip a hand under the petticoats of a pretty neighbor as he strolled with her in his garden, and now and then break the routine of a busy day for an orgiastic hour with any one of several easy-going ladies. Yet he was full of moral sentiments, detested profanity, and could honestly cry "God forgive me!" while still reeking from a lewd embrace. He was a reluctant libertine, periodically binding himself by vows to refrain from pleasures, and scolding himself when he fell from grace —not because of his moral conscience but because pleasure took him away from business and his life's ambition to be rich.[3]

Some apologists have tried to explain Pepys' libertinism as the result of a surgical accident. On March 26, 1658, when he was twenty-five years old, he was "cut for the stone," a painful and dangerous operation in a day when instruments were crude and chloroform and asepsis unknown. For years afterward he celebrated his survival with a solemn annual feast. Modern surgeons have guessed that in the course of the operation Pepys' "procreative power was permanently destroyed by interference with the seminal vesicles and ducts," and that after his recovery his "extraordinary incontinence . . . may really have been due to the continued irritation of the old scar in his perineum." In addition, they suggest that Pepys' "long spells of sedentary office work and his rather gross habits of life . . . tended to foster his sexual feelings."[4]

These arguments are half-way plausible, although one might wonder at the term "extraordinary incontinence." Let the surgeons keep their own diaries as long and as fully as Pepys did! Granted that Pepys was sterile—at least his wife was childless, and, as far as we know, no by-blows resulted from any of his adulteries—there is still no assurance that this sterility resulted from a surgical blunder. He had been married and childless for two years and five months before he was "cut for the stone." Further, the theory that his libido was stimulated by genito-urinary itches may explain his desires but not his adulteries. Pepys' world agreed with the Apostle Paul: if men lacked the gift of continence, "let them marry, for it is better to marry than to burn." Clearly Pepys lacked the gift of continence, yet he was married. Why, then, was he promiscuous?

The fact is that Pepys could be continent for long periods. At the height of his concern for business, or when he had bound himself by vows to abstain from pleasure, he could live an almost ascetic life. He was most unchaste when he was least busy, when "a wanton and idle humour" was upon him. But even then he was no impatient lecher driven by mad satyriasis; indeed, he was often timid with women, afraid to try an unbacked jade, and regretting too late his lack of boldness. And while consummation was devoutly to be wished for, he could be patient and satisfy himself with mere erotic play.

Mr. Pepys was a normal, reasonably healthy male animal, ruled, as all men are, by passions and appetites. He gave way to lechery because of his innate love of beauty and pleasure, because of the temptations of an easy-going, loose-moraled society dominated by a libertine King and Court, and because of tensions which developed between him and his wife. This is the story of his private life.

# II

# Better to Marry

## 1633
---
## 1660

Mr. Pepys' kinfolk, descended from the ancient family of the Pepyses of Cottenham, in the fen country six miles north of Cambridge, were numerous, respectable, and undistinguished. (The name is usually pronounced "Peeps.") By dint of industry and thrift they had climbed from the dikes and ditches of the fens to solid, middle-class positions as yeomen, reeves, bailiffs, barristers, and men of business. Some, by virtue of place or property, were entitled to sign themselves "gent.", and at least one, Paulina, Samuel Pepys' great-aunt, became a lady when she married Sir Sidney Mountagu of Hinchingbrooke, near Huntingdon. Samuel's father, John Pepys, born at the manor of Impington in 1601, was the youngest of three brothers and three sisters. At fourteen he went to London, apprenticed himself to a tailor, and in due time became a master. In 1626 he married—somewhat beneath him—Margaret Kight, a washmaid. On his mother's side Samuel had a host of relations whom he once described as "a pitiful rout." His mother's brother, William Kight, was a Whitechapel butcher; a brother-in-law, Thomas

Fenner, was a blacksmith; and two of her nieces, Kate and Mary Fenner, had married brothers: Anthony Joyce, a leather-seller, and Will Joyce, an alehouse keeper.[1]

Samuel Pepys was born on February 23, 1633, in his father's house on the east side of Salisbury Court, near St. Bride's Church, in London. He was the second born but the oldest survivor of eleven children. Three others reached maturity: Thomas (b. 1634), who followed his father's trade; Paulina (b. 1640); and John (b. 1641), who took holy orders. The Pepyses were decent, industrious, and reasonably pious. The father was a meek, patient man, who worked hard but throve little; the mother was improvident and quarrelsome.

Samuel came into a troubled world, with the conflict between King and Parliament rising to a climax. He was seven years old when the Long Parliament met, bent on revolution. When he was nine the Civil War began, and his family sent him to the grammar school at Huntingdon, sixteen miles northwest of Cambridge, perhaps because it was a place of safety. Four years later, when the Royalists had been defeated and King Charles I was a prisoner, Samuel came back to London, helped his father by delivering clothes to customers, and attended St. Paul's School, where he studied Latin, Greek, Hebrew, and geography. In those days he was "a great Roundhead," and afterward he remembered with distress that when he was fifteen he had witnessed the execution of the King and had boasted to his comrades that if he were to preach over the dead monarch his text would be, "The memory of the wicked will rot." Eleven years later his sentiments had veered to the other extreme, but so had those of most of his countrymen.[2]

When he was seventeen, Samuel won a Cambridge scholarship in the gift of the Mercer's Company. With the aid of this and other scholarships he attended Magdalene College,

Cambridge, from March, 1651, until he took his bachelor's degree in March, 1654, at the age of twenty-one. While he was studying Latin and Greek (and perhaps shorthand) in his chill monastic cell beside the River Cam, reading the classics and acquiring a love of books and music, the Long Parliament was dissolved, Oliver Cromwell became Lord Protector, and England fought a war with the Dutch. Only one item of personal information about young Pepys remains on the books of his college: on October 21, 1653, he and a companion were solemnly admonished for having been "scandalously o'erseene in drink."[3]

A few memories scattered through the *Diary* tell us a little about Pepys' youth. From boyhood he seems to have been captivated by feminine beauty. For example, there was a London neighbor, pretty Elizabeth Whittle, of whom he had "a great opinion" when he was a boy, in his enthusiasm going so far as to make an anagram on her name. Then there was Mrs. Hely, whom he met while visiting his well-to-do cousin John Pepys, at Ashted on Epsom Downs. With her he had his "first sentiments of love and pleasure in women's company, discourse, and taking her by the hand, she being a pretty woman." (Since "Mrs."—the simple abbreviation for "Mistress"—was a title applied as well to maids as to wives, Mrs. Hely's marital status is unknown.)

At Cambridge Pepys admired fair Betty Archer, whose memory he cherished for years. His amorous bent in his college days led him to try his hand at a prose romance which he planned to call "Love a Cheate." Ten years later he came across the unfinished manuscript, marveled at his early skill, and carelessly tore up the pages. In spite of his taste for beauty, the chances are that Pepys kept his youthful virginity, although he is darkly reticent about Betty Aynsworth, a Cambridge bawd, whose drinking-shop he used to visit with

his cousin, George Barnardiston of Cottenham. Betty taught
Pepys to sing a lewd song with the refrain "Full forty times
over." There was fun to be had at college even when the
cold hand of Puritanism lay heavy over England.[4]

Soon after leaving Cambridge the young scholar entered
the service of his first cousin once removed, Sir Edward
Mountagu of Hinchingbrooke, eight years his senior. Mountagu had chosen the Parliamentary side in the Civil War
and was now a member of Cromwell's Council of State, a
Commissioner of the Treasury, and General-at-Sea—i.e., Admiral. He had lodgings in Westminster at Whitehall Palace
(once the King's and now Cromwell's official residence), a
brick-and-stone huddle of buildings sprawling along the bank
of the Thames where the river takes a great southward bend.
Nearby was the ancient Westminster Palace with its Great
Hall (given over to shops and law courts); the "Parliament
Chamber" where the House of Lords set; and St. Stephen's
Chapel, home of the House of Commons. Behind these rose
the grandeur of Westminster Abbey. It was only a short walk
from Whitehall up King Street to Charing Cross, where one
turned eastward to the City.

It seems likely that Pepys had a chamber assigned to him
in Mountagu's lodgings. He served his kinsman as a kind of
steward, looking after things when the General was absent at
sea or in the country; receiving money and paying bills, overseeing the servants, and running errands all up and down
London. It was a job without a future, but at least it was a
cut above tailoring. Anyway, Pepys had friends and a powerful patron; he was at Whitehall, the center of government,
and there was always a chance for a good civil post.

When he was twenty-two Pepys met his future wife, Elizabeth, the fourteen-year-old daughter of a French émigré,
Alexander Marchant, who called himself Sieur de St. Michel.

Elizabeth's background was as romantic as Samuel's was staid. At the age of twenty-one, St. Michel, scion of a noble family in Anjou, turned Protestant. Disinherited by his father, the High Sheriff of Bauge, he went to England in 1625 as a gentleman carver in the train of the French princess, Henrietta Maria, betrothed to King Charles I. Some time after the royal marriage his career as a courtier came to an end when he struck an attendant friar in the course of an argument about religion, and the Queen dismissed him from her service. After that the handsome soldier of fortune tried his luck in Ireland, where he wooed and won a well-dowered young widow, the daughter of an Irish knight. Hoping to recover some part of his father's estate, St. Michel spent his wife's dowry on an ill-fated expedition to France. He was captured by the Dunkirkers (Spaniards), robbed of his money, and imprisoned for several months. Back in England, he proceeded to raise a family. Only two children reached maturity: Elizabeth (born in Somersetshire on October 23, 1640), and her younger brother Balthazar (born ca. 1641).

When Elizabeth was eight or nine years old, St. Michel, commander of a company of English foot sent to assist the French in the siege of Dunkirk, took his family with him to the continent. They lived in Paris for about three years, then, while her husband was off somewhere about his affairs, Madame St. Michel fell under the influence of "deluding Papists," who promised that if she would desert her Protestant husband they would give her a handsome allowance, place Elizabeth in a nunnery, and get little Balty appointed a page to the Papal Nuncio. Elizabeth, who then leaned strongly toward Catholicism, spent twelve days in the convent of the Ursulines before St. Michel heard what was happening, came storming back to Paris, collected his family, and herded them all over to England.

When Pepys first met Elizabeth (perhaps at the French Protestant Church in Threadneedle Street), the St. Michels were living in genteel poverty in Westminster. St. Michel, a man bred only to the sword, had turned his mind to "whimsies and propositions of perpetual motions, etc., to kings, princes, and others." He invented processes for curing smoking chimneys, purifying water, molding bricks, and raising sunken ships—all of them worthless. Too grand a gentleman to go to work, he lived by his wits, the charity of friends, and four shillings a week from the French Church.[5]

By the standards of the seventeenth century Elizabeth was no child but a woman, ripe for marriage. The Commonwealth had raised the age of consent from twelve to fourteen; the usual marriage age for girls was fourteen to sixteen. (At seventeen or eighteen a spinster was getting to be a little long in the tooth.) Elizabeth was extremely handsome, a brunette with an oval face, fair skin, a cupid's-bow upper lip, and well-developed breasts. Throughout the nine years of the *Diary* there are many testimonies to her beauty. Once, for example, in Pepys' presence, Mountagu (then Earl of Sandwich) said to old Sir John Minnes, the Comptroller of the Navy, "Sir John, what do you think of your neighbor's wife? Do you not think he hath a great beauty to his wife? Upon my word he hath." Pepys was "not a little proud." He might not have been so pleased had he known that "my lord" had once attempted Elizabeth's virtue, through the solicitation of his standard-bearer, Captain Ferrers.[6]

Beauty may fire the heart, but it rarely boils the pot. Elizabeth had not a penny of dowry, a fact which in after years was to stand out as a frequent cause of irritation. Of course, Francis Osborn had not yet written his famous *Advice to a Son* (1656), a book which Pepys later read and re-read, and could "never enough admire for sense and language." Perhaps, had he been forewarned by his "father Osborn" (as he called the writer), he might never have committed matrimony—at least not with Elizabeth.

Osborn had a very low opinion of marriage as an institution: at best it was "a clog fastened to the neck of liberty by the juggling hand of policy." If a young fool insisted on marrying, at least let him not marry for love alone; he should be certain of getting a good estate with his bride. "The best of husbands are servants," said Osborn, "but he that takes a wife wanting money is a slave to his affection, doing the basest of drudgeries without wages." And again, "I have heard a well-built woman compared, in her motion, to a ship under sail; yet I would advise no wise man to be her owner if her fraught be nothing but what she carries between wind and water." The worst of all follies was to marry a great beauty. All the gallants were likely to come buzzing about, seeking "a lick at your honey-pot . . . nor can you . . . decently restrain her from the concourse without making demonstration of jealousy towards her, by which you confess yourself a cuckold in your own imagination already." Pepys was to discover that Osborn was right in every detail.[7]

In addition some sober friend should have pointed out to Pepys the fact that Elizabeth was not only a dowerless beauty but a gentlewoman, proud of her aristocratic French-Irish lineage and brought up in the genteel tradition to look down upon yeoman and citizen. Whatever Pepys' claims to gentility might be (and they were distinctly dubious), he was by birth a citizen and a tailor's son. In moments of conflict Elizabeth was all too likely to remember that she had lowered herself socially by marrying him.

Someone should have warned Pepys, too, that Elizabeth was hopelessly untrained in the skills demanded of a citizen's wife. She could read and write (although her spelling was

atrocious and she considered punctuation the thief of time),
and she was bilingual by virtue of her heritage and her
residence in France, but she knew little or nothing about
housekeeping, she could not keep accounts, and she had never
been taught the simple virtues of thrift and frugality. Indeed,
from her aristocratic world and the feast-or-famine ways of
her feckless family, she had learned only waste and extravagance. Brought up to decorate a salon, she wanted fine society,
servants, ease, and pleasure. Pepys needed a woman to satisfy
his sexual needs, keep his house, cook his meals, and mend
his breeches.

But if there was ever a battle between Pepys' practical
commonsense and his innate love of beauty, it must have
been brief: he was headlong in love, sick with love, his whole
soul enraptured by a pretty face and a voluptuous figure. He
was an impetuous wooer, a lively, spirited young man with
very taking ways (including, no doubt, his ability to play
on the flageolet), and he would not be balked of his heart's
desire. Since Elizabeth cherished his love letters for many
years, we must presume that she returned his love.

As for her parents—true, although Pepys was well-man-
nered he was not quite a gentleman, and his pay was pitifully
small; but he was clever, well educated, and well connected.
Very likely he boasted of his kinship to the great Sir Edward
Mountagu. Anyway, the St. Michels had very little choice;
at a time when marriage went by barter and purchase, the
portionless daughter of a poor French exile had very few
chances. At least young Pepys was a solid fellow and a sturdy
Protestant. St. Michel hoped that in time his son-in-law
would "quite blowe out those foolish popish thoughts" which
had possessed Elizabeth in her childhood. To this wish (as
brother Balty wrote many years later), Elizabeth replied,
"Dear father, though in my tender yeares I was, by my low

fortune in this world, deluded to popery by the fonde diddly
[foolish swindle] thereof, I have now a man to my husband
soe wise, and one soe religious in the Protestant religion
(joyned with my riper yeares which gives me more understanding) to ever suffer my thought to bende that way any
more." Yet her thought did "bende that way" often in her
years as a wife, sometimes to her husband's deep concern.[8]

On October 10, 1655, two weeks before Elizabeth's fifteenth
birthday, the two were married according to the rites of the
Protestant church. Pepys had a thin gold ring for his bride,
and Elizabeth had a new gold-laced petticoat. After the ceremony the couple and their families ate their wedding dinner
(with a great deal of "kindness" and "bridal respect") at a
tavern on Fish Street Hill. But they were not legally married
according to the laws of republican England. On December 1
they went through a civil ceremony presided over by a city
magistrate at St. Margaret's Church, Westminster.[9]

Since Pepys could not afford a house of his own, he took
his bride to his chamber in Sir Edward Mountagu's lodgings
at Whitehall. There they began their married life, and Pepys
long remembered with gratitude that Elizabeth, "poor
wretch" (his term of endearment), made the coal fires and
washed her husband's soiled clothing with her own hands. It
was nearly three years before they were able to move to a
small house in nearby Axe Yard, just a few doors down King
Street from Whitehall, and keep a maid, and even then they
had to scrimp and save. They lived on a strict budget of
twenty shillings a week—equal to about as many dollars at
today's prices—for everything, including rent and taxes.
Elizabeth had to account for every farthing spent, "even to a
bunch of carrot and a ball of whiteing." Prosperity blessed
the young couple only after Mr. Pepys was appointed Clerk
of the Acts of the Navy in 1660.[10]

The mutual adjustments of a newly married couple are difficult enough without the complications of cramped quarters and poverty. Not long after the wedding something happened, a mysterious affair referred to by Pepys (who hated to be reminded of this period) as "our differences." Since the differences resulted in certain papers being given to Mr. Pepys, senior, for safekeeping, they must have been very serious. Perhaps the young couple quarreled about money. Elizabeth never knew the value of a shilling, and her husband was so obsessed by the need to increase his "crumb," as he called his small savings, that, especially in these early days, he was downright miserly.

More probably Pepys was jealous. Elizabeth was indiscreet, flirtatious, and fond of displaying her full-blown charms. It seems that one Captain Robert Holmes, a handsome swashbuckler in a gold-laced suit, had come buzzing about, seeking a lick at Sam's honey-pot. No doubt Elizabeth's vanity was tickled by her conquest, but Pepys, plagued by a deep sense of insecurity, went into a passion of jealousy—his "old disease" Elizabeth called it later. The quarrel was long and bitter, and may have brought about a temporary separation. But divorce was impossible in seventeenth-century England; friends on both sides were eager to mend matters; and in time husband and wife came together again. Since Pepys was a methodical young man, who liked to have agreements written out in full, it is quite likely that the papers delivered to his father were his and his wife's promises of future good behavior.[11]

The early squall foreran a stormy marriage. The honeymoon was hardly over before Pepys began to learn how much bitter he had to take with his sweet. Regrettably, he is our only source of information about Elizabeth, who kept no diary and left no letters. We do not know her side of the

story and are forced to see her only through her husband's
eyes. (We do not know even how he addressed her; in the
*Diary* she is merely "my wife.") His statements and opinions,
often recorded in the heat of anger, were prejudiced by his
mood of the moment, but the picture which emerges from
the pages of the *Diary* is remarkably consistent. The lines are
distorted and the colors too glaring, but the portrait is at
least convincing.

It seems that Elizabeth was careless, untidy, and indolent.
Much to her husband's annoyance, she commonly left her
belongings lying around, and, even when she had two or
more maids to help her, she seemed incapable of either neatness or good taste in dress. She was only occasionally interested in housekeeping and cleanliness, paid little heed to the
cooking and serving of meals, and could not keep her household accounts properly; whenever they refused to balance she
quietly fudged them. She was forever quarreling with maids
and companions, sometimes descending to petty bickerings
or the exchange of blows. A legion of maids marched through
the Pepys' household in the more than nine years covered by
the *Diary*; some left by choice, most were discharged by their
passionate mistress for trivial or trumped-up reasons.[12]

Intellectually Elizabeth never quite grew up. She lacked
education, she had little curiosity, and her reading was limited to French popular romances: de Gomberville's *Polex-
andre,* Calprenede's *Cassandra* and *Cleopatra,* Scudery's *Le
Grand Cyrus* and *Ibrahim,* and the like—six-decker yarns
about the adventures of incredible lovers in improbable situ-
ations. Her conversation was confined to the gossip of the day
and the repetition of long stories taken from her latest novel.
Yet she could be a good companion when she chose to bestir
herself. Pepys was interested in everything; he was always
"with child" to see and learn something new. His reading

ranged from plays and pornography to such weighty volumes as Camden's *Britannia*, Fuller's *Church History of England*, Hooker's *Ecclesiastical Politie*, and books on philosophy, science, mathematics, geography, travel, and naval history. He loved books, bought them, cherished them, and had them bound in fine bindings. He too loved to gossip, but he liked also to talk about politics, science, history, morality, and religion. Intellectually Pepys and his wife were poles apart.

In one of the most important functions of her gender Elizabeth was a failure. Sexual harmony cannot of itself make a happy marriage, but sexual discord can break one. It is clear that Elizabeth failed to meet her husband with ardor in bed; in fact, she rarely found pleasure in intercourse and therefore was sometimes reluctant to satisfy him. In such a situation the modern tendency is to blame the husband as selfish and inept, and to sympathize with the frustrated wife. But the tough-minded seventeenth century took sexual compatibility for granted, and accepted no excuses for a wife who failed to do her marital duty. Admittedly the chief aim of marriage was procreation, but its second purpose was as "a haven to such as are in jeopardy of their salvation through the gusts of temptation to lust." The ideal wife and husband (assumed to be equal in ardor) were expected to yield "due benevolence one to another" to the end that fornication should be unnecessary. If the wife got no pleasure from the act of love, so much the worse for her. If she failed in her duty she could not complain when her husband sought pleasure elsewhere. According to this standard, Elizabeth, by failing to yield "due benevolence" to her husband, left him open to the temptations of lust.[13]

She was only partly to blame. During a considerable part of her adult life she suffered monthly from what modern physicians have labeled "spasmodic (neuralgic or obstructive) dysmenorrhea." Incapacitated by pain, she would take to her bed and sometimes remain there for days. Even more serious was a recurrent abscess in the groin which had given her trouble since the earliest days of her marriage. When it was active it caused her excruciating pain until it worked its way out, and even when it was dormant she sometimes suffered a good deal after relations with her husband. Although Pepys sympathized with her, he was annoyed by her frequent ailments and selfishly concerned about his own deprivation. Thus he wrote once when he came home to find Elizabeth "ill in pain a-bed" that he was troubled and "not a little impatient." And again, "my wife has been so ill of her old pain [the abscess] that I have not known her this fortnight almost, which is a pain to me."[14]

Elizabeth pained him in other ways, too. Very soon after the wedding Pepys discovered that she had a temper and a will of her own, and that unless he asserted his authority, his wife, "who ought in right reason to serve and obey," would command. Many of their quarrels resulted from Elizabeth's attempts to get her own way; sometimes Pepys had to strike her or pull her by the nose to enforce obedience. In his own home a seventeeth-century husband was king; a wife's revolt was treason, and her failure to obey was a felony deserving corporal punishment. Our ancestors thought it right and proper for a husband to beat his wife on occasion, believing heartily in the proverb,

> A woman, a dog, and a walnut tree,
> The more they're beaten, the better they be.

The clashing of strong personalities is not the proper music for love, but fortunately marriage is not a daily battle; one has to stop at times, if only to bind up wounds. In the early years of their marriage, after their "differences" were over, the Pepyses' quarrels usually "ended all in love," and there were long stretches of happiness between skirmishes. They had very little money, but they had privacy in their little chamber; they talked, read, played, and worked together; they went out to dinner with friends and kinsmen, walked to church on Sunday, and took pleasant little excursions on the Thames or into the green fields only a stone's throw from Westminster.[15]

In those days Pepys had time for everything. He would rise early in the morning, dress, and sally forth for his breakfast, a flagon of ale at the nearest Westminster tavern. While Elizabeth did her housework and marketing, he would idle away an hour or two among the haberdashers and booksellers of Westminster Hall, perhaps buying gloves, scarves, and books for the Mountagu family at Hinchingbrooke. After that he might wander eastward to the City, strolling along the Strand where the mansions of the great stood in a stately row, with gardens sloping to the river.

London, still a roaring medieval town within its ancient walls along the north bank of the Thames, was a never-failing delight to Pepys. The narrow, twisting streets, the housetops almost meeting overhead, the gilded signs, the shops with 'prentices bawling their wares, the street-vendors with their musical cries, the carts and drays and the crowds of shoppers with here and there a pretty face to catch a roving eye—all these (plus the stink of garbage and offal) were a part of Mr. Pepys' daily life.

Sometimes he hunted out tailors, mercers, or cutlers to make purchases or pay bills for Sir Edward. Sometimes he visited the booksellers at St. Paul's, or went to the Royal Exchange in Cornhill, where all the merchants congregated, and gathered news to send his patron. At noon he had his big meal of the day at an ordinary—a tavern which served food at a fixed price. After dinner, if the tide was right and he was near the Tower or London Bridge, he took a boat back up the river and was rowed through the traffic of barges, wherries, and sailing vessels, past the wharves and warehouses of the City, to Westminster Stairs and home. Usually, then, he was free to take Elizabeth on an outing, to visit his family, or to burn daylight in a tavern, drinking, arguing, or singing with friends. At night he would have a bite of supper with Elizabeth, write letters, read, or play on his flageolet or flute, say prayers, "and so to bed."

It was a pleasant life, if one could ignore the political rumblings underfoot. In January, 1655, Cromwell had angrily dissolved his first Parliament. Thereafter he tried to rule alone, plotted against by Royalists and Levelers alike— the diehard right and the fanatic left. England, parcelled out among eleven major-generals, lived under what amounted to martial law. Overseas King Charles the Second and his followers wandered about with shabby clothes and empty pockets, still hoping for a glorious restoration. But "His Highness" Oliver Cromwell was all-powerful, a king in everything but name. The monarchy which called itself a republic seemed destined to last forever.

In March, 1658, Samuel Pepys was "cut for the stone," not in a hospital but at the house of a kinswoman, Mrs. Jane Turner, in Salisbury Court. He had fully recovered by the first of May, and in the summer he took a new job as clerk to George Downing, one of the Tellers of the Exchequer. (He continued to act as Mountagu's agent.) On the strength of his additional fifty pounds a year salary, Pepys rented a small house in Axe Yard and hired a maid, Jane Wayneman. He had hardly moved in when, on the night of September 3, at the height of a great storm, Oliver Cromwell died.[16]

His son Richard, an amiable country gentleman, succeeded

him—"the vulture died, and out of his ashes rose a tit-mouse." In April, 1659, a cabal of army chiefs chased the titmouse back to his country hedges and restored the last remnants of the Parliament of 1648—"the Rump," as it was derisively called. In the ensuing months the Rump went out; a Committee of Public Safety took over; the generals struggled with each other for power; and the Royalists made overtures to various leaders, among them Admiral Mountagu, then with his Fleet on a diplomatic mission in the Sound—the straits between Denmark and Sweden. It seems very likely that in May, 1659, when Mr. Pepys sailed to the Sound in a little ketch, the sealed dispatches he carried included cipher letters from the Royalist party.[17]

On January 1, 1660, Pepys wrote the first lines in his diary: "Blessed be God, at the end of the last year I was in very good health, without any sense of my old pain, but upon taking of cold. I lived in Axe Yard, having my wife, and servant Jane, and no more in family than us three." At the end of the year the Rump Parliament had been restored again; Mountagu, suspected of Royalist plotting, had been relieved of his command and was biding his time at his country house, Hinchingbrooke; General George Monck, commander-in-chief of the army, was brooding in Scotland; and the cry of all England was for a freely elected Parliament. Behind the cry lay weariness of anarchy and experiment, and a deep longing for the old ways of King, Lords, and Commons.

At heart Pepys was a royalist, but he had grown up in the chill climate of canting republicanism. He hardly knew where to turn in the veering winds of the spring of 1660. Politically he was conservative, distrustful of change; but his chief concern was to stay on the winning side and make a living. He envied "the happiness of them that have estates of their own," and dreamed of the day when he too might have an estate.

At this time he was a moral conservative too, and not a little tainted by Puritanism. He objected to profanity and ribaldry, and he could be shocked by the merriment of the guests at a wedding supper, or by the freedom a rakish friend took with a pretty lady as she lay in bed in the morning. But he was showing signs of change, just as rigid Puritanism itself was changing and breaking down. At twenty-seven Pepys was just beginning to dabble in the lesser forms of vice—sins so venial as hardly to deserve the name—gambling a little, drinking too much now and then, and occasionally kissing and "playing the fool" with a pretty maid. Of course kisses meant little in an age when a hearty buss was the common salutation between a man and a woman. Even the fanatics had failed to outlaw the custom. And a little amorous dalliance—an arm about a waist, or fingers tickling a bare neck, or playing with the palm of a white hand—was expected by a pretty maidservant, a barmaid, or a shopgirl. But Pepys was careful never to let his wife see him playing the fool.[18]

Politically the tide turned for Pepys in February when General Monck, with his troops in control of London, declared for a free parliament. That night the happy citizens built bonfires everywhere, and from the windows of a Westminster coffee house Mr. Pepys saw "the City from one end to the other with a glory about it, so high was the light of the bonfires, and so thick round the City, and the bells rang everywhere." There was increasing talk about the King's return. "Everybody now drinks the King's health without fear," said Pepys, "whereas before it was very private that a man dare do it."

In March, when Admiral Mountagu, called out of retirement and restored to his old office, asked Pepys to serve as his secretary at sea (at a salary of two hundred pounds a year), hinting that the King would soon be back, bringing pelf and preferment to the faithful, he became an ardent royalist. He hated to leave Elizabeth, but the chance for advancement was not to be missed. Hiring a boy and a clerk, Pepys sent his wife to board with friends (William Bowyer's family) at Huntsmore, near London, made his will and locked up his house. On March 23 he joined his ship and settled down to his secretarial work. For a month the Fleet lay in the Downs, while Mountagu awaited developments at Westminster. On May 1, in a mood of general rejoicing, the newly elected Parliament declared for the King. On May 12 the Fleet sailed for Holland bearing Parliament's invitation to the King to come home and all would be forgiven—plus a very welcome gift to his Majesty of fifty thousand pounds.[19]

A spectator at a great drama, Pepys enjoyed every day to the fullest. He was proud when he received a letter addressed to "Samuel Pepys, Esquire," a title to which he had little claim. He was delighted by the respect accorded him by the officers of the Fleet and by the pieces of gold which poured in as rewards for writing out commissions and doing small favors. In the space of a month he increased his small savings from forty pounds to one hundred pounds. The voyage to Holland brought him to new sights: tall, dark King Charles the Second, the royal family, famous cavaliers, and noble ladies—"a very splendid Court"; the Dutch cities, canals, churches, people, and a world of curious customs.

At the Hague he was a tireless tourist, "with child" to see everything new and strange. Although he had a keen eye for pretty women, he passed up two chances to exercise his latent libertinism. One night a friend, Charles Anderson, took him "to a Dutch [bawdy] house, where there was an exceeding pretty lass, and right for the sport." Later that night Anderson went back to lie with the lass, while Pepys slumbered sadly at his inn. At Scheveling the next day he lay down for a short nap in a chamber of an inn, "where in another bed there was a pretty Dutch woman in bed alone." Although he had "a month's mind" to attempt something with the sleeping beauty, his native timidity restrained him. At last she rose and began to dress herself "after the Dutch dress," while Pepys walked about and tried to talk to her. He nerved himself to kiss her hand, but without Dutch courage to support him he "had not the face to offer anything more."[20]

There was glorious weather and a favoring wind for the short voyage back to England. On May 25 the King landed at Dover, where a mighty crowd waited to welcome him home. The Mayor of Dover gave his Majesty a rich Bible, "which he took, and said it was the thing that he loved above all things in the world." The crowd cheered, the church bells rang, and everybody was happy.

Because Pepys and his master the Admiral—soon to be Earl of Sandwich—had to stay with the Fleet, they did not see the King's procession through London on his birthday, May 29. Another diarist, John Evelyn, witnessed the "triumph of above 20,000 horse and foot, brandishing their swords, and shouting with inexpressible joy; the ways strewed with flowers, the bells ringing, the streets hung with tapestry, fountains running with wine; the Mayor, Aldermen, and all the Companies, in their liveries, chains of gold, and banners; Lords and Nobles, clad in cloth of silver, gold, and velvet; the windows and balconies, all set with ladies; trumpets, music, and myriads of people flocking, even so far as from Rochester, so as they were seven hours in passing the city, even from two in the afternoon till nine at night." Evelyn stood in the Strand, watched the procession with his heart full of joy, "and blessed God."[21]

# III

# The Climate of Pleasure

## 1660

---

## 1662

Hᴉꜱᴛᴏʀɪᴀɴꜱ ʟɪᴋᴇ to say that when King Charles the Second entered London, all England deserted the bread-and-water of Zion for the flesh-pots of Egypt. Puritan repression, they argue, led to Restoration excess; under good King Charles the sons of Belial were let out of jail. They had a glorious time.

This is all well enough, but the change was not quite so immediate as it has been pictured. There was dancing in the streets the night the King rode through London (and bonfires and heavy drinking), but no open orgies. Even under the Puritan Commonwealth, London had been a rough, disorderly city, given to drunkenness, blasphemy, and uproar; the return of King Charles added little to its normal brutality. The rank lechery for which the Restoration is infamous came later, inspired as much by the King's aphrodisiac example as by reaction to repression.

Some changes came quickly. Good people were free to enjoy again the innocent pleasures outlawed by the Commonwealth: dancing, singing, bell-ringing, wrestling, May-poles, church-ales, wakes, fairs, and such religious festivals as Christmas and Easter. The rough and reckless returned to drinking, gambling, cock-fighting, sword-fighting, and bear-and-bull baiting. The gentry had their balls, bowling, tennis, horse races, and playhouses once more. These pleasures were all open enough now, and no doubt, after years of gloom and doom, many a good soul reveled to excess.

More important is the fact that sinners of all classes came out of hiding to dance in the twilight of merry England. Hardest hit by Puritan laws, offenders against sexual morality had been driven underground for at least ten years. By an Act of 1650, any married woman, convicted of being "carnally known by any man other than her Husband (except in Case of Ravishment)" was doomed to suffer death without benefit of clergy, along with her partner in crime. To this strict application of a verse in *Deuteronomy* (22:22) two provisos left slender loopholes: the man might be forgiven if he could show that he did not know the woman was married; and the woman might be spared if her husband was supposed dead, or had been absent abroad for the space of three years or more.

The penalty for simple fornication was lighter, but severe enough. Any man who had "carnal knowledge of the body of any Virgin, unmarried Woman, or Widow" could be jailed for three months. So, of course, could the woman. Bawds—men or women—found guilty of "wittingly keeping a common Brothel or Bawdy-house" could be sentenced on the first conviction to be whipped, pilloried, branded on the forehead with the letter B, and jailed for three months. On a second conviction the punishment would be death.[1]

Fortunately (since venery, like necessity, has no law) the Commonwealth's bark was worse than its bite. From 1650 to 1660 in Middlesex County (which included London) twenty-three women and fourteen of their fellow sinners were brought to trial for adultery. Of these only one woman was found guilty. She may have been executed, but the facts are not clear. During the same period five women and three of their bedfellows were tried "for fornicacion." One woman was found guilty, but there is no record of her sentence. One man was cited for "keepinge a notorious disorderly house . . . where bawdry is suspected to be committed," but there is no evidence that he was ever brought to trial. This is a very small bag of game for ten years in wicked, populous London. Middlesex constables and jurors were either more realistic or more tenderhearted than Puritan legislators. Nevertheless, the threat of punishment hung constantly over the would-be sinner's head; its effect was not to deter him but to make him more careful.[2]

With the Restoration, the Act of 1650 was nullified. Sinners were free to sin, and bawds to profit from lechery, so long as no one broke the peace. Adultery, which was commonly defined as "the lying of a single or married man with another man's wife, and not the lying of a married man with a single woman," became a matter for civil rather than criminal law. The onus of sin was thrown on the married woman, whose misbehavior could upset the economics of wedlock and perhaps produce a bastard to inherit an estate. In 1675 one indignant writer, who sought to have the death penalty restored, complained that "all the remedy the injured husband hath by our law is to sue a divorce in the spiritual court, and to be cousened with a separation *a mensa & thoro*, a crafty invention against the plain gospel." Therefore, he said, "the crime grows" upon the present age; "it is common, and this age gives it the soft and gentle French names of gallantry and divertisement, in apology for it."[3]

After 1660, for the diversion of rakes and roués, bawdy-houses multiplied throughout London and its suburbs, with notable clusters in East Smithfield, Moorfields, Whetstone's Park, Covent Garden, Lewkenor's Lane, Fleet Alley, and Dog and Bitch Yard. Almost any coffee house or alehouse could be a bawdy-house in disguise, with trollops on call; and the playhouses were notorious for the whores who sought their customers in the pit, and for the demi-mondaine actresses who were also for sale at slightly higher prices.

The true brothels were kept by bawds whose names became famous in Restoration annals: Madam Cresswell, Damaris Page, Mother Temple, "Lady" Bennet, Madam Moseley, and Betty Buley. Every year on Shrove Tuesday the London apprentices, ordinarily good customers, amused themselves by riotously assembling to pull down bawdy-houses. Once in Mr. Pepys' presence, the Duke of York "complained merrily that he hath lost two tenants, by their houses being pulled down, who paid him for their wine licenses fifteen pounds a year." The apprentices themselves protested that "they did ill in contenting themselves in pulling down the little bawdy-houses and did not go and pull down the great bawdy-house at Whitehall."[4]

The label was well deserved. The King and most of his younger courtiers were skeptical-minded voluptuaries, sworn enemies to chastity and virginity, living for the pleasure of the moment and gathering rose-buds as fast as they bloomed. Even before his return to England, King Charles had run through a long string of mistresses, among them Marguerite de Carteret, Lucy Walter, Elizabeth Killigrew, Catherine Pegg, and Eleanor Needham (described by Evelyn as "the King's seventeenth whore abroad"). Shortly after his return he acknowledged Barbara Palmer (née Villiers) as his mistress, creating her husband Earl of Castlemaine in the peerage of Ireland, with inheritance only to the children born of

Barbara's body. In the course of time Lady Castlemaine's reign at Whitehall was challenged by two actresses, Moll Davis and Nell Gwyn. Eventually the King added at least two more ladies to his harem: Louise Keroualle (created Duchess of Portsmouth) and Hortense Mancini, Duchess of Mazarin. In addition to all these, there came by night into the King's private bedroom a succession of nameless women, "clean and unclean," picked up by his Page of the Backstairs and processed for his pleasure.[5]

Like master, like men. Libertinism became so much the fashion at the Restoration Court that Lord Chancellor North, a sober lawyer, was seriously advised "that he should keep a whore . . . because he was ill looked upon for want of doing so." His morality was construed as a reproach to the Court. It was taken as a matter of course that gentlemen should keep mistresses and frequent bawdy-houses. Sir Charles Berkeley, Captain of the King's Guard, was heard to say that he would not suffer a Guardsman to be absent from his lodgings at night without leave, " 'not but that,' says he, 'once a week or so I know a man must go [to a bawdy-house], and I am not for denying it to any man.' " Members of Parliament were men, too; once when an important bill was to be voted on, the King ordered the Lord Chamberlain "to send to the playhouses and bawdy-houses, to bid all the Parliamentmen that were there to go to Parliament presently." Bawdy-houses, bawds, keepers, and whores were socially acceptable as sources of good clean fun; without their stage copies Restoration comic writers would have been at a loss for jokes.[6]

Secure in the King's protection, courtiers, wits, poets, gamesters, soldiers, and politicians seduced maids, wives, widows, and other men's mistresses, ran riot in the streets by night, broke windows, fought duels, beat the watch, and reeled drunkenly to bed at dawn. One evening Mr. Pepys and his actor-friend Henry Harris went for a stroll in Vauxhall Gardens on the Surrey bank of the Thames, a wooded area laid out with walks and groves and shady arbors for private meetings. In one of the walks they fell into the company of Henry Killigrew, Frank Newport, and some other young courtiers, and listened wide-eyed to their "mad, bawdy talk." The group was called "The Ballers," a band of hectors who met frequently with the procuress "my Lady Bennet and her ladies," and danced with them naked and committed "all the roguish things in the world" with impunity. It was cursed loose company, Pepys thought, but "worth a man's being in for once, to know the nature of it, and their manner of talk, and lives." Woe betide a constable who arrested a courtier for committing roguery! He was likely to find himself laid by the heels for interfering with the amusements of gentlemen![7]

On June 9, 1660, when Pepys got back to London at last after his voyage to Holland, he was too busy to notice any changes in the moral climate of his world. He became aware of them only gradually, over a period of years. Re-united with his wife, he stayed at his father's house in Salisbury Court while his own place in Axe Yard was being readied, resigned his post in the Exchequer, worked steadily as Mountagu's secretary, and hoped for the reward his cousin had promised him. His duties were even heavier than at sea; Mountagu now had two additional posts to add to all his other offices: Clerk of the Privy Seal and Master of the Wardrobe.

Late in June Pepys was appointed a Commissioner of the Navy and Clerk of the Acts, with a salary of three hundred and fifty pounds a year and almost unlimited pickings. Even after he was sure of the post, he had to fight off or buy off rival claimants, at last agreeing to pay one hundred pounds a year to the former incumbent, old Thomas Barlow. Then he had to get his patent made out, engrossed, passed, and sealed, paying out some forty pounds in gifts and fees to greedy clerks. In July "my Lord," too grand in his new dignities as Earl of Sandwich, Viscount Hinchingbrooke, and Baron of St. Neot's to execute a mere clerkship, appointed Pepys as a deputy Clerk of the Privy Seal. This proved to be temporarily a very lucrative job. The King was making hundreds of appointments, and each new office-holder had to have his patent sealed, paying a fee to the Clerk in attendance. (The Clerks worked in rotation, one month at a time.)

One of the perquisites of Pepys' office as Clerk of the Acts was a house near the Navy Office in Seething Lane. Late in July he hired a clerk, Will Hewer, and a boy, also named Will, and moved his goods and his family to his new house. Will Hewer turned out to be an honest, intelligent man and a lifelong friend. The boy Will proved to be a thief, and was soon replaced by a third Will, brother to Pepys' maid, Jane Wayneman.[8]

The Navy Office, just west of Tower Hill, was at the corner of Seething Lane and Crutched Friars, opposite the churchyard of the parish church, St. Olave's. From the Office the houses of navy officials and clerks ran east along Crutched Friars and south along Seething Lane. Pepys' new lodgings (a house by courtesy) formed part of a long, two-story brick row facing on Seething Lane, just a step from his office. Usually he walked there from his back door through the gardens of the houses between. Because previous occupants of the building had carved off rooms almost at will, it was not always easy to tell which chambers belonged to which house. The section allotted to Pepys had at least eight rooms.

From Seething Lane Pepys entered his new home through a hall or "entry," a part of which had been partitioned off to form a small room where the boy, Will Wayneman, slept. The entry led to a parlor and a large, cheerful kitchen equipped with a wood-burning range and a fireplace with a spit for roasting meat. Somewhere in the ground floor labyrinth was the bedroom of Will Hewer, Pepys' combined clerk and valet. Then there was the communal "house of office"—the privy—which emptied into a vat in the cellar. The vat in turn was emptied periodically through the kitchen by "night-men" with buckets. Even Pepys, accustomed to the stinks of London, found the process nauseating.[9]

Ordinarily the Pepyses ate in the kitchen. Stairs from the parlor led to the second floor and the dining room, which usually served as a living room and was used for its proper purpose only when there were guests. (Once Pepys came home, rushed headlong upstairs to the dining room, and surprised Lady Sandwich "doing something upon the pott.") There were three bedrooms on the second floor, one of which Pepys took for his study. At first, because of a shortage of furniture, master, mistress, and maid got along comfortably together in one bedroom, Jane sleeping on a trundle bed. They were quite cosy. One night, while Elizabeth was away, Pepys went to bed early, "reading myself asleep while the wench sat mending my breeches by my bedside." When they moved in, the Pepyses called the spare bedroom "the Nursery," but no children came to fill it. Later, when they hired a second maid, Mary, to help Jane, it became "the little green chamber" where the maids slept.[10]

Pepys had hardly settled in before he began making some badly needed improvements. For the next year and a half there were workmen in the house almost constantly, cutting a door from Pepys' study onto the roof ("the leads," where he loved to walk with Elizabeth of a summer evening), re-flooring the dining room, plastering and whiting the kitchen, painting walls, hanging draperies, setting up shelves and bookcases in the study, and building a new set of stairs from the parlor to the second floor. Even under Pepys' watchful eyes they worked slowly, but when they had finished, the house was neat and fine, with gilding in the parlor; green serge hangings, gilt leather chairs, a new chimney piece, and gilded picture frames in the dining room; pictures on all the walls, and pewter sconces for candles on the stairs and in the entry. But no amount of repairs could get rid of the trouble-some mice. Pepys tried mousetraps and added a cat to his domestic menagerie, which already included Elizabeth's little black dog Fancy (badly house-broken), a pet monkey, and two cages of canaries.[11]

Overseeing all this work took time, but to Pepys, who loved neatness and beauty, it was a pleasure, and, after the first month or so in his new job, he had time to burn. In August, 1660, he worked hard, spending his mornings at the Navy Office and his afternoons at the Privy Seal. At the end of the month Lord Sandwich's share of the Privy Seal profits was more than four hundred pounds; Pepys, who did the work, netted one hundred seven pounds. He saw nothing wrong with this division of the spoils. It was the way of the world for the lord to get more than the commoner.[12]

After the first of September, Pepys' duties were much lighter. He knew very little about the work of the Navy, but his fellow officers, Treasurer Sir George Carteret, Surveyor Sir William Batten, Comptroller Sir Robert Slingsby, and Commissioner Sir William Penn, were veteran administrators and easy-going gentlemen, content to meet two or three

mornings a week to transact business. For the moment Pepys
was satisfied to keep accounts and records, the work for
which his previous experience had fitted him. Except for the
Lord High Admiral, the Duke of York, who never meddled
in office affairs, he had no superior to mark his coming and
going. He fell into easy habits, rising late, drinking his cus-
tomary morning draught of ale or whey, going to his office
for a leisurely morning, coming home to dine at noon or
eating at a tavern with friends, lazing away an afternoon
reading, practicing on his lute, overseeing his workmen, or
going to a play. Late at night, after a light supper of bread
and cheese, or whatever was in the house, he would call his
household to prayers—"and so to bed." For the first time in
his life he had money to spend as well as to save; life was
good and Mr. Pepys was merry.[13]

In the main his merriment was innocent enough. Bright-
eyed and alert, he ran about London, eager to see new sights
and to taste new sensations. He visited Southwark Fair, across
the river; marvelled at a procession of bishops in Westminster Abbey; saw Thomas Harrison, the first of the regicides to
suffer death, drawn, hanged, and quartered at Charing Cross
("he looking as cheerful as any man could do in that condition"); watched the pageant on Lord Mayor's Day (October
29); carried Elizabeth to Whitehall to see the Queen-Mother
("a very little plain old woman"); went often to the theatre;
and bought books, clothes, and furnishings for his house. He
was living like a gentleman (even wearing a sword), and like
a gentleman of leisure he continued to live during the first
eighteen months of service in his new post.

The high tide of pleasure was the day of the King's coronation, April 23, 1661. The day before, from a window in
Cornhill, Pepys and his wife had watched a long, splendid
procession file through the City from the Tower to West-

minster: barons and knights in gorgeous raiment sprinkled with diamonds, the harsh-featured King "in a most rich embroidered suit and cloak," looking very noble, and so much silver and gold in the glittering cavalcade that Pepys' eyes were dazzled. The City was in its best array, "the streets all gravelled, and the houses hung with carpets [tapestries] before them made a brave show."

On Coronation Day it was everyone for himself. Pepys rose at four o'clock, hurried to Westminster Abbey and climbed up to a seat on "a great scaffold across the north end." There he sat patiently until eleven, while the vast nave, decked out in red, filled up with a packed mass of people, including the peers in their rich Parliament robes and the Dean and Prebends of Westminster, some in cloth-of-gold capes. Then came the King in his robes with the sword and scepter borne before him, and followed by a train of servants in scarlet and silver and ecclesiastics in white and gold. There was a sermon and a service which Pepys could not hear and then, in the choir before the high altar, the unctuous ceremony of the crowning which, to his grief, he could not see. There were great shouts of joy, proclamations and challenges by the Garter King-at-arms, barons kneeling before the King to do homage, and silver medals flung up and down to the crowd. But Pepys had to hurry out to find a house of office.

The rest of the day was a mad scramble of excitement. At the coronation dinner in Westminster Hall, Pepys, scurrying about among the tables where the great were seated, managed to get four rabbits and a pullet, sharing them in an empty booth with his friend John Creed. Later he found Elizabeth in the throng and kissed her and the pretty woman with her. There was a gay supper with friends and too much wine to drink. Late at night there was an encounter at a bonfire in Axe Yard with a tipsy crew who insisted that Pepys and his party drink the King's health on their knees. With Elizabeth safely stowed to spend the night with a friend, Pepys wandered out to the Yeoman of the Wine-cellar's house, where he found more revellers drinking the King's health, "till one of the gentlemen fell down dead drunk, and lay there spewing." Very late, Pepys got into bed in a room at Lord Sandwich's lodgings, "but my head began to hum," he said, "and I to vomit, and if ever I was foxed it was now." The next morning he awoke with his head "in a sad taking," but a day of such wonder and joy was cheap at the price of a headache.

The first of these years devoted to pleasure and merriment was marred by two small outbreaks of Pepys' amorous nature. On a Sunday afternoon in August, 1660, by chance he met an old friend, Betty Lane, a seamstress with a booth in West-minster Hall, took her to Lord Sandwich's new house in Lincolns Inn Fields, and gave her a bottle of wine in the garden. Afterward he took her to his now empty house in Axe Yard (which he was offering for lease), where he was "exceeding free in dallying with her, and she not unfree to take it."

The other outbreak was with Diana, the wanton young daughter of Mrs. Crispe, next-door neighbor to the Pepyses when they lived in Axe Yard. At an alehouse gathering one evening in the following September, Diana, with her head full of wine, became very loving toward Mr. Pepys. Two days later he was standing in the doorway of the Axe Yard house when Diana came tripping by, temptation in every wiggle. Pepys took her upstairs in his empty house, and there, he said, "did dally with her a great while, and found that in Latin 'Nulla puella negat.'" The motto—no maiden refuses —is misleading; for all of Pepys' dallying we may take it that

Diana was at least technically true to her name. His mild flirtation with her went on intermittently for another week or so, but there were no more private meetings.[14]

For the next two years, although Pepys was free enough with his kisses, he dallied only in his own dells. With no need to hurry off to work, he fell into the morning habit of lying long a-bed, "talking and sporting" with his wife, when conditions were favorable. In a house full of maids and clerks, morning, with everyone else downstairs at work, was the best time for intimacy. Unfortunately, either because of Elizabeth's indifference, or because of her frequent ailments, these occasions seem to have been too far apart for a man of Pepys' ardent temperament. Well-fed, he was content; starved, he grew restless and unhappy, and looked at other women with lascivious eyes. Had he been as insensitive as most husbands, Pepys would have possessed his wife when he chose, indifferent to her moods or feelings; but he had too much sensibility to demand his rights of a wife who was indifferent or indisposed.

For example, on April 2, 1661, he sent Elizabeth and his sister Paulina (then serving as Elizabeth's maid) to stay at his father's house in Salisbury Court while a new set of stairs was being built at Seething Lane. Pepys slept at home, seeing his wife only occasionally at dinner or supper. After a week of such an unnatural life, he was ready for anything. In the course of a stay at Chatham on Navy affairs, he fell headlong in love with pretty Rebecca Allen, daughter of Captain John Allen, kissed her freely, and was troubled to part with her at last. Back in London on April 11, he was still a temporary bachelor, and his libido mounted daily. One rainy night after supper at his father's house, he badly wanted to stay and sleep with Elizabeth, but she gave no sign that she was aware of his need. He pretended to be willing to go home;

she seemed willing to have him go; so off he went "in a discontent," too timid to make his wishes known. But Elizabeth, who knew well enough what he wanted, decided to be kind after all. "She, poor wretch," said Pepys, "followed me as far in the rain and dark as Fleet Bridge to fetch me back again, and so I did, and lay with her tonight, which I have not done these eight or ten days before."[15]

Pepys was not gifted with continence, but in these months his timidity and good taste kept him safe from sin. Yet whores fascinated him, and occasionally his lean diet of sex made him think of resorting, like other gentlemen, to a bawdy-house. One day in August, 1661, his friend Peter Luellin, a clerk of the Privy Council, coaxed him into a "pitiful alehouse in Bartholomew Fair," where, upon request, "a dirty slut or two come up that were whores." But Pepys found them revolting; he hurried to get away as quickly as he could for fear of being seen in their company.[16]

His pleasure (and perhaps his sublimation) came largely from plays, company, and wine. (He rarely worried now about expenses; in February, 1661, he found himself worth three hundred and fifty pounds, plus all his household goods.) Plays were his greatest delight. In the twelve months from January 1 to December 31, 1661, he went to the theatre a total of seventy-six times. He enjoyed the music and dancing, the acting of Betterton, Hart, Lacy, and Mohun, the silken legs of actresses in boys' clothing, the sight of beautiful faces and white bosoms on stage and in the side-boxes, the spectacle of the dark, sardonic King surrounded by glittering courtiers in velvet and satin, and the chance to rub his upstart elbows with the world of fashion. The two theatres were the social centers of the Restoration upper classes, places to which one resorted of an afternoon to see a play, to court a mistress, or simply to be seen. Most mere "citizens" stayed away.

On domestic occasions, at weddings, christenings, and funerals, Pepys' company was sadly plebeian: his own kinfolk and his friends from former days, clerks, butchers, turners, weavers, and small tradesmen. He took little joy in their mean company, preferring to associate with his colleagues in the Navy Office, with other bureaucrats and officials, with musicians, singers, and men of science, politics, or war. He took delight in showing off his possessions to these gentry and their wives, and in talking with them about books, music, and domestic and foreign affairs. Sometimes he entertained a group of friends at dinner. At one of his annual March feasts in celebration of being cut for the stone he had such pretty comestibles as "a brace of stewed carps, six roasted chickens, and a jowl of salmon, hot, for the first course; a tanzy [a pudding] and two neats' tongues, and cheese the second"—all for six people.[17]

Of course every gentleman drank wine, at meals and between meals, and by the pint. Pepys' jolly colleagues, Batten and Penn, two lusty old sailors, were notable topers and irresistible in their cups. On their trips downriver with Pepys to inspect shipyards or pay off crews, they lived luxuriously at the King's expense, working to the tune of bacchic laughter. The quantity of wine Pepys drank under their tutelage was staggering. Day after day he would conclude an entry with "drank a great deal of wine," or "to bed, my head akeing mightily through the wine that I drank today," or "and so to bed, very near fuddled." Wine made him merry and carefree; he danced like a May-fly in the sunshine of pleasure, gradually forgetting the moral chrysalis of his youth.[18]

A break in Pepys' pleasant life came in the summer of

1661, when Robert Pepys of Brampton, near Huntingdon (his father's oldest brother), died on July 5, leaving his property to Samuel after his father's death. Robert's step-sons, Tom and Jasper Trice, promptly entered claims against the estate on their mother's behalf, and Thomas Pepys of London, the second oldest of the Pepys brothers, claimed his right as heir-at-law. The resultant quarrels and litigation cost Pepys quite a sum of money and many a headache.

The estate itself, a house and some rented properties, was a great disappointment. But after many family conferences Samuel's father, tired, sick, and old, decided to retire to Brampton with his wife and his daughter Paulina, who had proved to be too "proud and idle" for domestic service. Tom, the second son, an aimless, tongue-tied young man, who could not even find himself a wife, took over his father's tailoring business. John, the youngest, was still at Cambridge.[19]

At the end of August Pepys took stock of himself and his situation and was not happy. "I find myself lately too much given to seeing of plays, and expense, and pleasure," he said, "which makes me forget my business, which I must labour to amend. No money comes in, so that I have been forced to borrow a great deal for my own expenses, and to furnish my father, to leave things in order. I have some trouble about my brother Tom, who is now left to carry on my father's trade, in which I have great fears that he will miscarry for want of brains and care." There were just too many people dependant on Pepys: his brother John, a mild, gentle young man with no drive or ambition; Paulina, too homely and bad-tempered to get a husband unless Pepys supplied her with a large dowry; and even Elizabeth's brother Balty, who needed help and yet had little education and no trade. Pepys himself had no security, no prospects of a pension, no insurance of any kind against disaster. If he lost his health or his job he had only his savings (now some six hundred pounds) to fall back on. In case of his death Elizabeth would have no one to turn to, certainly not her own penniless family. The lesson was clear: Pepys must get to work and build up an estate.[20]

But dulled ambition would not be spurred. Pepys continued in his usual merry courses, going to plays as often as before, letting music, good company, and fair ladies take up his time, and drinking so much wine that sometimes he was afraid to say prayers at night lest his servants see that he was drunk. The affairs of the Navy Office went on somehow: ships were paid off or readied for sea; Lord Sandwich sailed with a Fleet to bring home the new Queen from Portugal; Sir Thomas Allen's Mediterranean Fleet was reinforced for a war against Algiers; and Comptroller Slingsby died in October and was replaced by old Sir John Minnes. Working with only half his mind, Pepys continued to dance and play, occasionally scolding himself for his folly, but unable to stop the merry-go-round.[21]

On the last day of the year he applied the brakes. Suddenly sober as he looked at his personal accounts and feared to cast them up, he took "a solemn oath to abstain from plays and wine." It had some effect. In the first two months of 1662 he saw only six plays and restricted his drinking to a glass of wine with each meal. But he made no serious attempt to break himself of his idle ways. He still lay long a-bed in the mornings, sleeping, or sporting with his wife. He spent hours every day singing, composing music, or practicing on his lute or flageolet; sitting for his portrait, jaunting abroad with his family; overseeing the workmen who were forever improving his house; and being "very merry" with friends. On March 1, when he finally balanced his accounts, he was shocked to discover that in the last six months he had spent two hundred and fifty pounds—his net salary for a year as Clerk of the Acts. He was worth only five hundred pounds, while only six months ago he had been worth six hundred pounds. Resolving that thenceforth frugality must be the motto of his household, he bound himself by oaths to refrain from all expensive pleasures.[22]

Bad habits die hard. In spite of his vows, Pepys saw ten plays in the next three months. He tried to work, but there were too many delightful distractions. He excused himself with the universal plea of idlers: "I do think it best to enjoy some degree of pleasure now that we have health, money, and opportunity, rather than to leave pleasures to old age or poverty, when we cannot have them so properly." This was very pretty, but at the end of May Pepys found that he had increased his nest egg by only thirty pounds. For an estate he needed at least one thousand pounds, which, invested in land, would provide a bare living. (If he had two thousand pounds, he once told Elizabeth, he would be a knight and keep his coach.) But at his present rate of gain it would take him years to reach even his minimal goal. His job was precariously subject to the whims of kings and courtiers, and he was twenty-nine years old, approaching what the seventeenth century considered middle age. Obviously he must work harder, learn his business, save every penny, and find out new ways of making money.[23]

The very next working day he was "up early about business." Thereafter he settled into a new pattern of life, rising at four or five o'clock, working in his study or office until noon, often staying with his affairs all the afternoon and far into the night, and drinking only small beer. Four weeks of this and the pattern was set: "business," he reported, "is a delight to me, and brings me great credit, and my purse encreases too."

For every gain there must be a loss. Farewell to the long, indolent mornings (except for an occasional Sunday) spent lying in bed with Elizabeth "merry and pleasant," and farewell to music, games, pleasure jaunts, and the theatre—he made and kept a vow to see no plays until Michaelmas, September 29. Pepys had found his occupation. He threw himself headlong into the work of the Navy Office, inquiring the prices of tar, oil, deal boards, and bunting, learning all he could about ships, and studying arithmetic, beginning with the multiplication table! Aided by a new Commissioner of the Navy, William Coventry, the Duke of York's secretary, he began poking his long nose into abuses and mismanagement. He learned that it was "impossible for the King to have things done as cheap as other men," but he did all he could to save the King's money, and succeeded in thoroughly annoying his indolent colleagues. Because it was no longer profitable he resigned his deputy Clerkship of the Privy Seal, and a few days later learned that Lord Sandwich had got him appointed to the Commission for Tangier (part of Queen Catherine's dowry), a position of honor and a new source of profit. By the end of the year, in spite of great expenditures for his house and furnishings, he was worth six hundred and fifty pounds in cash.[24]

Left to her own devices, Elizabeth had begun to mope, but her husband saw nothing amiss. She "has lately had but little of my company," he wrote, "since I began to follow my business, but is contented therewith since she sees how I spend my time." The new regime was hard on Pepys, too. His frustrated lust for pleasure threatened to break out in a new direction. On the last day of June he came early to his office to find the doorman's maid sweeping out, and "God forgive me!" he said, "What a mind I had to her, but did not meddle with her." A month later, just three days after he had sent Elizabeth to stay at Brampton while he was building a third story on his Seething Lane house and everything was "all in dirt," he heard that Sir William Penn's maid Betty had left him. "I was in hopes to have had a bout with her before she was gone," Pepys complained, "she being very pretty." He had also, he confessed to his diary during this summer of bachelorhood, "a mind" to his own maid, Jane Wayneman, "but I dare not for fear she should prove honest and refuse and then tell my wife." Jane was a constant temptation: "Dined at home and can hardly keep myself from having a mind to my wench, but I hope I shall not fall to such a shame to myself."[25]

Caution and the remnants of middle-class morality won the day. Pepys was continent for two months; his only slip from strict virtue was an hour or two spent dallying with Lord Sandwich's housekeeper, Sarah, a veteran at the game. On September 27 his house was ready for occupancy; Elizabeth came home; and that night Pepys "had her company with great content and much mutual love," slightly marred by her stories of bickerings at Brampton. Two days later his oaths expired; he saw three plays in quick succession, and then renewed his vows until Christmas.[26]

To Pepys the course of the future was clear: he would continue as the industrious apprentice, renewing his vows as they expired (with an interlude for a play or two), staying close to his business, and rising in the world's esteem. He would save his money and acquire property, not to leave to children—he had accepted the likelihood that Elizabeth would never give him a son—but to provide for himself and his family. Elizabeth would continue to serve as a dutiful wife, keeping his house with "care and thrift and innocence" so long as he kept her "from occasions of being otherwise." Of course he would remain the master in his house.[27]

He failed to take into account Elizabeth's growing dissatisfaction with the life she was now leading, his own dangerously suppressed itch for pleasure, and the changing moral climate of the age which had already affected him more than he knew. He could see the effect on others—on his friend John Creed, for example, with whom he had gone to an alehouse one Sunday in 1661, a man who, he said, "twelve months ago, might have been got to hang himself almost as soon as go to a drinking-house on a Sunday." But he could not see the change in himself.

Like most men, Pepys took his morals from his surroundings. There were Puritans a-plenty in Restoration London, but his way of life brought him into daily contact with the ungodly. In his world love was equated to lust, and sex was a subject for bawdy jests. At the theatre he saw plays dealing lusciously with sex intrigues, seductions, and rapes, while in the pit of the theatre whores paraded, openly soliciting custom. On stage, at Court, and in private houses he met women in gowns cut dangerously low (out-of-doors the exposed territory was covered by a gorget, whisk, or neckerchief). At night in the jolly West End taverns, men and women openly kissed and toyed, and many a whisk was rumpled or petticoat lifted. In Pepys' circle ladies received male callers in their bedrooms of a morning (sometimes permitting them liberties), or dressed by the fireside, careless of who might see. (Once his distant cousin, Jane Turner, took occasion while dressing to show Pepys her leg, "which indeed is the finest I ever saw," he said, "and she not a little proud of it.")

But all this was nothing to the scandalous goings-on at the King's Court. When Pepys first began to hear about the depravity of Whitehall he was shocked, but his curiosity was aroused. His friends found him an eager listener, avid for gossip about the Court, where "the vices of drinking, swearing, and loose amours" abounded, and the pox (venereal disease) was "as common as eating and swearing."[28]

Pepys was not a courtier, but his business took him to Whitehall Palace almost daily. By virtue of his office he could go alone or take his wife to a play at night in the palace theatre. As a loyal subject he was free to crowd into the Banqueting Hall when the King dined in ceremonial state, or stroked the ulcers of the scrofulous. He could wander at will in St. James's Park, where the King and his cronies strolled and made bets on which drake would tup which duck in the canal. Friends brought Mr. Pepys still closer to the center of contagion, leading him through the Stone Gallery at Whitehall into private apartments where he marveled at paintings and tapestries, watched great lords at gaming tables, and ogled maids of honor in décolleté gowns. He came to feel himself almost a courtier, and to make excuses for sin. When he heard the story of the Duke of York's attempt on Lady Chesterfield's virtue, and her husband's abrupt flight to the country with the lady in tow, he said, "it is the effect of idleness, and having nothing else to employ their great spirits upon." He touched pitch only at second hand, but he was still defiled.[29]

Symbolic of his pollution was his love for Barbara, Lady Castlemaine, the King's chief mistress. Although he never so much as touched her hand, he enjoyed her in imagination. She was a great beauty, with a queenly figure, dark auburn hair, deep blue eyes, and red lips. She had the clear complexion and oval face of a Raphael Madonna, but beneath the innocent surface was flaming youth incarnate. Even age could not tame the hey-day in her blood.

At fifteen Barbara became the mistress of the dissolute Earl of Chesterfield. At eighteen she married Roger Palmer (later Earl of Castlemaine), a young man of wealth and good family. At nineteen she became the mistress of King Charles the Second; according to some gossips he spent his first night in London in her bed. Her daughter Anne (later acknowledged by the King) was born exactly nine months after the blessed Restoration.[30]

Pepys first heard of Barbara one July night in 1660, when he was writing letters in Lord Sandwich's Whitehall lodgings. From next door came the strains of music; the King and his brothers, the Dukes of York and Gloucester, were entertaining "Madame Palmer, a pretty woman that they have a fancy to, to make her husband a cuckold." Pepys did not know that the King had already supplied Mr. Palmer with a handsome pair of horns.

In Whitehall Chapel, three months later, Pepys observed with a frown that "the Duke of York and Mrs. Palmer did talk to one another very wantonly through the hangings that part the King's closet and the closet where the ladies sit." He was still Puritan enough to be shocked by unseemly behavior. Again, at the Cockpit Theatre in Whitehall, on April 20, 1661, he noted that there were many "great beauties" present, but the most beautiful was "Mrs. Palmer, with whom the King do discover a great deal of familiarity." Princes should not behave like costers on an outing.[31]

As time passed, Barbara's beauty won Pepys' susceptible heart. He saw her often, usually at the theatre, and rarely failed to comment on her beauty. Once she was in a box at the Theatre Royal, and he sat where he could fill his eyes with her beauty, "which much pleased me." On another occasion he said that he could never "enough admire her beauty." He made no secret of his admiration. Elizabeth, too, was forced to approve Barbara's beauty (with what twinges of envy we can guess), and Pepys' patroness, the Countess of

Sandwich, twitted him for his steady homage, "calling her 'my lady,'" he said, "and 'the lady I admire'."[32]

But his feeling for the glorious strumpet was more than a connoisseur's admiration; gradually he became deeply infatuated. He found it strange that the King was bewitched by "this pretty Castlemaine," not realizing how completely he too was under her spell. She was his "dear Lady Castlemaine," and with all his heart he wished her well. When the King married and Lady Sandwich was "afeared that my Lady Castlemaine will keep still with the King," Pepys' written (but unspoken) reply was, "I am afeared she will not, for I love her well." He was no judge of women's undergarments, but one day when he walked through the Privy Garden and saw the Palace washing hung out to dry, with "the finest smocks and linen petticoats of my Lady Castlemaine's, laced with rich lace at the bottom, that ever I saw," he stopped to gaze with a rich sense of intimacy. It "did me good," he said, "to look upon them." When Barbara quarreled with her husband and left him for good, baggage and bag, Pepys recorded the event, adding, "but strange it is how for her beauty I am willing to construe all this to the best and to pity her wherein it is to her hurt, though I know well enough she is a whore." At a pageant on the river he stood near Barbara on Whitehall Stairs and saw very little of the show. "I glutted myself with looking on her," he said. When he saw her portrait at Sir Peter Lely's house he was in ecstacies—"a most blessed picture; and that that I must have a copy of." Three years later he bought copies of Faithorne's print of the lady's head—"a very fine picture, and like her"—mounted one in a handsome frame and had the print varnished and the frame gilded—an icon of Venus.[33]

Although he never said so, we may take it that Pepys envied the King his costly courtesan; his ideal of sexual happiness was not a harem but Lady Castlemaine, the un-attainable. For at least five years she was the focus of his erotic fancy, and his search for womanly perfection followed always the same subconscious pattern of desire. But in 1662, only two years after the Restoration, although he had changed with the moral climate of his age, his fornications yet were but fantastical. Without further pressures and temptations he might have been content all his life (as most men are) with dreams and visions, reveling only in imagination, and taking pleasure from time to time in the casual embraces of his dutiful wife.

# IV

# An Apprentice Libertine

$$\frac{1662}{1663}$$

IN THE AUTUMN of 1662 Elizabeth's discontent deepened as the nights grew longer. With her husband at work all day and often until late at night, and with two maids to do all the housework, her life became a chronicle of wasted time. After all, Pepys had not consulted her when he made his vows to abstain from expensive pleasures, and she neither shared nor understood his driving urge to be rich; yet she suffered the greater hardship. He went off every morning into a man's world: to the Navy Office, the Royal Exchange, Westminster Hall, the Houses of Parliament, and Whitehall Palace; to taverns where he ate, drank, and talked with all sorts of interesting people; or farther afield to Deptford, Greenwich, Woolwich, or Portsmouth. He came home with news, gossip, and the strutting glory of daily achievement. Elizabeth had to stay at home and console herself with her maids, goodhearted creatures, but ignorant and dull. She measured out her life in kitchen ladles. Even the monthly washing day, when the maids rose before dawn and kept the house in a steamy turmoil until dark, was a great event.

She began to pester her husband for a companion, a superior domestic with whom she could be on more nearly equal terms, someone able to read aloud, sing, dance, set hair, trim petticoats with ribbons and lace à la mode, and carry her fan when she went visiting. It was not seemly for a lady to go out alone; either her husband took her, or she towed a genteel maid in her wake. But in his busy life, Pepys had no room for wifely foibles; what Elizabeth needed, he thought, was work. He feared the expense of a companion and the temptation for Elizabeth to go in for extravagant fancies. She was flighty enough without a giddy maid to put notions in her head. By now Pepys had his crumb up to six hundred and fifty pounds—roughly $13,000 in modern purchasing power—and each month he managed to put aside a few more pounds toward the estate he must have. There could be no frivolous expenses. He listened absently to his wife's complaints and promptly forgot them.[1]

He was a happy man in October, with "no crosses, but only much business" to trouble his mind. The whole world, he thought, was smiling upon him. At the Navy Office he was growing in power and importance, winning the envy of his colleagues. The new third floor of his house was almost finished, needing only plaster and paint. As for his domestic life, he wrote one day of "lying a great while talking and sporting" with his wife in the morning, and concluded, "we have been some years now, and at present more and more, a very happy couple, blessed be God." He was mistaken: Elizabeth was not happy. Secretly she told her brother Balty about her desire for a companion. Balty, a gay spark with a wide acquaintance, recommended two young women, the Gosnell sisters, who had been gently bred and well educated—that is, they could read, write, sing, dance, embroider, and perhaps speak a little French. On November 1, while Pepys was at home for his noon-day meal, the sisters showed up by Elizabeth's appointment. Although he was much taken with them, especially with the younger, Winifred, who was "pretty handsome" and sang very well, Pepys refused to engage them.

That night the Pepyses had a violent quarrel. Elizabeth was angry because her plot had failed, and Pepys because she had negotiated behind his back. They were both sullen and unhappy the next day. After long brooding, Elizabeth wrote out the whole story of her discontent in a letter which she sent to her husband at his office. Pepys received it, but in his angry mood tossed it into the fire unread, and so failed to profit from Elizabeth's "sound counsel." The next day, still sullen but calmer, the two reasoned out their differences, listening to each other's arguments and keeping their tempers. Elizabeth urged her husband to give Winifred Gosnell a trial. If he disliked her, he could "put her away," and try one of Mr. William Bowyer's less desirable four daughters, humble young women who would cost very little. Partly because he realized that Elizabeth lived a very lonely life, and partly because he was attracted by Winifred Gosnell's "musique and dancing," Pepys agreed to a trial period.[2]

This was only one of many quarrels caused by the conflict between Pepys' frugality and Elizabeth's extravagance. They quarreled for other reasons that autumn and winter: because of Elizabeth's carelessness with her possessions; her sluttish housekeeping; her bad spelling; and her "deadly hate" for her chambermaid, Sarah (successor to Mary the First), who was soon discharged as a liar. But these were trivia and quickly forgotten; the real trouble was a fundamental difference in values. Pepys was all for saving money and getting ahead in the world. He knew that if his uncle, Thomas Pepys, succeeded in getting possession of the Brampton estate, he would have to provide for his father, mother, and sister—and probably brother John as well. Elizabeth, gifted with a child's faith in the future, was eager to spend money, be a lady, wear a velvet gown, and make a show. Pepys wanted to add to his "crumb," Elizabeth, to eat it.[3]

Winifred Gosnell arrived on a cold, snowy day in December and seemed "like to prove a pretty companion." She sang very well indeed, and Mr. Pepys was delighted. Four days later she was gone. Fantastic Balty had told her a pack of lies about Elizabeth's way of life: that she went to plays and to Court daily, and gave her maids all sorts of liberties. Mrs. Gosnell was disappointed; she was too ambitious to settle down to the staid routine of a citizen's household. Trumping up an excuse, she packed her things and trudged off to seek her fortune elsewhere. Sarah left the same day, and went to work for Sir William Penn. Jane Wayneman, promoted to chambermaid, was replaced in the kitchen by Susan, "a good well-looked lass."

Five months later Pepys was surprised to see Mrs. Gosnell at the Duke's Theatre, as an attendant lady in *Hamlet*. Thereafter, from time to time, he saw her in various singing and speaking roles. At her best she was never more than a mediocre actress, yet she seems to have remained a member of the Duke's Company for at least thirty years.[4]

Pepys was sorry to see her leave his household. She had brought a touch of color into his drab family, and he was beginning to see what a dreary life Elizabeth, "poor wretch," had to endure without a companion. Still, perhaps her departure was God's providence to keep him from "running behind in the world." He tried to bring Elizabeth to his stoic way of thinking, and consoled her as well as he could, even buying a copy of Ovid's *Metamorphoses* in translation and reading from it aloud at night. Fortunately, according to his vows, the Christmas season left an interlude for pleasure and plays. He took Elizabeth to five plays (and saw another alone); to Whitehall to see Queen Catherine in her presence chamber, surrounded by Maids of Honour in velvet gowns; to dinner at the house of Dr. and Mrs. James Pierce (spending the night at Lord Sandwich's lodgings in Whitehall); and to dinner with John Creed at brother Tom's house. On January 6, after a delightful vacation, Pepys decided to go back to work again. "I do find my mind so apt to run to its old want of pleasures," he said, "that it is high time to betake myself to my late vows."[5]

This was all very well for Pepys, who could arrange his life as he chose, but Elizabeth, staring at the empty days ahead, saw only moping solitude. Her bitterness found voice one January morning as the two lay abed wrangling about some of the departed Sarah's gossip and loose talk. Pepys was in a thoroughly irritated mood when Elizabeth, with a fine lack of tact, chose to bring up once more her need for a companion. Calling Jane to fetch her a bundle of papers, she pulled out a copy of the letter she had sent her husband in November. Dismayed, Pepys had to lie there and squirm while she read it aloud. "It was so piquant, and wrote in English, and most of it true, of the retiredness of her life and how unpleasant it was," that his cheeks burned with shame. To cover his confusion he first begged her and then ordered her to destroy the letter, arguing that since it was in English it was "in danger of being met with and read by others." When she refused, his temper flared into action. "I forced it from her and tore it, and withal took her other bundle of papers from her, and leapt out of bed and in my shirt clapped them into the pocket of my breeches [which hung near the bed] that she might not get them from me, and having got on my stockings and breeches and gown, I pulled them out one by one and tore them all before her face, though it went against my heart to do it, she crying and desiring me not to do it." Out of the wreckage of documents, letters, and mementos he saved only a bond, his marriage license, and the first love letter he had ever written to Elizabeth. All the rest he burned.

It was the worst quarrel they had ever had; never before had both been "so heartily angry." Although there had been provocation on both sides, it was Pepys who had lost his temper and therefore had to sue for peace. He bought it with apologies and the promise of a new moiré gown, and the battle of the sexes ended that night with the combatants "mighty friends," and going happily to bed. Yet Pepys predicted gloomily as he recorded the episode in his journal, "I doubt the heart-burning will not soon [be] over."[6]

Certainly Elizabeth was not one to forget and forgive in a hurry, but for the moment she was bent only on getting her way. Almost at once she consulted brother Balty again, and less than a week after the battle she had another candidate to propose: Mary Ashwell, daughter of "little Mr. Ashwell," one of Pepys' old associates in the days when he was an Exchequer clerk. It took Elizabeth just a month to wear down her husband's resistance and get his permission to hire Mary.[7]

He might have put up a better fight, but he was "overcharged with business" because of the work he had to do for the Tangier Commission, to which he had been appointed the previous August. Then, too, his Uncle Thomas was suing the Brampton tenants for their rent; the Trices' suit was still impending; his latest attempt to get brother Tom a wife had failed; Jane Wayneman was leaving his service (to be replaced by Mary the Second); and at the end of January his savings had fallen to six hundred and forty pounds! Moreover, some time earlier the Principal Officers of the Navy (all Justices of the Peace in Middlesex) had com-

mitted a rogue named Field to prison for slandering them.
Field, claiming rightly that their jurisdiction did not include
London, the city in which the offense was committed, was
seeking legal reprisals. Since the other officers were all members of Parliament and therefore immune to civil suits, Field's
wrath fell on Mr. Pepys' defenseless head. In addition, his
fellow Commissioners, lazy, venal Sir William Batten, Sir
William Penn ("a cheating fellow"), and Sir John Minnes
(an "old doter"), all seemed bent on frustrating Pepys' noble
efforts to serve the King. He felt himself abused, the only
honest man in a world of knaves.[8]

On February 6, 1663, he came to an "agreement upon very
hard terms" with his uncle and was happy to have his father
left in possession of Brampton even at the cost of twenty-five
pounds a year to Uncle Thomas. Two weeks later the trouble
with Mr. Field came to a ridiculous climax when the august
Clerk of the Acts spent an entire day hiding in Sir William
Batten's house from bailiffs intent on his arrest at Field's
suit. The arrival of a solicitor with a release set him free
temporarily, but he had had a bad scare which made him
think soberly of his precarious state: "God knows in what a
sad condition I should be in if I were truly in the condition
that many a poor man is for debt." Two days later the bailiffs
were satisfied, and he was free from further danger of arrest.
In his joy he decided for once to break his vows, take Elizabeth to a play, and pay the forfeit (give to the poor a sum
equal to half the cost of his pleasure). After all, it was his
birthday, "being this day thirty years old, for which let me
praise God." The play was *The Slighted Maid*; Mr. Pepys
was delighted by the sight of little Moll Davis dancing in
boy's clothes, "she having very fine legs, only bends in the
hams, as I perceive all women do." At night, to climax the
holiday, he took his wife to the Court Theatre for a bad

performance of Dryden's *The Wild Gallant*. Here his only pleasure was the sight of beautiful Lady Castlemaine.[9]

Mary Ashwell joined the Pepys household in March. She was a pretty girl, humble enough for her station, and eager to please. She was ingenious at all "fine work," skilled at cardplaying, musically inclined, with a nice touch on the harpsichord, and, above all, "a merry jade." With a pretty, intelligent girl to talk to, Pepys found his home more attractive and was even lured into taking up his music again. Elizabeth came out of her retirement. She began making visits, playing the great lady with Ashwell at her side. In April she started dancing lessons with Mr. Pembleton, a darkly handsome young man (but married), who came to the house daily. A large empty room on the third floor, almost directly above Pepys' study, became a temporary dance hall. Even through his closed door he could hear the rhythmic shuffle of feet and the murmur of voices.[10]

One of Pepys' financial problems was finally solved. On May 1, taking stock of the Brampton estate, he found that after all debts and annuities were paid his father would have a clear fifty pounds a year to live on, no small sum in those days. It was costing Pepys only seventy-five pounds a year or so to run his own large household, feeding seven people, while Elizabeth's proud parents were scraping along on twenty pounds a year. Pepys' savings had mounted to seven hundred pounds. He could easily have afforded aid to both sets of parents, but so long as they were fed and sheltered he saw no reason to spoil them with luxuries. He was not mean, merely provident; his fattening purse was their insurance against destitution.[11]

Now only an occasional squall riffled the surface of domesticity. One day early in May Pepys scolded Elizabeth for "neglecting the keeping of the house clean." She replied with unwifely impudence: when Pepys, taunting her with her lack of dowry, called her "beggar," she retorted with "prick-louse"—i.e., tailor. The next day there was another falling out, this time because Pepys would not leave a pleasant chat with Ashwell to talk with his wife alone. She complained that he would "rather talk with anybody than her," and Pepys noted in his diary, "by which I find I think she is jealous of my freedom with Ashwell, which I must avoid giving occasion of." There was a new coldness between Mrs. Pepys and her maid which foreshadowed trouble.[12]

The dancing lessons continued, and Pepys enrolled himself as a pupil, thinking that skill in country dances and corantos might be "very useful for a gentleman," but he rarely found time for the lessons. As the days passed, Elizabeth became more and more absorbed in her dancing, even having Pembleton come twice a day—"a folly," Pepys growled. He came home late one afternoon and ran up to the third floor, where he found his wife and her teacher alone, "not dancing but talking," and immediately his old fears awoke. From talking to something worse was an easy step—perhaps the couple had already taken it! Elizabeth was alone all day except for her maids, who usually stayed in the lower rooms of the house. Opportunity was easy, and dancing masters—especially such smooth, handsome fellows as Pembleton—were traditionally expert at cuckolding middle-class husbands. Pepys knew how attractive Elizabeth was to other men. On the street, he could see their eyes turn to follow her, and, of course, there had been "the old business" of Captain Robert Holmes' attempt on her chastity. Scold himself as he would, reminding himself that this was only his old disease of jealousy and that he had no real cause for doubt, he could not kill his suspicion. At bedtime he even watched to see if Elizabeth had worn drawers that day as she always did. He was ashamed of his doubts and spying, and all the more so as he told himself that upon a small temptation he could be false to Elizabeth, and therefore ought not to expect "more justice from her"— a surprisingly honest statement. But reason could not wither the growth planted in his mind.[13]

Mutual distrust makes an unhappy marriage. Elizabeth knew by experience how easily her husband's jealousy was aroused, and it may be that she chose to play the fool with her dancing master only to get even with Pepys for his obvious interest in Ashwell. On the other hand, she was just twenty-three, there was little love in her life, and Mr. Pembleton was young, handsome, and courtly—a proper man, framed to make women false.

Although Pepys never learned the whole truth about his wife's relations with her dancing master, for the next month he suffered the tortures of the cuckold, picturing Pembleton kissing Elizabeth, caressing her, even leading her to a bed—! He was afraid to say anything for fear of making a fool of himself. When he was home in his study while a lesson was going on, he listened to the footsteps overhead, his heart leaping whenever they stopped. On an outing with Pembleton he had to look on in silence, his gorge rising, when the master took Elizabeth by the hand. He could say nothing even when he learned that Pembleton had dined one day with Elizabeth in his absence, and at church as he watched the dancing master "leer" at Elizabeth all through the sermon. This was lechery, not courtesy—no mere harmless flirtation. His suspicions were fed by the change he saw in Elizabeth: she was getting to be ever more headstrong and spirited. One night at supper he checked her for using the word "devil," and she answered so scornfully that had not Ashwell been present he would have struck her. It was a melancholy situation for a man who saw himself losing command over his wife. It was all the fault of the dancing, he thought, "her mind is taken up from her business and finds other sweets besides pleasing of me, and so makes her that she begins not at all to take pleasure in me or study to please me as heretofore."[14]

Stubbornly Pepys clung to the illusion that whenever Elizabeth wore drawers her intentions were chaste. In this respect he had an advantage possessed by few English husbands of the age. Except for stage dancers, whose twirling petticoats disclosed thighs and legs, most Englishwomen wore as their only undergarment a short-sleeved linen smock, or shift, open at the breast and falling to the knees. A gust of wind or a fall could result in spectacular effects. Once one of the Pepys' maids, Jane Gentleman, getting into a boat, "did fall down and show her arse." Elizabeth's modest habit was exceptional. Pepys followed still the donning of the drawers with fresh suspicion, but those close-mouthed garments told him nothing.[15]

One morning he came home from his office unexpectedly and found Pembleton and Elizabeth in circumstances so suspicious that he could not bring himself to describe them even to his diary. His fears, now wrought to the height, seemed to be confirmed by the fact that Elizabeth was sending everyone out of the house for the afternoon, when Pembleton would come again. In such agitation that he hardly knew what he was doing, Pepys hurried through some of his affairs that afternoon and ran home, where he found Pembleton and Elizabeth dancing and, as he feared, no one else in the house. He joined in the dancing lesson for a turn or two, and then, summoning the commander of one of the King's yachts to sit in a little room downstairs until he returned, he ran back to his office, dispatched the rest of the day's business in haste, and sped home again. "I think," he said, "if they had any intention of hurt I did prevent them doing anything at that time." Ostentatiously he stayed in his study the rest of the afternoon, tormented by raging suspicion. After Pembleton had gone he stole softly up to the third floor "to see whether any of the beds were out of order or no, which I found not." He kept away from Elizabeth that evening; when she tried to talk to him about business he "construed it to be but impudence." Late at night, when he came to write up his diary, he summed up the day: "By many circumstances I am led to conclude that there is something more than ordinary between my wife and him, which do so trouble me that I know not at this minute that I now write this almost what either I write or am doing. This is my devilish jealousy, which I pray God may be false, but it makes a very hell in my mind."[16]

Farewell the sweet sleep of yesterday! At three o'clock the next morning Pepys woke from uneasy slumbers and lay tossing and turning for an hour. Then Elizabeth woke up and wanted to know what ailed him. He began "to tax her discretion in yesterday's business," and she retorted by blaming his old disease of jealousy. Pepys denied the countercharge and returned to the attack, but Elizabeth admitted nothing. "After an hour's discourse," he said, "sometimes high and sometimes kind, I found very good reason to think that her freedom with him is very great and more than was convenient, but with no evil intent, and so after awhile I caressed her and parted seeming friends, but she crying in a great discontent." The talk failed to clear the air; Pepys thought his wife honest and feared she was not; he had no proof one way or the other.

Fortunately this was the last day of the scheduled series of lessons. When Pepys got home that afternoon after a visit to Lord Sandwich, he found Elizabeth "in a musty humour."

Pembleton, she said (in front of Ashwell!) had come in the morning and she had sent him away; she refused to be alone with him again. Later that day Pembleton came for the last time, and Pepys, summoned from his office, joined in a country dance. He did his best to keep a smiling face, and, after Pembleton had been paid off, even invited him to supper and was painfully merry. He saw—or thought he saw—that Pembleton knew all about his jealousy, "which I take very ill," he said. It was another black mark against his foolish wife.

All this excitement and brooding over what might have passed between Elizabeth and the dancing master had made Pepys reckless and had set off his hair-trigger libido. The next two days, with his mind full of sex and jealousy, he took Elizabeth to two plays in succession, paying his forfeits to the poor as usual. After the second play he sent Elizabeth off on her own, did several small errands, and walked home through the City with his mind in a turmoil. On a sudden impulse he made a detour through Fleet Alley, a noisome little lane just north of Fleet Prison, where a pair of excitingly pretty strumpets flaunted their wares at their doors. "God forgive me!" said Pepys, "I could scarce stay myself from going into their houses with them, so apt is my nature to evil after once, as I have these two days, set upon pleasure again." But timidity was stronger than desire.[17]

Even with the lessons ended and Elizabeth on her good behavior, Pepys could have no peace of mind until she left for Brampton in mid-June, according to an earlier plan. Every time he saw Pembleton his jealousy boiled up. The slightest variation in Elizabeth's daily routine aroused his suspicion; he questioned the boy, Will Wayneman, when Elizabeth sent him on errands; and he still watched every morning to be sure that his wife wore drawers. On June 9

Pembleton came for an extra lesson. Pepys was home; he let Elizabeth, Ashwell, and Pembleton go upstairs to dance, while he stayed in his own chamber. "But, Lord!" he said, "how I listened and laid my ear to the door, and how I was troubled when I heard them stand still and not dance!" Pepys was one too easily jealous, and, being wrought, perplexed in the extreme.[18]

But Mrs. Pepys had her own complaint against her husband. One morning, "lay long in bed talking with my wife, and do plainly see that her distaste (which is beginning now in her again) against Ashwell arises from her jealousy of me and her, and my neglect of her, which indeed is true, and I am to blame." Jealousy on both sides was intolerable; constraint, suspicion, and self-pity led to endless wrangling, so that Pepys wrote wearily, "It troubles me to see that every small thing is enough now-a-days to bring a difference between us." The day before Elizabeth left for Brampton the two had a long and serious talk with inconclusive results. "I do see great cause every day," said Pepys, "to curse the time that ever I did give way to the taking of a woman for her, though I could never have a better, and also the letting her learn to dance, by both which her mind is so devilishly taken off her business and minding my occasions, and besides [she] has got such an opinion in her of my being jealous, that it is never to be removed, I fear." Worst of all was the fact that Elizabeth knew of his jealousy. Now she had a deadly weapon against him, and one which, ironically, he had given her himself. His only defense was patience.

On June 14 Elizabeth and Ashwell left for the country, Pepys "kissing her often, and Ashwell once." That night he was lonely and unhappy. He concluded his entry for the day with, "sad for want of my wife, whom I love with all my heart, though of late she has given me some troubled thoughts." Love is a mixture of heaven, hate, and habit; the greatest of these is habit.[19]

But even habit was of little use to Pepys in the critical summer of 1663. A variety of forces—his long suppressed love of pleasure, his too-lean diet of sex, his slow moral decay, the sensuality induced by the Pembleton affair, and now Elizabeth's absence—all combined to push him into lechery. Yet for two weeks after his wife's departure he lived an exemplary life, rising "betimes" (often as early as four o'clock), pursuing the dull routine of business, gathering news, and discussing with his friend Commissioner Coventry the folly and knavery of his other colleagues. Since he had taken an oath to refrain from plays until Christmas, he had no safe amusements to divert him. Time hung on his hands, and the erotic excitement of the Pembleton affair found no normal outlet. Once he confessed, "I have used of late, since my wife went, to make a bad use of my fancy with whatever woman I have a mind to, which I am ashamed of, and shall endeavour to do so no more." Surely Lady Castlemaine, who had "all the tricks of Aretin that are to be practised to give pleasure," had her place in his imaginary revels![20]

It is possible that Betty Lane also figured in his fancy, although he had had very little to do with her in the three years since he had found her "not unfree to take" his dallying in his empty house in Axe Yard. He must have seen her almost daily. She kept a haberdasher's shop in Westminster Hall, Red William's grand old banqueting hall which in the seventeenth century was a place of resort for all London. Near the entrance to the cavernous building was the Court of Common Pleas; at the far end were the Courts of Chancery and the King's Bench, side by side. All around the walls were the booths of stationers, booksellers, milliners, haberdashers, and sellers of toys and trifles. "On your left hand," said a

contemporary, "you have a nimble-tongued painted sempstress, with her charming treble, inviting you to buy some
of her knick-knacks; and on your right a deep-mouthed crier,
commanding impossibilities, *viz.*, silence to be kept among
women and lawyers." All the world wandered in and out in
a tumult of "clamour, squalling, and bawling." The Hall was
a popular place for assignations, and a gallant without a lady
was likely to find some "painted sempstress" accommodating.[21]

Betty Lane was no child, but the chances are that she was
much younger than Pepys. She was coarsely pretty, buxom
and earthy, a free-hearted girl whose chastity one had to take
on trust. She was much sought after by gallants, one or two
of whom had proposed marriage. But she was still single, and
her family seems to have consisted only of a younger sister,
Doll, who later played a minor role in Mr. Pepys' private
life.

On June 29 Pepys was in the Hall on business. That done,
he started to leave, but catching sight of Betty at her booth
he decided on impulse to try the substance instead of the
shadow. After some good-natured banter, she agreed to meet
him at a near-by wine-house for dinner. There he took her
into a private room, ordered lobster and wine, and made love
to her, kissing her and tousing [handling] "her all over, making her believe how fair and good a skin she has, and indeed
she has a very white thigh and leg, but monstruous fat." Betty
enjoyed his caresses, which were made easy by the feminine
clothing of the period; loose smock, low-cut gown, and full
petticoats offered few obstacles to roving hands. How far he
might have gone with her he did not know; today he was
content to feel his way. Pleased with his game, he failed to
notice that the room had a window on the street. "Somebody," he wrote later, "having seen some of our dalliance,
called aloud in the street, 'Sir, why do you kiss the gentle-

woman so?' and flung a stone at the window." That ended
the session.

For the moment Pepys' libido was dulled if not sated.
Betty went complacently back to her booth, and Pepys to his
office and the daily routine. For the next few days he trod
the dreary treadmill, hearing occasionally from Brampton,
playing a little on the viol, helping Will Hewer with his
Latin, and sporting in his fancy at night. The boy, Will
Wayneman, had run away, to escape a whipping, and only
Pepys, Hewer, and the cook-maid, Hannah, were left in the
big house. It was a cold, wet summer, with very few chances
for exercise and outings. Life was dreadfully dull.[22]

Pepys was bored and restless, weary of work and eager for
pleasure. If he had wanted only sex he could have gone back
to Fleet Alley and taken his chances with strumpets and
venereal disease. Other men did so—respectable gentlemen
and noble lords—and made light of the usual consequences:
the mercury treatment, "diet drink," and sweating tubs
which were supposed to cure "the pox." One was hardly
considered a man until he had contracted the pox at least
once, and "pox on it" was a common oath among gentlemen.
But Pepys was too cautious to risk disease.

Probably he did not know himself exactly what he wanted:
sex, excitement, gaiety, romance, or a combination of all.
(What he needed was a long vacation.) He tells us the results
of his thoughts, but not the processes; his actions this rainy
summer seem to have resulted more from whim than plan.
So, ten days after his tousing bout with Betty Lane, he went
out in a heavy shower to a little alehouse near Blackfriars,
and there, on impulse, kissed three or four times the maid of
the house, a pretty, modest lass, "and, God forgive me, had
a mind to something more." Later that day, at loose ends and
still in a ruttish mood, he remembered that some time ago a

certain Mrs. Bagwell, wife of a carpenter in the Navy Yard
at Deptford, had called upon him to ask a favor for her husband. Whatever it was, he had granted it, because Mrs.
Bagwell was a very pretty young woman. Suddenly he decided
to go downriver to Deptford and muster the yard, "pur-
posely," he said, "God forgive me, to find out Bagwell . . .
that I might have some occasion of knowing him and forcing
her to come to the office again." He would have denied indignantly that he had anything evil in mind. All he wanted—he
would have said at this stage in his apprenticeship—was
liberty to kiss and dally. Yet he knew now that he could
touse Betty Lane as much as he pleased. Was he seeking something which he felt vaguely had passed him by, something
visionary and strange, some lyric love, half angel and half
whore, someone like Lady Castlemaine? If so, he never found
her.

By land it was only four miles to Deptford from London
Bridge. Often Pepys walked the distance, or took a boat to
Redriffe on the south bank where the river began a great
loop to the north, and thence cut across on a footpath through
the fields. It was much longer down the winding, rain-swept
river, but the ebbing tide lent speed to the boat. Deptford
was a pretty little village: a church and a cluster of tree-shel-
tered houses along the waterfront and around the King's
Yard; a sprinkling of cottages inland; and a few country
mansions, notably Sayes Court, owned by the virtuoso, John
Evelyn. Pepys mustered the yard (called all the workmen together) and found Bagwell, as he had hoped. After the muster
the young carpenter hurried home and back with his wife
to thank the great Mr. Pepys for his former kindness. Pepys
was pleased with pretty Mrs. Bagwell. "I spoke little to her,"
he said, "but shall give occasion for her coming to me."

Unfortunately, no occasion appeared, and there was little

sustenance in merely looking at a pretty face now and then
in the course of official visits to Deptford. Pepys saw the Bagwells twice more that summer. Once at their urgent invitation he visited their little house, drank wine with them, and
kissed the pretty wife, "a virtuous, modest woman." On another occasion they waylaid him to beg his help in getting
Bagwell a better appointment, "which," he said, "I shall
pretend to be willing to do for them, but my mind is to
know his wife a little better." But this could be only in the
dim, unlikely future. Meanwhile Pepys' hunger for erotic
pleasure was pressing, and the nightly play of fancy was not
enough.[23]

Everything conspired to increase his appetite. Wherever
he went he found pretty women with enticing ways and
bosoms fashionably bared or visible through neckerchiefs of
transparent lawn. The beauties of the Court were the most
tempting of all, and the farthest from his reach. One day at
Whitehall he watched the King and Queen with the "Ladies
of Honour" returning from a gallop in Hyde Park. All the
ladies seemed beautiful to Pepys, even the toothy little Queen
in her "white laced waistcoat and a crimson short pettycoat,
and her hair dressed à la negligence." Prettiest of all was
Mistress Frances Stuart "with her hat cocked and a red plume,
with her sweet eye, little Roman nose, and excellent *taille*."
The King was supposed to be in love with her (rumor said
that she was his mistress), and for the moment, approving
his Majesty's choice, Pepys was false to his own true love,
Lady Castlemaine. That night when he went to bed he be-
trayed her grossly, fancying himself "to sport with Mrs.
Stewart with great pleasure."[24]

It was a far cry from Maids of Honor to Betty Lane, but
in Pepys' hungry mood a chicken on the table was better than
peacocks in the park. On July 15, after his office work was

done, he went by water to Westminster Hall. "God forgive me," he said, "[I] had a mind to have got Mrs. Lane abroad, or fallen in with any woman else, in that hot humour." But Betty could not leave her stall, and he met no other light of love fit for his purpose. He went home in a sad state, yet grateful that he had not fallen in with any company "to occasion spending time and money." That night when he went to bed he drifted in his fancy back to Whitehall and sported with the Queen!

Three days later he was at Westminster Hall again, this time to pick up some bands (collars) ordered from Mrs. Lane. While she went to fetch them from the starchers, Pepys chatted with little Betty Howlett, the daughter of a neighboring haberdasher, who was growing up fast and seemed likely to become "a mighty handsome wench." She was so like the Elizabeth St. Michel of eight years ago that he jestingly called her his "wife," adding to himself, "I could love her very well." In his mood of the moment he could have made love to a statue.

Betty Lane returned with the news that the bands were not yet done and accepted Pepys' invitation to go to the Crown Tavern in Palace Yard. There they had a cozy dinner and a bottle of wine, with kisses for dessert. Betty's plump body gave promise of pneumatic bliss; she allowed full freedom to Pepys' roving hands, and docilely used her own hands as he bade her, but, in spite of strong temptation, she still refused him "the last thing of all." Pepys toused and tumbled her until his bands were ready and then walked home— nearly three miles—arriving "all in a sweat with my tumbling of her and walking." That night as he set down the details of the episode he was heartily ashamed of his lechery and resolved never to engage with Betty again.[25]

He stuck to this resolution for a fortnight, a dull period

highlighted only by a pleasant week-end trip to Epsom in fine weather with John Creed, Deputy-Treasurer of the Fleet. The outing cost him twenty shillings, a justifiable expense, he thought, since it was for his health. (Betty Lane was cheaper and more fun.) But the holiday excursion failed to satisfy his deeper needs. On August 4 he went in search of Mrs. Lane, or any other light lady with whom he could be merry in his fashion. He found none ("blest be God," he said), and went home to have supper with his brother John, who had come to London for a visit.[26]

The next afternoon he tried Mrs. Lane again and found her free to join him in food and games. By agreement they met at Westminster Stairs, took a boat across the river, and walked to the King's Head Tavern overlooking Lambeth Marsh. Pepys was learning to seek out taverns where he would not be known.

After a variety of meats and drinks, said Pepys, "I did so touse and handle her! but could get nothing more from her though I was very near it; but as wanton and bucksome as she is she dares not adventure upon the business [a seventeenth-century euphemism for coition], in which I very much commend and like her." Still, erotic play was fun, and Pepys thoroughly enjoyed his outing. In a great sweat with his tousing and tumbling, he took a coach home, and spent the evening with his brother John discussing Des Carte's philosophy.

It was not entirely for her virtue that Pepys commended Betty. A prudent man himself, he admired prudence in others, even when it cost him consummation. Although with Betty he had no fear of the pox, there was always the chance of pregnancy. He wanted his fun, but he had no mind to pay for the support of a bastard.

Pepys' season of sports a-field ended on August 12 when

Elizabeth came home without consulting her husband and with only two days' notice. With John in the house there were not enough beds, and Pepys had to scurry out and buy one. Moreover, because he had planned to have all his floors relaid, Elizabeth's presence at this time was most inconvenient. He was annoyed and apprehensive. During the summer word had reached him of quarrels between Elizabeth, her maid, and the family at Brampton. Elizabeth had written that on one occasion Ashwell had given her "the lie to her teeth." When the mistress had boxed the maid's ears for impertinence, Ashwell had had the temerity to strike back.[27]

Pepys' fears were justified: Elizabeth's first words were complaints about his family and Ashwell. He did his best to soothe her, was very kind and loving, and at last took her off to bed where he "entertained her with great content." But the next morning she proposed seriously that Ashwell be dismissed at once. Pepys insisted on hearing the girl's side of the quarrel. After a judicious weighing of the evidence he concluded, "I do perceive she [Ashwell] has received most base usage from my wife, which my wife sillily denies, but it is impossible the wench could invent words and matter so particularly, against which my wife has nothing to say but flatly to deny, which I am sorry to see, and blows to have passed, and high words even at Hinchingbrooke House among my Lady [Sandwich's] people; of which I am mightily ashamed."

To make matters worse, John Pepys, senior, who had come to town with Elizabeth and was staying at Tom's house, was so bitter at his daughter-in-law that Pepys had a deal of trouble persuading him to come to dinner. It was evident that Elizabeth had behaved very badly at Brampton, quarreling with everyone in sight. But there was nothing Pepys could do; right or wrong, she was his wife and he had to stand by her. Gloomily he wrote, "I find my wife has got too great head to be brought down soon, nor is it possible with any convenience to keep Ashwell longer, my wife is so set and convinced, as she was with Sarah, to make her appear a Lyer in every small thing that we shall have no peace while she stays." Two days later, very reluctantly, he gave Ashwell notice to find another place.[28]

Life became still more irksome when Pembleton, the dancing-master, appeared at church again, reviving all Pepys' old jealousy. He even came to the house one day while the carpenters were at work and all was dirt and confusion, to see if Elizabeth wanted more dancing lessons. Pepys got rid of him in a hurry, but the jealousy lingered on. One Sunday, when Pepys was at church alone, he saw Pembleton come in, look about the congregation as if seeking somebody, and leave. Pepys was on pins and needles until the service ended, but when he got home at last he found "all well and no sign of anybody being there." Pleasantly relieved, he spent the rest of the day "with great content playing and dallying" with Elizabeth.[29]

There were a few such moments of felicity in the late summer, but there were also frequent quarrels, heart-burnings, and domestic problems. Elizabeth was often tired and peevish with all the work she had to do cleaning up after the carpenters, and once she accused her husband of constantly making improvements in the house only to "keep her within and from minding her pleasure." There was just enough truth in the accusation to hurt. Hannah, the cook-maid, was charged with theft, and left "in a huff." Three days later a parish child, Jinny, was hired. After she had been cleansed of her lice and dressed in new clothes, she promptly ran away. Susan the Second, another little girl, replaced her, and, after Ashwell left on August 25, was for a week the only domestic in the household. Mr. Pepys had to shop for his dinner himself, "having never a maid to do it." For sixpence he bought a prime leg of beef, and Elizabeth agreed that it was well worth the money! On August 31 a new chambermaid, Jane Gentleman (Jane the Second), came to relieve the situation.[30]

In mid-September an episode on the road to Brampton brought Pepys and his wife close together for a moment. For Pepys it was a business trip, but at supper the night before his departure he said casually, "Well! shall you and I never travel together again?" Elizabeth took this as an offer, and the next day she jogged along contentedly with the party bound for Brampton. At Ware, as the result of drinking cold beer when she was over-hot with riding, she became deathly sick, and her husband was beside himself with fear. "I thought she would have died," he said, "and so in great horror, and having a great tryall of my true love and passion for her, called the mayds and mistress of the house, and so with some strong water [brandy], and after a little vomit, she came to be pretty well again." But Pepys soon forgot the incident, and for the remainder of the expedition, although Elizabeth was occasionally "good company," for the most part she was just an encumbrance.[31]

Even though he now had his wife to turn to, Pepys' summer of libertine apprenticeship was not yet ended. For more than a month he was continent, and early in September, when Betty Lane greeted him in Westminster Hall and hinted that she would like to have his company again, he said, with a touch of his old austerity, "methinks if she were very modest, considering how I tumbled and tost her, she should not." But most of the pressures upon him were still operating, his home was not a happy place, and he found it hard to give up the excitement of stolen kisses and dangerous caresses. He took another walk through Fleet Alley one day "out of an itch to look upon the sluts there," but he found them entirely too sluttish for his taste. His urge to sport with buxom Betty ("which is my great vanity upon me at present," he said) grew upon him daily. Twice that September he hunted for her vainly in Westminster Hall. On the third try (telling Elizabeth that he had to go to Deptford) he found her, took her again to the King's Head in Lambeth, wined and dined her, and afterwards sported with her beside a window with a broken pane through which a cold wind blew. "Did what I would with her," he said, "but only the main thing, which she would not consent to, for which God be praised."

That night, when he got home late after writing letters at his office and found Elizabeth still hard at her house-cleaning, his conscience smote him for abusing "so good a wretch." It was only God's justice, he reflected, "to make her bad with me for my wronging of her, but I do resolve never to do the like again." Three days later he came down with a bad cold in his head and ear, "which God Almighty in justice did give me while I sat lewdly sporting with Mrs. Lane the other day with the broken window in my neck." God tempers the wind to the shorn lamb, but not to the wolf.[32]

# V

# Wives and Maids

## 1663
## 1664

For THREE MONTHS Pepys feared God and honored the King by working for him—taking time out in October for a bout with colic and constipation. His virtue won him increased credit, responsibility, and cash. Discovering that most of the tradesmen and officials who dealt with the Navy Office were glad to pay for favors received, he worked out his own code of honest graft. Too cautious (and, indeed, too honest) to sell his favors in advance, he refused to be, as he put it, "so squeamish as not to take people's acknowledgement where I had the good fortune by my pains to do them good and just offices." If the acknowledgement was slow to come, he was quick to hint. His savings mounted so rapidly that by the end of 1663 he was worth in money only, not counting the value of his household goods, "above eight hundred pounds."

He wanted to save more, but in October he came to a compromise with Jasper and Thomas Trice, paying them one hundred pounds to drop their suit against the Brampton estate. Then he had to spend a good deal on his beloved house, on clothes for himself (fifty-five pounds in October), and even on clothes for Elizabeth (twelve pounds). He was vexed to see his neighbor, Lady Batten, in a velvet gown, when he could not afford to dress Elizabeth in such luxury, but Batten, he argued, had "a good estate besides his office" as Surveyor of the Navy. Pepys could easily justify spending so much money on himself: his old clothes were so shabby that he had been "forced to sneak like a beggar." Now when he went abroad he was spruce and fine in a black cloth suit trimmed with scarlet ribbons, a black cloak lined with velvet, and a new beaver hat. This was as it should be; he had to face the world every day and put up a front, dressing like a gentleman, while Elizabeth went out so rarely that one good gown was enough. In November, when Pepys had his hair cut short and bought a periwig, his excuse for the expense was not comfort (like most men of his time he suffered from lice and nits) but that gentlemen were now wearing periwigs, and he had to be in the mode. The brown, curly wig, flowing to his shoulders, made such a change in his appearance that the Duke of York insisted he hardly knew him.[1]

There were other little changes that winter. For one, the household in Seething Lane became overwhelmingly feminine. Pepys had refused to take the runaway Will Wayneman back, even though the boy's sister Jane came to plead for him, and he had no new boy in mind. In October his personal clerk, Will Hewer, ordinarily a steady, sober fellow, suddenly began taking an interest in the maids, corrupting them "by his idle talk and carriage." For their protection and his he had to be got out of the house, although Pepys begrudged the twenty pounds a year for his maintenance elsewhere. On November 14, with expressions of regret on both sides, Hewer left to take lodgings nearby in the house of Mrs. William Mercer. Now Pepys was the only man in his house. At the end of the year his household consisted of his wife; a pretty chambermaid, Jane Gentleman; a good-natured cook-maid, Besse; and the "little girle," Susan. The whole family slept on the third floor, Elizabeth and Samuel in their fine new "red chamber" with adjoining dressing rooms, and the maids close by. Pepys bought a bell to hang by his bedchamber door to wake the maids in the morning. The first time Elizabeth used it, the girls slept placidly through its clamor. Pepys bought a bigger bell.[2]

Without Mary Ashwell life was dull; there was no music and little laughter, but at least Elizabeth was not tempted to expensive pleasures. Gradually Pepys wore her down and brought her into subjection again. Once in October she began to whine about her lonely life, but this complaint, Pepys noted sagely, came as usual from "her lack of something to do, for while she was busy she never, or seldom, complained." He exerted himself to keep her busy, and even persuaded her to take up the study of arithmetic, with himself as tutor. The project lasted some two months, during which she learned to do simple addition, subtraction, and multiplication. Then she grew bored with numbers, as she did with anything requiring mental effort.[3]

There were a few quarrels, one a truly violent battle in early November. Obsessed by her belief that all maids were liars, Elizabeth announced triumphantly that she had caught Jane in a fib. When her husband disagreed, high words followed on both sides. At last Pepys retreated to his study with Elizabeth close on his heels, spitting out the venom of a neglected wife—"calling me perfidious and man of no conscience, whatever I pretend to, and I know not what, which troubled me mightily, and though I would allow something to her passion, yet I see again and again that she spoke but somewhat of what she had in her heart." But Pepys was learning husbandly wisdom; he kept his own temper, and gradually Elizabeth quieted down. That night, "though we went to bed with discontent, she yielded to me and began to be fond, so that willing myself to peace, we did before we sleep become very good friends, it being past 12 o'clock, and so with good hearts and joy to rest." The double bed has saved many a marriage.[4]

Moments of pleasurable union were few. One reason for their rarity this winter was the recurrence of Elizabeth's old abscess. At first her surgeon, Thomas Holyard, looked grave, and talked of an operation, but Elizabeth was so terrified at the prospect that he decided a "fomentation," although slower working, would do. From mid-November to Christmas Elizabeth was a semi-invalid. Deprived of the satisfactions of sex, Pepys found compensation in peace. He spent as much time with his "poor wife" as he could, dining at her bedside, telling her the news of the day, or teaching her arithmetic. With his fortunate gift for living only in the present he was able to report one day, when Elizabeth was practically recovered, how pleased the two were "with one another's company, and in general enjoyment one of another, better we think than most couples do." Both could be good company when they had nothing to fight about.[5]

The chances are that all through the autumn Pepys' libido was buried under the weight of his many cares. The period of Elizabeth's illness happened to coincide with his estrangement from his patron, Lord Sandwich. Forgetting his quality, the noble earl had formed a liaison with a woman of low degree, Mrs. Betty Becke of Chelsea. The Court gossips and scandalmongers (who would have approved an affair with a lady of quality) were amused that my lord had fallen so low as to lie with "a common courtizan." Much more important was the fact that by neglecting his business and his attendance at Court (cardinal crimes in everyone's eyes) the besotted earl was jeopardizing his career and the welfare of his family.

On November 17, after long deliberation, Pepys sent his patron a dignified letter of warning and advice. This was not a case of the pot calling the kettle black: Pepys' concern was for appearances, not morality. He had a stake in Sandwich's career. He was not yet strong enough to stand on his own bottom, and if the earl fell completely out of favor with the King, Pepys would be left exposed to the slings and arrows of greedy place-hunters. Moreover, Sandwich was Pepys' debtor in the sum of seven hundred pounds!

When he received the letter, Sandwich was furious, and for a while it seemed that Pepys had suffered the loss of his patron's favor. But the letter got results: Sandwich accepted his advice and deserted the Chelsea "slut." After some weeks of assiduous, humble courtship, Pepys felt safe again.[6]

Pepys' own lust may have been buried, but it still panted after Betty Lane. He could hardly wait until his oaths were out and he could enjoy at least a brief period of plays and pleasures. At Westminster Hall one December day he met Mr. Hawley, formerly his fellow clerk in the Exchequer and for three years Betty Lane's suitor. Pepys encouraged him to press his suit, "while God knows," he said, "I had a roguish meaning in it." Like cynical Dorimant, in Etherege's *The Man of Mode*, he knew that marriage was a great corrupter of maids. Anyway, he felt sure that some day he would overcome Betty's resistance, and conception would be no blessing if she was still unmarried. Pepys did not know that he was sterile. Once in a long while his wife awakened his dormant hopes of having a child of his own. One morning Elizabeth "was mighty earnest with me," he said, "to persuade me that she should prove with child since last night, which, if it be, let it come, and welcome." As usual Elizabeth was mistaken.[7]

With the dawn of 1664, Pepys' vows ended, and he turned happily to fun and games. On Friday and Saturday, January 1 and 2, he took his wife to the first plays they had seen in more than six months. Stimulated by the holiday spirit, the music, and the pretty, impudent actresses, his love of pleasure came back in full force. From plays to erotic dallying was an easy step; on Monday he ran to Westminster Hall to seek out Betty Lane. Failing to find her, he—or rather his sober self—rejoiced; but his lustful urge brought him back again on the following Saturday. This time he found her free for an outing, and after the usual badinage he took her to the Bell Tavern in King Street for food and fondling. But with Betty the moon was in the ascendant, and Venus could not shine. "Could not do as I used to do," said Pepys, "yet nothing but what was honest. . . ."

A week later he tried again, and this time achieved "the main thing." The details of the meeting are hidden behind his editors' Three Dots, but the result is clear enough. His entry for the day concludes, "So home to supper and to bed, with my mind un peu troubled pour ce que fait today, but I hope it will be la dernier de toute ma vie."

The sudden shift to French, the language of love, was not simply for concealment; anyone able to read Pepys' cipher was likely to understand French. It was as if, in the revulsion of satiety, his sober self, then dominant, could not bear to discuss the subject in plain English. We see him late at night in the quiet of his study, in a shaggy purple gown with gold buttons and loop lace, his pen poised over a page in his journal in the light of a flickering candle. Now he is Pepys the diarist, the meticulous, objective recorder of events, quite a different man from the amorous fellow who toused, struggled, sweated, and finally consummated that afternoon in the plump arms of buxom Betty Lane. Pepys the recorder, the respectable businessman, can indeed hope devoutly and without hypocrisy that his first adventure in adultery will be the last in all his life—but Pepys the successful libertine, forced into silence by the sputtering quill, knows better.[8]

In a world without contraceptives, fear follows on the heels of fornication. Pepys discovered that lifting a petticoat was no light matter. For two worrisome weeks he avoided Westminster Hall. At last, when business took him there, he sought out Mrs. Lane, "of whom," he said, "I doubted to hear something of the effects of our last meeting about a fortnight or three weeks ago." To his great relief, Betty said nothing to confirm his fears. All was well this time.[9]

If his conscience troubled him at all, he made no mention of the fact; his concern seems to have been only for a possible by-blow. His natural caution taking control, he decided that for his sake Betty must marry. (He never for a moment doubted that she would remain easy of access, married or single.) Although she had once told him "flatly no, she could not love" Mr. Hawley, her faithful suitor, Pepys started a vigorous campaign to bring the two to the altar. Hawley was eager, of course, but Betty, who seemed at first willing enough, ended by doggedly refusing to consider him. Late in February Pepys gave up his campaign. For his own safety he resolved "to avoid occasion of further ill" with Betty unless she married, and took a silent oath never to be alone with her for more than fifteen minutes at a time.[10]

Although it cost him some pain, he kept his stern vow, seeing Betty Lane only twice in the following four months, and always in company. One day at her lodgings he ate a lobster with her. Fortunately "her body was out of temper for any dalliance," but to avoid even the appearance of evil Pepys kept her landlord Mr. Swayne and his wife in the room.

On another occasion he took her to the Swan Tavern in the Palace Yard, where, although he had a great mind "to be playing the fool with her," he was careful to keep the chamber door open and to call in, one after the other, the master and mistress of the house to drink with him. "So that," he said, "as I did nothing so they are able to bear witness that I had no opportunity there to do anything." His caution was not excessive; he knew his amorous disposition all too well. He knew, too, that a paternity suit could ruin his reputation for respectability, ruin his credit with the Sandwich family, and perhaps—because clerks dared not imitate openly the manners of their betters—could cost him his job. As for Elizabeth—but the mind shrinks from the prospect of her fury![11]

Except for an occasional play and his stolen moments with Betty, Mr. Pepys stuck to his business all through the winter. Now and then his overactive libido gave him some bad moments. For example, one night from his coach going up Ludgate Hill he saw two gallants and their footmen tugging at a pretty wench, a seller of laces and ribbons who had often attracted Pepys' eyes. "They seek to drag her by some force," he said, "but the wench went, and I believe had her turn served, but, God forgive me! what thoughts and wishes I had of being in their place." Of course, gallants—gentlemen of quality, estate, and leisure—were privileged as Pepys was not.[12]

In January Pepys rewrote and swore to his rules against wine, plays, and costly pleasures. This time he vowed to see not more than one play a month at the public theatres until he had spent a total of fifty shillings—enough for ten plays for two people. If and when his savings mounted to one thousand pounds, he would reconsider this arrangement. After these commendable decisions he returned to his work with such diligence that by the last of February he was worth "eight hundred and ninety and odd pounds, the greatest sum I ever knew." Part of this sudden rise in fortune came from his salary, but more from grateful tradesmen. The great timber merchant Sir William Warren, for instance, sent him a pair of gloves for Elizabeth wrapped up in a paper with "forty pieces in good gold." Pepys opened the package in the privacy of his study, joyfully hid the gold, and gave Elizabeth the gloves. He was so happy that he could hardly eat his dinner. He had good reason to celebrate his thirty-first birthday on February 23, finding himself "in a fair way of coming to a better esteem and estate in the world" than he had ever hoped for.[13]

Although a golden sun continued to shine upon him, spring brought trouble and grief to Pepys. The unhappiest event of the season was the death on March 15 of his brother, poor, feckless Tom the tailor, who had long been ailing—of a consumption, said some, while others whispered "the pox." Pepys' grief was genuine but short-lived. It lasted through all the painful arrangements: the laying-out; the details of burial in the middle aisle of St. Bride's Church and the sexton's cheerful "I will justle them together but I will make room for him"; and the ordeal of the funeral—one hundred and fifty guests who had "six biscuits a-piece and what they pleased of burnt claret." His grief turned to anger when he learned the full account of Tom's failures and follies. The tailor died intestate, leaving his affairs in confusion, debts amounting to more than his whole estate, and a bastard daughter, an infant named Elizabeth, the survivor of twins begotten on the body of a former maidservant, Margaret.[14]

Pepys was "vexed to think what a rogue" his brother had been, but the news that Tom had fathered a bastard, while unpleasant, disturbed him only because of possible publicity

and expense. Affairs between master and maid were common-
place enough, and so were their biological consequences. The
typical London housemaid was naive, ignorant, and vulnera-
ble. Nine times out of ten she was a homely slut; beauties
rarely grow in slums. Her wages were pitiful, usually three or
four pounds a year plus food, lodging, and weekday clothing.
Since she could never hope to save enough for a dowry, her
only chance of marriage was with a male domestic or some
ne'er-do-well as hard up for a wife as she for a husband. She
was virtually a slave, working from early dawn until the
family retired for the night, and patiently enduring beatings,
kicks, and abuse. Her starved heart snapped at the most per-
functory love-making. "Beware of the solicitations of the
flesh," a contemporary moralist warned her, "for they will
undo you, and though you may have mean thoughts of yourself, and think none will meddle with such as you, it is a mistake; hungry dogs will eat dirty puddings; and I myself have
known a brave gallant to fall foul with the wench of the
scullery, when some others would have hazarded their life
for one sole enjoyment of that incomparable lady his wife,
[whom] he so ingratefully slighted." It was really unsporting
to seduce a housemaid, but poor, foolish Tom, wifeless and
tempted, had seduced his Margaret ("an ugly jade!" cried
Pepys) to the shame of his family. It was truly a roguish
business.

Margaret had disappeared. The infant Elizabeth, at the
cost of five pounds, had been committed to the care of one
Cave, a poor pensioner of St. Bride's parish. Pepys made no
attempt to see the child or to provide for her. Let the parish
raise her; he was concerned only to avoid expense and scandal. He was no more brutal than other men of his day.
Usually gentlemen provided for their own by-blows only
when forced to do so by the authorities; it would have been

sentimental and quixotic for Pepys to subsidize his brother's bastard. In his view she was no kin to him and had no place in his world. Moses himself had declared that "a bastard shall not enter into the congregation of the Lord," and what was good enough for Moses was good enough for Pepys.[15]

In addition to Tom's tangled affairs, most of which fell, as usual, on his busy brother's shoulders, Pepys had troubles at home and abroad. Jane Gentleman left the Pepys' service, Besse was promoted to chambermaid, and little Susan did the cooking until June, when Jane Birch (Jane the Third) came as cook-maid. The business of the Navy Office grew daily more complex; the incompetence of Penn, Batten, and Minnes was a constant annoyance, and there was serious talk of war with the Dutch. The merchants of London were eager for it, but, said Pepys, "for my part I dread it." With the addition of his work for the Tangier Commission, and now for the Corporation of the Royal Fishery to which he had recently been appointed, Pepys was so occupied with public affairs that he could hardly find time for his private accounts. His eyes were beginning to suffer from the long hours he spent writing by candle light. But his hoard grew steadily larger; at the end of May he was worth nine hundred and thirty pounds.[16]

As usual, Elizabeth, now healthy and restive again, was the domestic storm center. At twenty-six she was still a great beauty (in spite of the occasional loss of a tooth), and Pepys lived in daily fear of marauding gallants. Early in the spring her indiscreet conduct with Will Hewer roused Pepys' jealousy, a demon which could not be exorcized even by his frank admission that he had no real grounds for suspicion, nor could he, miserable sinner that he was, "expect her being so true to me as I would have her." He continued jealous of Pembleton, too, discouraging Elizabeth from going to church lest she see him there. "God help me!" cried Pepys, "this is nothing but my ridiculous folly."[17]

He could guard against the enemy from without, but he never suspected his uncle (his father's half-brother), old William Wight, a prosperous fishmonger whose children had all died young. Uncle Wight visited Elizabeth time and again when her husband was absent, kissed her earnestly, praised her beauty, and promised wonders in his will if she should ever give her husband an heir. One day he proposed co-operating with her to get a child. "For all he knew," he said, "the thing was lawful." He offered to make the child his heir and to give Elizabeth in advance five hundred pounds in either money or jewels. If Pepys ever feared that his wife might open her lap to saint-seducing gold, her conduct should have reassured him: she gave the lecherous old fellow "a very warm answer," turned him out of doors, and sent for her husband at once. But since there was still a chance that Mr. Wight might remember his nephew in his will, Pepys curbed his anger and decided to say nothing. He was cool to his uncle for months.[18]

Elizabeth was hardly to blame for her beauty, and, although she was often flirtatious and indiscreet, she was surely chaste. But her quick temper and sharp tongue were hers to control; she used them as weapons, alternating with tears. When Pepys refused to let her buy lace to decorate an old gown, offering instead to buy her a plain new gown, she flounced away in a pet. By and by, still raging, she went to his office—"and coming to me tells me in a spiteful manner like a vixen and with a look full of rancour that she would go buy a new one and lace it and make me pay for it, and then let me burn it if I would after she had done with it, and so went away in a fury." An hour later, "her stomach coming down," the two were friends again, but Elizabeth got the lace for her old dress. When the gown was finally brought back, "new laced," Pepys, wincing at the cost, admitted that it became Elizabeth nobly.[19]

All through the spring and summer of 1664 Elizabeth fought sporadically against her husband's domination. She discovered a new weapon: whenever she wanted to hurt Pepys she talked of being secretly a Catholic and declared her resolution to die in the Catholic faith. Pepys took her seriously; "indeed," he said, "a small matter, I believe, would absolutely turn her, which I am sorry for." Ordinarily the Pepyses' quarrels would have ended in bedtime love, but that season, at first because Pepys had another siege of colic, then because Elizabeth had a bad cold, they slept in separate rooms. Anger lasted longer. Lying in their lonely beds, husband and wife tasted the sweet poison of self-pity.

According to the seventeenth century, Elizabeth was always at fault. It was her duty to be humble and to submit herself in all things—including religion—to her husband's will and pleasure. When Pepys reproved her or restrained her liberty he was acting as a wise husband should; when he struck her he was only following the common practice of his time. Yet he was always ashamed after he used force. Once when he came home tired and irritated after a frustrating day, he found Elizabeth dressed as if she had been out. He inquired suspiciously; she resented his question and gave him a short answer; he resented her tone and wrung her nose. She burst into tears of pain and rage. Pepys apologized, pretending that he had acted in thoughtless haste.[20]

When Elizabeth rebelled she lost all discretion. After dinner one Sunday with Pepys' friend John Creed as a guest, there was a great dispute over whether or not the Pepyses should go to a christening to which they had been invited. For good reasons of his own, Mr. Pepys decided in the negative. But christenings were jolly occasions, with cakes, wine, and good company, and Elizabeth was already dressed in her best. She proposed going by herself. No, said Pepys, she would stay at home. She complained—still in front of Creed! —that he kept her always within doors. Pepys was vexed "to the guts," but he kept his temper and insisted on obedience. Later, to console her for her lost pleasure, he took her and Creed down to the Halfway House—halfway between Redriffe and Deptford in the peninsula formed by the northward loop of the Thames—"where without any the least cause [Pepys' version!] she had the cunning to cry a great while, and talk and blubber," shaming her husband before his friend. That night Elizabeth was sorry—"coming to my bedside and doing all things to please me, and at last I could not hold out, but seemed pleased, and so parted."[21]

With Pepys it was a matter of principle that he be master, no matter how trivial the issue. When he got home after dinner one day to find that Elizabeth, "of her own accord," had bought a pair of earrings, he was furious. The price, twenty-five shillings, was secondary; the important fact was that his wife had spent money frivolously and without consulting him. Pepys scolded, and Elizabeth retorted with every weapon in her well-stocked arsenal, using language so "foule" that Pepys, who detested loose talk and profanity, was shocked. She even taunted him with their old "differences" when they were first married, knowing how he hated to be reminded of that episode.

Through all the din he made his ultimatum heard: return the pendants or see them destroyed. Then he stormed out of the house, waited until Elizabeth sent her maid to return the earrings, intercepted the messenger and sent her back. Satisfied that Elizabeth acknowledged hs authority, he was content to let her keep the trinkets. But he could not get her foul words out of his mind, and that night, when she came to his bedside repentant and eager to make up, he would not be appeased. He rose the next morning still angry.[22]

What with business, sickness, death, and quarrels, the Pepyses' love life was distinctly minimal. On July 9, two days before Elizabeth was due to leave for a month's stay at Brampton, she tried to make things up to him. "So home," wrote Pepys, "to my wife to supper and to bed, where we have not lain together because of the heat of the weather a good while, but now against her going into the country." There was some thought of a repeat performance the following night, but Pepys was not well "and so had no pleasure at all with my poor wife." The next morning Elizabeth set out for Brampton with her maid Besse, leaving her husband to the care of Susan and Jane Birch—"and my poor wife I shall soon want, I am sure," said Pepys.

He was slow to take illicit advantage of his month of freedom. He had a great deal of routine business on his hands; besides he was negotiating a contract for the victualing of Tangier by which he hoped to make three hundred pounds a year, and he had to defend himself from the anger of Lord Chancellor Clarendon, who objected to having the trees in Clarendon Park chopped down for the use of the Navy. Pepys had thought them royal property; now it appeared that the Chancellor had an interest in them, and he had to apologize as gracefully as he could. Moreover he had no lady of easy virtue in view. (Except, of course, his dream love Lady Castlemaine, "whom I do heartily adore," he sighed.) He had put Betty Lane out of bounds, and the modesty of Mrs. Bagwell, wife of the Deptford carpenter, still daunted him. Yet his long pent-up urge for erotic pleasure was bursting at the seams.[23]

A week after Elizabeth's departure Pepys took one of his

two periwigs to his barber, Jervas, in Palace Yard, Westminster, to have it "cleaned of its nits." Jervas had a very
pretty young maid, Jane Welsh, who had been in his service
for some time. Pepys had often seen her and lusted for her.
She was a "good-natured as well as a well-looked girl," and,
as far as he knew, still a virgin. Pepys liked his women to be
pretty and pliable, but above all he liked the face of innocence—his lyric love should at least look like an angel.

He knew very well that housemaids were dangerous toys.
Occasionally his mouth had watered at one or another of his
own maids—tempting creatures, flitting about the house at
night in their smocks and bare feet—but he was always afraid
to make advances lest the abigail prove honest and tell his
wife. For much the same reason the maids of his friends
and neighbors were taboo; caution was the keynote of Pepys'
amorous campaigns. And if he needed stronger warning of
the danger of meddling with maids, he had it in the example
of his brother Tom.

But today he was at leisure and in a sportive mood; Jane
Welsh was temptingly pretty; and Palace Yard was a safe
three miles from Seething Lane. It was unlikely that Jane
would know anyone in Pepys' circle. Anyway he took the
chance: pretending to send the girl on an errand, he intercepted her en route "and took her into a little alehouse in
Brewers Yard, and there did sport with her, without any
[carnal] knowledge of her though, and a very pretty innocent girl she is."

This was a harmless enough beginning, and it is quite
likely that at first Pepys intended no more than a little dalliance with the barber's wench. Perhaps he promised himself
more pleasure with Jane in the near future; if so, an item of
news two days later changed his plans: he heard that Betty
Lane was married. This was "great news" indeed! Now his

oath against being alone with her was pointless; if the new Mrs. Martin became pregnant by his endeavors, she had a husband to legitimize the child. "I must have a bout with her very shortly," Pepys exulted, "to see how she finds marriage."

At Betty's lodgings the very next day he had his bout— kissing and tousing only—and met the brand-new husband, who came in by and by. Mr. Martin, a ship's purser, seemed to be "a sorry, simple fellow." Pepys suspected that he had married Betty only "to make a prize of her." If so, he was due for a shock: she had only her shop and her trade. Apparently she intended to keep on working. Marriage had not changed wanton Betty; privately she urged her lover to set a time for a meeting next week when Mr. Martin would be out of town.

But Pepys could not contain himself so long. Once started on a course of erotic pleasure he could not check his headlong rush. On Saturday afternoon, "in an idle and wanton humour," he roamed through Fleet Alley again, and was strongly tempted to accost a pretty wench who stood in the doorway of a bawdy-house. Instead he took coach for Westminster Hall, found Betty at her booth, and "plotted with her to go over the water." At their old trysting place, the King's Head Tavern near Lambeth Marsh, he plied her with food and drink (at a cost of five or six shillings), kissed and toused at will, and had his "pleasure of her twice."

He should have been sated, but he had been continent far too long; his lustful cravings were still unappeased. Setting Betty back on the Westminster shore, he journeyed a-foot to Fleet Alley. "Not knowing how to command myself," he said, he entered the house he had marked down. If the place was typical Pepys found himself in a dirty-windowed room, flavored with the stink of stale beer and sour humanity, furnished with tables, chairs, and a handful of fire in a rusty grate, and presided over by a slovenly bawd who sold ale, wine, Nantes brandy, and female flesh. But Pepys had eyes only for the prostitute who had caught his fancy, "a most lovely woman," whose nickname, he learned, was Cocky. He spent some time drinking and talking with Cocky, but, either because of his recent exploits with Betty Martin or because he "had no courage to meddle with her for fear of her not being wholesome," he pretended to be too poor to pay her price. After a while he made his escape, walked to his office to write some letters, and then "home and to bed, weary of the pleasure I have had to-day, and ashamed," said his sober self, "to think of it."[24]

For the next few days, with the erotic fever still boiling in his veins, Pepys was torn between conflicting desires. Now that he could have Betty Martin almost at will, he was no longer so ardent for her. Her easy availability made her less desirable, and in post-coital revelation he saw clearly her vulgarity and impudence. She was coarse fare, and only salt desire could make her savory. Although he would never give her up—indeed, she became in effect his steady mistress—she would be thenceforth no more than a "ready" or "convenient" to satisfy his lust.

But the image of innocent Jane Welsh, who was still a romantic mystery, lingered in his mind. When he learned that Jervas himself intended to deliver his de-nitted periwig, Pepys was sorely disappointed. He had hoped that Jane would bring it to him at a time when he could have her in his house alone and try her long-preserved virginity. On the other hand, Cocky of Fleet Alley—the painted face of mercenary vice—was a powerful lure. Whores excited Pepys and frightened him at the same time; danger added spice to wickedness. Perhaps in his heated imagination innocent Jane and wicked Cocky added together to make up his ideal love. Certainly he wanted both, but at this moment Cocky more.

Once again he walked through Fleet Alley past the house where Cocky did business, fearful of being recognized, dreading disease, afraid of the cost, yet almost helpless in the grip of desire. This time his "sense of safety and honour" won, and he went on to Jervas's, where he found a child's funeral in progress and Jane very busy. Four days later a providential rain as he detoured through Fleet Alley on his way home gave him an excuse for seeking shelter in the now familiar bawdy-house. He found Cocky at liberty, but the jade, misled by Pepys' earlier plea of poverty and his present reluctance to show the color of his money, "would not offer to invite me to do anything," he said, "but on the contrary saying she had no time," cooled his ardor. Pepys spent an hour with her, talking and drinking, and saw how she managed to increase the reckoning "by still calling for things that it come to be six or seven shillings presently." Betty Martin was safer and much cheaper.[25]

On August 6 Elizabeth returned from Brampton and, although Pepys was very glad to see her, he realized that his holiday was over. He returned to his usual round of work, visits, a play now and then, squabbling with his colleagues, and preparing for a war with the Dutch. At the end of July he had reached and passed his thousand-pound goal and was clearly "worth one thousand and fourteen pounds." Prosperity encouraged him to expand his household again. Late in August he hired a new "boy," Tom Edwards, nineteen or twenty years old, an excellent singer who had been trained for four years in the King's Chapel. In September he engaged, as a companion for his wife, Mary Mercer, the pretty seventeen-year-old daughter of Will Hewer's landlady, Mrs. William Mercer, "a decayed merchant's" widow. Mary played the harpsichord and sang fairly well. One night Mr. and Mrs. Pepys, Mercer, and Tom "sat till eleven at night, singing and fiddling." Home became a very pleasant place, and Elizabeth, happy with her new maid, stopped complaining for a while.[26]

But Pepys could not banish the romantic image of Jane Welsh. Even a tavern meeting with Betty Martin in mid-August was no help; he had his "pleasure" of her, but found her an impudent jade, already with child (by her husband), and full of sad stories about worthless Mr. Martin and pleas for the Clerk of the Acts to get him a better place. "But I will have no more to do with her," said Pepys. "Let her brew as she has baked, seeing she would not take my counsel about Hawley."[27]

Twice in late August Pepys made excuses for dropping in at Jervas's, "willing to have any opportunity to speak to Jane," but each time she was either absent or busy. On his third visit early in September he found her free and begged for an assignation. She told him a strange story: her master and mistress, she said, "had a mind to get her a husband," and therefore refused to let her go abroad alone except during sermon time on Sunday afternoon. As always in the presence of beauty, Pepys' common sense deserted him. (In another situation he said once, "a strange slavery that I stand in to beauty, that I value nothing near it.") It did not occur to him to wonder at this curious concern for a mere housemaid, or why the Jervases guarded her so jealously. It was enough that Jane agreed to meet him Sunday afternoon, "come sennight," at Westminster Abbey—an odd place for an assignation but close to Palace Yard and Jervas's shop. From the Abbey Pepys could lead the little housemaid to a nearby tavern or across the river to Lambeth and caress her in privacy. Elated at the prospect of new pleasure, Pepys hurried home, "doing errands by the way."[28]

On the appointed Sunday afternoon (September 11), he walked to Westminster at his usual rapid pace and by three o'clock was at his post in the Abbey cloisters. The waiting lover always dreams, and the flame of desire, fanned by anticipation, burns higher as he waits. But Pepys waited three hours—far too long. At six o'clock, chilled and vexed to the heart, he gave up and headed for home. But he took care to pass by Jervas's on his way, and there at the door of the shop stood the truant Jane. Pepys begged for a drink, and went into the empty house with her. He does not say that he was angry or that he scolded her. She made some sort of an excuse—so trivial that he failed to record it—and promised to meet him in the near future. Completely under her spell, Pepys left her at last, going away like a reluctant schoolboy, "contented," he said, "with my speaking with her." Surely he was in love.[29]

What had started out as a casual affair was becoming a dangerous whirlpool in the subcurrent of Pepys' private life. On Monday he was back at the barber's shop again, dodging in and out until he found Jane alone. In an upper room of the house he "drank with her, and staid two hours with her kissing her, but nothing more." She refused to go out with him that afternoon, but promised to meet him Sunday at the same trysting place. If her strange conduct disturbed him he made no note of the fact; indeed, at this time he was curiously reticent about his feelings toward Jane. Had Betty Martin behaved so capriciously he would have cursed her for an impudent jade, but he had never loved Betty.

Sunday, September 18, was another disappointment. Pepys waited for Jane at the Abbey until five o'clock, and then took his injured pride home to supper and to bed. On Monday he

could hardly wait until he was free to go to Jervas's again.
This time there were no excuses; suddenly Jane was "cold
and not so desirous of a meeting as before." Here Pepys is
oddly laconic; we have to imagine the girl's off-hand dismissal of her gentlemanly suitor, his pleading, and the blow
to his ego. Twice Pepys had been balked of his hopes by a
jilting little maid, who now made it clear that she wanted
nothing to do with him. That night as he recorded the day's
events, his sober self took charge. "It is no matter," he wrote,
"I shall be the freer from the inconvenience that might follow thereof, besides offending God Almighty and neglecting
my business." In failure he turned quite humanly to God.

Condemned to virtue, Pepys did his best to forget Jane
Welsh, seeing her only occasionally at the barber's shop. He
turned again to his wife, and gave her so much attention
that once more she was convinced that she was pregnant.
Pepys no longer cared. "I neither believe nor desire it," he
said, "but God's will be done." Yet, "after all her merry
discourse of being with child," Elizabeth was pathetically
mistaken. Her husband was more interested in property;
making a valiant effort he got back to his "good temper of
business again" with the usual result: at the end of September
in spite of great layings out on clothes, his hoard had
mounted to one thousand two hundred and three pounds,
"for which the Lord's name be praised."[30]

Pepys' life and purse were full enough, but he still yearned
for the barber's wench. Her apparent innocence fascinated
him; her resistance stimulated his desire. Besotted, and blind
to what was going on under his nose, he suffered in silence,
lost to pride and manhood. As the winter drew on he found
new excuses for haunting the barber's shop, where at least he
could see his love ("my Jane," he called her) and sometimes
speak to her. Although there were times when he had some

hopes of her, including two more fruitless Sunday afternoons spent in the cold cloisters of the Abbey, his love still went unrequited.

One day he failed in another attempt to persuade her to an assignation. That night his amorous self broke out in a despairing cry which his recorder self insisted on phrasing in French, "Je avait grande envie envers elle, avec vrai amour et passion." In the crucible of imagination his great desire for her had transmuted lust to true love and passion.[31]

If he had known then the facts he was to learn later, disgust might have saved him many a heartache. Jane had never cared for him. The Jervases were guarding her so closely only to keep her from the embraces of a worthless sweetheart, one Harbing, a poor little fiddler, with whom she was as besottedly in love as Pepys was with her. In spite of their watchfulness, "innocent" Jane had lain several times with her beggarly lover in the barber's house while the family was away—perhaps at those very times when Pepys was waiting and freezing in Westminster Abbey. He had been no more than a stalking-horse for a back-stairs intrigue.[32]

But these revelations were yet to come. In the autumn of 1664 Pepys was restless and emotionally unsatisfied. If he could not have Jane Welsh, there was modest Mrs. Bagwell who came from Deptford time and again to plead for her husband's advancement. She too was pretty, and, because she was a wife, much safer game than a maid. Pepys should have been content with his conquest of Betty Martin, but two beds were better than one.

# VI

# The Carpenter's Wife

$$\frac{1664}{1665}$$

DID PEPYS SEDUCE Mrs. Bagwell? Certainly he thought he did. As with Jane Welsh, her apparent modesty aroused his interest, and her resistance excited him. His success with her at last inflated his male ego. But it is equally possible that it was she who seduced Pepys, with the tacit consent of her husband.

In this affair the conduct of the Bagwell family fits neatly into a well-worn pattern. At the top level of Restoration society almost any nobleman was willing to sacrifice his wife, sister, or daughter on the altar of his own ambition. The husband who held his wife dear and cherished her chastity was remarkable, at least in Court circles. When the Duke of York fell in love with handsome Lady Robartes and wanted to take her for his mistress, the Court was astounded by the reaction of her husband, John, Baron Robartes, "an old, snarling, troublesome, peevish fellow," who selfishly insisted on keeping his wife for his own bed. He refused to bargain, spurning behind-the-scenes offers of the lord lieutenancy of his own county and the profitable management of the Duke's revenues in Ireland, and took his lady off to the wilds of Wales.

On the other hand, Roger Palmer, a well-to-do gentleman with a beautiful wife but no title, showed proper good sense. When Barbara Palmer became the King's mistress, Roger politely bowed out of the picture, and in return the King created him Baron Limerick and Earl of Castlemaine in the peerage of Ireland. Being a King's cuckold was not at all bad when cuckoldom paid off in estates or glittering titles. Of course one might have to acknowledge another man's children, but think of the drudgery saved!

On lesser levels of society many a courtier, officeholder, or mere citizen was willing to imitate his betters and climb to fortune over his wife's prostrate body. Cynical Henry Bulkeley, for example, a mere captain in the Irish Guards when he married Sophia Stuart (Frances Stuart's younger sister), conveniently overlooked his wife's affairs with powerful politicians. In due time—but not because of merit—he became Master of the King's Household and a Groom of the King's Bedchamber. Since the forkèd plague was destiny unshunnable, the wise man accepted his horns and made the best possible use of them. On the lowest level of all, that of the poor craftsman, cuckoldry was a very small matter indeed; virtue was a luxury too dear for hempen homespuns and rude mechanicals. The wives and daughters of the poor were fair game for any gentleman. The humble cuckold had no "honor" to lose, and could only hope to profit from his wife's shame.[1]

Young William Bagwell was a carpenter in the service of the Navy. He was industrious, childless, and poor, but he had a pretty young wife, a pretty little house on the outskirts of Deptford, a fair measure of ability, and a deal of ambition. His first berth seems to have been in the *Dolphin*, a little

5th rate warship of only 149 tons and 16 guns. Since a carpenter's pay varied with the rating of his ship—from two pounds a month in a 5th rate to four pounds in a 1st rate—Bagwell naturally wanted promotion to a bigger ship. But according to the custom of the seventeenth century, promotion went by patronage rather than merit; as Pepys himself once put it, "How little merit do prevail in this world, but only favor"—knowing the right people. The officers of the Naval Commission (among them Mr. Pepys) could bestow favors; ergo, the Bagwells must solicit the kindness of an officer.[2]

At some unspecified time, perhaps early in 1663, Mrs. Bagwell had visited Pepys at his office to ask for and get a small favor for her husband. The Clerk of the Acts never forgot a pretty face. On July 9, 1663, he journeyed down to Deptford to find her and to lay the groundwork of a better acquaintance. He saw her twice more at Deptford that summer; once he visited the Bagwell's little house, drank wine with them, and tasted Mrs. Bagwell's lips. Intending only to have an excuse for the wife to come often to his office, he promised Bagwell a better place in the service.

For the next six months—the autumn and winter of 1663-1664—Pepys recorded nothing about the Bagwells in his journal, yet during those months he was at Deptford a dozen times on business. If the Bagwells sought him out on his visits there, they failed to find him. Had Pepys been more interested in Mrs. Bagwell at the time, he would surely have made some excuse to visit her. The fact that he did not suggests that he was not bent on seduction. Of course, all that winter Betty Lane was much in his mind, and once or twice in his arms. Pepys was still an apprentice libertine; he had yet to discover how much fun it was to play the field.

It seems to have taken the Bagwells all those months to

realize that it was up to them to pursue the Clerk of the Acts and constantly remind him of his off-hand promise. The chances are that they had the counsel of two older people, Mrs. Bagwell's mother ("Bagwell's wife's mother," Pepys called her), and the carpenter's father, Owen Bagwell ("old Bagwell"), foreman of the Deptford Yards. These shadowy figures, who later played disreputable roles in the little comedy, would have been wise in the ways of the world, well aware that the way to promotion was paved with gifts to bureaucrats.[3]

Just as places at Court were bought and sold, so were posts in the civil and military services. The Commissioners of the Navy profited considerably from their powers to appoint and recommend. It was said, for example, that one Mr. Falconer, in order to get his place as Clerk of the Rope Yard at Woolwich, had given two hundred pounds to Commissioner Coventry and a gold watch to Commissioner Sir William Penn. The venality of Surveyor Sir William Batten was notorious. "Hardly anybody goes to see or hath anything to do or hath anything done by Sir W. Batten but it comes with a bribe," Pepys declared indignantly. Yet Pepys himself trafficked in places. John Downing, an anchor smith, gave the Clerk fifty pounds to get him the post of smith in the Navy Yard at Deptford, and one Mr. Viner gave him a diamond ring worth ten pounds as a reward "for helping him to be a purser." In a burst of generosity, Pepys gave the diamond to Elizabeth.[4]

According to his peculiar ethics, Pepys was as honest about place hunters as he was about favor-seeking merchants. He argued that when he secured a post for a good man, both the man and the King were gainers. If the new appointee then gave Mr. Pepys a present, he too was a gainer, and everyone was happy. But he would not recommend the clearly unfit. When Betty Martin was besieging him with requests to get her husband, the purser, a position as lieutenant in the Navy, he was polite but firm; in his opinion Martin was an ass, unfit for command. Pepys' honesty even made him go so far as to refund a gift if something went wrong. After Mr. Downing had been appointed smith at Deptford, he found himself unable to take the position. Pepys gave him back his money, with what agonies we can imagine.[5]

Unfortunately, meritorious though Bagwell was, he had no money; his only wealth was his wife's beauty. Here we must guess at the counsel given by the worldly-wise elders of the family. To judge from their conduct later, they were completely unscrupulous, saying, in effect, that if Mrs. Bagwell was not too nice she could make her husband's fortune. Let her act as suitor for the carpenter's promotion, venturing her person if need be. A few liberties granted to that fine gentleman Squire Pepys might work wonders. If perchance he had a fling at her, what was the harm? No one outside the family would ever know, and young Bagwell could paint his imaginary horns with his wife's guilt. Perhaps, as envoy from Deptford to Seething Lane, Mrs. Bagwell was sent, like a good seventeenth-century ambassador, to lie abroad for the good of her lord and master.

Her diplomatic campaign started on February 27, 1664, when she arrived unexpectedly at Pepys' house "to speak for her husband." The house in Seething Lane was no place for dalliance with Elizabeth hovering about; anyway Mrs. Bagwell was such a modest-seeming young woman that Pepys was daunted. He could not bring himself "to offer anything uncivil to her." Contenting himself with stroking her under the chin, he sent her away with fair promises.

With these the Bagwells were content for three months.

Then, on May 31, Mrs. Bagwell made an ambassadorial call at Pepys' office. This time the Clerk of the Acts had her alone in his inner office "a great while," with every opportunity for tousing and tumbling. But again she seemed so modest that he "durst not offer any courtship to her." In a rare burst of altruism he decided to do her husband a courtesy, not for her sake but for Bagwell's, "a man that deserves very well."

Another three months passed—the summer marked by Pepys' adultery with Betty Martin and his lust for Cocky of Fleet Alley. Without Mrs. Bagwell to prick the sides of his intent he had done nothing for her husband. He had thought of her occasionally, but now his heart was set on Jane Welsh, the barber's wench. On September 7 the persistent envoy called again.

By this time, as the result of his summer experiences, Pepys was becoming skilled at the fine art of venery. Hoping that Mrs. Bagwell would return, he was prepared, the next time she called, "to discourse with her of pleasure," to sound her out, try her modesty with words and please himself with kisses. Although he liked her well enough, he was not in love with her. She was a pretty woman, therefore to be wooed. Unfortunately, visitors interrupted his tête-a-tête before it had fairly begun. Pepys was disappointed. Later that day he consoled himself with a trip to Bartholomew Fair, where he saw the best dancing on the ropes that he had ever seen in his life.

On October 3 Mrs. Bagwell came for the fourth time. Only that morning Pepys had visited elusive Jane Welsh, for whom his heart truly yearned. Transferring his frustrated passion to the carpenter's wife, he took her into his private office and kissed her so ardently that she appeared to be offended. She rebuked him, pointing out that if he treated every female visitor so, it would be a "stain" to him. "But," concluded Pepys that night, "I do not see but what she takes it [the kissing] well enough, though in the main I believe she is very honest"—i.e., virtuous. Perhaps she was.

She was back again on October 20, driven, we have to assume, by the family need for Bagwell's promotion. But she must have felt some measure of erotic excitement. She was an inexperienced young woman, stirred by her first timid ventures into the wicked world of London and by the flattering attentions of a gentleman. For two months Pepys had been continent, building up his appetite; Mrs. Bagwell arrived at the biological moment. Ignoring diplomatic immunity, he took her into his office, kissed and caressed her, and did as much tousing as the place permitted. What with his good words "and promises of getting her husband a place" she began to yield a little, to be "every day more and more coming." Now Pepys could "discourse with her of pleasure" and tempt her to further love-making in a cozier place, some alehouse or tavern. He persuaded her to give him an assignation a fortnight thence, when he would be free for an afternoon of dalliance. Surely, unless Mrs. Bagwell was an innocent or a fool, she must have guessed at the price of her husband's preferment.

If she had any doubts about that price they were dispelled on November 3, when she met Mr. Pepys at the Royal Exchange and followed him to Moorfields, a mildly disreputable suburb north of the City. His choice of this district, with which he was not familiar, was probably due to caution. He was well known in the dives about Westminster, whither he had often taken Betty Martin; it would never do to let Betty learn that she had a rival. Choosing a tavern at random, Pepys led the carpenter's wife to a private room where they ate and drank together, and talked of ships, and shoes, and many private things.

Later that night Pepys wrote, "I did there caress her, but though I did make some offer did not receive any compliance from her in what was bad, but very modestly she denied me, which," his fading sober self concluded, "I was glad to see and shall value her the more for it, and I hope never tempt her to any evil more." A truly virtuous woman would have been so outraged by Pepys' "offer" as to blister him with scorn and walk out in a rage. Instead she "modestly" denied him. Was she holding aloof, waiting for an offer, a bargain? Or did Pepys—a common fault of timid lovers—talk too much?

Five days later back came Mrs. Bagwell to Pepys' office—the fly that begged to be caught. His record of this meeting is surprisingly laconic: "I to my office, where Bagwell's wife staid for me and together with her a good while, to meet again shortly." By the sequel we know that she agreed to another tavern assignation with him the same day "sennight," and to judge by his careful preparations for the meeting she must have given him hopes of success.

On November 15 Pepys rose from bed with his mind set on an afternoon of sinful pleasure. Forgotten were all past scruples and counsels of religion; he was a gentleman now, and therefore above conventional morality. Like his master King Charles, he thought that "God would not damn a man for a little irregular pleasure." Instead of wearing his newly purchased cloth suit lined with plush, he donned an old black suit as less conspicuous and more suited to Moorfields. After his morning office work he walked to the Royal Exchange in Cornhill where Mrs. Bagwell waited for him. At his signal she fell in behind him, following at a cautious distance to Moorfields and a little tavern hidden away at the end of an alley. There in a private room they dined and drank, and Pepys attacked her as he had Betty Martin, with

kind words, kisses, caresses, and tousing. It was a long afternoon; Mrs. Bagwell was not as easy as wanton Betty. She gave
Pepys "many hard looks" and many soft, pleading looks, too,
"and I think verily," he said with some surprise, "was
troubled at what I did." Nevertheless, in spite of her protests,
he gradually overcame her resistance. His exploring hands
quickened her soft flesh, and his urgent kisses broke down
the last barriers to his desire. "By degrees," he said, "I did
arrive at what I would, with great pleasure."

Then it was evening and a soft rain was falling. Pepys and
his new mistress walked together back into the City until
Mrs. Bagwell got her bearings; then they separated in the
dusk. That night Pepys' sober self was quiet; there were no
regrets, no words of shame or resolves never to sin again.

Who seduced whom? There is no doubt that Mr. Pepys
had a way with women. He was not a handsome man, but his
lively face with its sensual mouth was attractive enough, and
in his full regalia, with hat, periwig, and sword, he made a
fine figure of a Restoration gentleman. His vivacity and good
humor, his tenderness and cajolery, all combined with the
aura of sex to make him dangerous to women. It is quite
possible that Mrs. Bagwell, willing to give a few liberties in
exchange for her husband's promotion, was overcome by the
excitement of Pepys' kisses and caresses and succumbed after
a stubborn resistance. On the other hand, it is also possible
that she was encouraged by her family—including her ambitious husband—to put the powerful Clerk of the Acts under
so strong an obligation that he could not fail to make the
carpenter's fortune. Her struggling suggests modesty assailed
by strong temptation; her persistent courtship suggests her
hope for gain. Did she surrender or did she win?

Unfortunately Mrs. Bagwell remains a riddle, a woman
without personality. She talks but never laughs, and her

conversation is rarely recorded, perhaps because she had so little to say. All that Pepys tells us about her is that she loved her husband and was reasonably pious; after he had had his full meed of pleasure with her one day he was bemused by the fact that a woman who pretended to love God and her husband could yet be conquered. He tells us nothing else about her, not even her Christian name. She is always "Mrs. Bagwell," "Bagwell's wife," "la femme de Bagwell," or (mixing his languages) "la guniaca de ma minusier"—the woman of my carpenter. He was certainly never in love with her. He lusted for her body, but his attitude toward her as a person was quite properly that of a gentleman toward an inferior. When she appeared at his door one Valentine's Day and "had the confidence [impudence] to say she came with a hope to be time enough to be my Valentine," Pepys was annoyed. The pleasant little custom by which a lady claimed a gentleman as her Valentine, obliging him to buy her a gift, obtained only among social equals. Mrs. Bagwell was a carpenter's wife; Pepys could never meet her socially—only in bed. She was his new "convenient," a not unworthy substitute for Betty Martin. Of course he had no intention of abandoning that gravid damsel; like good King Charles the Second, Pepys never discarded; he merely added to his hand. Now he had a pair of queans.[6]

One day three weeks after his success with Mrs. Bagwell, Pepys was in Westminster Hall on business when Betty Martin plucked him by the cloak and coaxed him to follow her home. Although she was "great with child," she was not *hors de combat*; Pepys did what he would with her to his content. No doubt one of Betty's reasons for allowing him full liberty with her person was the hope that he would do something for her husband, who was then at Portsmouth as paymaster to a company of soldiers. On the other hand, she was a lass who loved the sport, a well-instructed amateur. Very likely Pepys was not her only lover.[7]

Certainly Pepys was no longer an apprentice at venery; he was now a fully chartered libertine. True, he had known carnally only two women in addition to his wife, but he was no mere holiday wencher seeking strumpets in the summer when his wife was out of town. He had learned that, with Elizabeth safely at home, he could carry on his affairs without danger of discovery, and without breaking his vows against plays and costly pleasures. They cost him very little in time and money—an hour or so now and then, or sometimes part of an afternoon, at the price of a few shillings for food and drink.

He had finally gotten the better of his conscience, that sober self which had earlier regretted sin and hoped for virtue; now it appeared only as he recorded his amours in a whimsical jargon of foreign tongues. But he never lost his initial timidity with women—"having not confidence, no[r] alcune ready wit"—and he never achieved the cynicism of more famous libertines who waged endless war on women and by conquest fed their egos as much as their lusts. Everlastingly romantic about women, Pepys grew progressively more disillusioned about their virtue, constancy, and emotional stability, but he still liked them, enjoyed their company at all times, and kept on looking for his ideal love.

His heart was large enough to hold many women at once—even his wife. Despite her real and fancied faults, he loved her too, although he rarely showed his affection. Yet careless, slovenly Elizabeth continued to give her husband cause for anger. At a dinner party given by the Pepyses for Dr. and Mrs. James Pierce the food was so badly served that Pepys woke the next morning still angry as he remembered. "Lay pretty long with some discontent abed," he reported, "even to the having bad words with my wife, and blows too, about the ill-serving up of our victuals yesterday." This time "all ended in love."

If not housework, then household accounts were at fault. Pepys always knew to a farthing where his money went, but Elizabeth cared not a fig for accounts. Whenever Pepys came to audit her jumbled records at the end of a month there was sure to be a quarrel. But Elizabeth defied her husband and refused to mend her ways. "I find she is very cunning," said Pepys one day when she could not account for a shortage of seven shillings, "and when she least shows it has her wit at work; but it is an ill one."[8]

An orderly man himself, Pepys could not bear disorder. On Monday, December 19, the Pepyses woke early and rang their bell for the maids. The resulting turmoil and confusion so annoyed Pepys that he began to pick at Elizabeth for failing to command her servants properly. "Thereupon," he wrote later, "she giving me some cross answer I did strike her over the left eye such a blow as the poor wretch did cry out and was in great pain, but yet her spirit was such as to endeavour to bite and scratch me." What with apologies, caresses, and butter and parsley for Elizabeth's black eye, Pepys made his peace.

Somewhat ruffled, he dressed and went out to a quarrelsome meeting of the Navy Commissioners at Whitehall. It was turning out to be a very bad day. He had made an assignation with Mrs. Bagwell for that afternoon. Four days earlier he had spent an entire morning exploring Moorfields, a region of walks, enclosures for fights and games, small shops, alehouses, bawdy-houses, quack doctors, and fortune tellers. He had found no very desirable resort, but one or two taverns, he thought, might serve his lustful purposes.

After dinner he hunted up Mrs. Bagwell at their trysting

place, the Royal Exchange, and took her to first one and then the other of the places he had picked, but in each she permitted him no liberties. "I think," he decided later, "it was chiefly not having a good easy place to do it upon." Alehouses were rarely equipped with couches, but where else could Pepys take his new mistress? She herself solved the problem very simply. That night Pepys went to bed all in a glow, with his mind running upon what he could do with his mistress the next afternoon. He had promised to come to dinner at the Bagwells' house in Deptford. The carpenter would be there, of course, but Pepys—or was it Mrs. Bagwell?—had a very simple plan for getting rid of him after dinner.

Tuesday was a scarlet-letter day. "Up and walked to Deptford," said Pepys, "where after doing something at the yard I walked, without being observed, with Bagwell home to his house, and there was very kindly used, and the poor people did get a dinner for me in their fashion, of which I eat very well." It was gracious of Mr. Pepys to eat the carpenter's coarse fare, and we may be sure that the humble mechanic appreciated the honor. It was as if the lord of the manor had condescended to dine with his poorest tenant.

"After dinner," said Pepys, "I found occasion of sending him [Bagwell] abroad" on some kind of a trumped-up errand. When the carpenter had left, Pepys took his mistress in his arms, kissed her ardently, and tried—perhaps too quickly—to lead her upstairs to bed. But Mrs. Bagwell's modesty died hard. In her own home, beset by fears and with no time for dalliance, she resisted instinctively. It was not a glamorous situation, not at all like allowing herself to be seduced in a tavern after all the excitement of a stolen meeting and the long build-up of kisses and caresses. This time Pepys had to contend with more than "hard looks and sooth"; he had to exert all his strength against hers. He was the stronger, and he did what he wished to his full satisfaction.

After an indecent interval the carpenter returned, and Mr. Pepys, having exercised his lordly rights, took his leave, strutting like a turkey cock. It was still only a little after noon. He walked all the way home by way of Redriffe and London Bridge, ate another dinner, and spent a long afternoon hard at work. He went to bed late that night, after recording the day's triumphs in a mixture of English and French, and with never a word of remorse or shame.[9]

He had still not kept his part of the bargain with Mrs. Bagwell; the price had been paid but the goods not yet delivered. It would be easy enough to excuse him on the grounds of pressing business and forgetfulness, but he was not too busy for a moment of pleasure now and then, and he never forgot a promise. More probably he was not yet sure of Mrs. Bagwell and chose to keep her dependent on his favor.

Yet he was a very busy man indeed in the winter of 1664-1665. In effect, hostilities with Holland had already begun, and trade stood still, giving way to war. Lord Sandwich was cruising the Channel with a squadron, harrying the Dutch shipping, and the Navy Office was bending every effort toward getting out a mighty Fleet in the spring. There were ominous signs of great and terrible things to come in 1665: a new star blazing in the December sky, accompanied by the noise of fires and cannon; and in March a still brighter comet, presaging war, pestilence, and famine. Pepys was too busy to worry; what with ships, supplies, sailors, contracts, finances, and his own private dealings, his mind was full. He rose betimes and often worked until one or two o'clock in the morning. He was too busy to take part in the Christmas festivities, usually going to his study to work at night, and leaving Elizabeth, Will Hewer, Tom Edwards, and the maids at their holiday gambols.

When he cast up his accounts on the last day of 1664 and found himself worth one thousand three hundred and forty-nine pounds, his joy compensated for lost pleasures. In the past year his income from all sources had totalled nine hundred and sixty pounds. Since his net salary as Clerk of the Acts was only two hundred and fifty pounds (one hundred pounds a year went to Mr. Barlow, the previous holder of his office), the rest, seven hundred and ten pounds, must have come from honest graft. He had increased his hoard that year by five hundred and twenty pounds. "The Lord make me forever thankful to his holy name," said pious Mr. Pepys. He was content: he had made and saved a great deal of money. Moreover, either the hare's foot which he had been carrying lately, or the pill of turpentine taken every morning, had helped his colic; his household was in good health and quiet for the moment; and he himself was rising in esteem and credit every day. On New Year's Eve, as soon as the clock struck one, he kissed his wife in the kitchen by the fireside and wished her a merry new year.

His vows ended with the old year, and on Monday, January 2, a clear day after a hard frost, he took a brief holiday. First he went to his barber's in Westminster, sought out Jane Welsh, gave her money as a Christmas present, and made an assignation with her (which, as usual, she failed to keep). Thence he wandered over to the Swan Tavern in the Palace Yard to sport a while with a new acquaintance, Sarah, a pretty bar-maid. Properly stimulated, he found Betty Martin in Westminster Hall, took her to her lodgings in Bow Street, and did what he wanted to with her "most freely," at a cost of two shillings in wine and cake. Sick of her impudence, but still in a holiday mood, he took a coach to Covent Garden and the house of Lord William Brouncker, recently appointed an Extra Commissioner of the Navy. Here, at a noble banquet, Pepys made a hit by reading aloud a copy of Lord Buckhurst's now famous ballad from the gentleman volunteers with the Fleet at sea, "To All You Ladies Now at Land." After a brief interlude at his bookseller's and a visit to his office, he went home, thinking to be merry with his wife. But Elizabeth had dug out something by Sir Philip Sidney on jealousy (probably from the *Arcadia*) and maliciously she insisted on his reading it. His holiday joy was spoiled. He spent the evening moodily playing cards with Elizabeth, and the next day he went back to work.

Gradually, as he found sexual independence, Pepys was growing farther away from his wife. He still loved her and occasionally desired her, but what with her moods and her various ailments she had come to be undependable as a bedmate. Now what he wanted at home was peace and order so that he could work quietly in his study, or spend a pleasant musical evening with his merchant friends John Andrews and Thomas Hill, and his boy Tom Edwards, singing four-part psalms. Elizabeth's wilfulness and her constant wrangling over maids or money spoiled many a home-coming for him. Once that winter, after a long argument with her about the cook-maid, Jane Birch, he complained bitterly how unfair it was "that all my trouble in the world almost should arise from the disorders in my family and the indiscretion of a wife that brings me nothing almost (besides a comely person) but only trouble and discontent." Certainly his household was ill-managed. Jane Birch left on February 2, 1665, and was replaced on March 29 by a new cook-maid, Alce. Besse the chambermaid left on March 6, and three weeks later Elizabeth hired another girl, Mary the Third. There was no end to the procession of maids.[10]

He felt himself justified in seeking erotic pleasure away from home. "Strangers," said his father Osborn, "are taken for dainties, wives as physick." Pepys' rare meetings with his newest dainty, Mrs. Bagwell, gave him not only sexual pleasure but self-assurance, the feeling of the dominating, conquering male. Besides, there was the excitement of secret meetings; ducking through dark lanes into taverns and ale-houses, deceiving a husband (who discreetly saw nothing), and embracing a pretty young woman who wore, if nothing else, the charm of novelty.[11]

Unfortunately it was not always easy to plan an amorous bout with the carpenter's wife. January weather made the trip up-river from Deptford hazardous, and if Pepys went down to visit her without preparation he could not be sure that her husband would be safely out of the way. Jane Welsh was much easier to see—his business took Pepys to Westminster almost daily—and his continued infatuation with the barber's wench made him spend time he could ill afford dancing attendance and vainly trying to get her to a tavern for dalliance. Even after Jane's duplicity was revealed with the shocking news that she had "made herself sure" to the fiddler Harbing by lying with him, Pepys still lusted for her. He was willing to share her with another man if he must; he would be content, he said, to "have now and then her company." Playing her own little game, Jane kept him dangling, promised again to meet him, and again left him to shiver through a Sunday afternoon in the Abbey.[12]

On January 23, his mind still "running too much after some folly," Pepys made a final trip to Jervas's to see Jane and learned that she had gone out. Sadly he went home to dinner. That afternoon he found patient Mrs. Bagwell opportunely waiting for him at his office. He wasted no time in preliminaries—"away she and I to a cabaret where she and

I have eat before, and there I had her company tout and had mon plaisir of elle." Back at his office later that day he made a vow to mind his business and let women alone for a month. He even included rules about kissing: the first kiss would be free; thereafter each additional kiss would cost him twelve-pence to the poor! His oath was aimed chiefly at Jane Welsh. As the result of his folly in pursuing her, both his business and his honor, he said, lay "a-bleeding."[13]

But he had not quite done with Jane Welsh. Four days later she came to Seething Lane to tell him that she had left her master and was going to her sweetheart, Harbing. Fearful of talking with her at his house, Pepys sent her away to wait for him at the Royal Exchange. There he found her later and took her across the river to the Falcon Tavern in the fields. At last he had his assignation with Jane, but it was a joyless meeting. He tried to persuade her to stay with Jervas and give up the sorry fiddler, "a fellow of no kind of worth in the world and a beggar to boot," but she would not be persuaded. "It was her fortune," she said, "to have this man, although she did believe it would be to her ruin." It was a strange, stupid thing to do, Pepys thought; he could never understand a woman who would give up everything for love.

After an hour or two of talk, Pepys took the girl back across the river, said goodbye, and went about his business. Jane followed her destiny. She took Harbing for her husband without benefit of clergy, discovered after some weeks that he already had a wife and child; and in her despair fled to Ireland, the last refuge of the self-defeated.[14]

Pepys was through with Jane Welsh, but he still had not kept his promise to Mrs. Bagwell. In February the carpenter's wife came to see him twice, humbly awaiting his pleasure and begging his favor. Her second visit came on a day when he had some time free and was in a mood for pleasure. He decided to put her off no longer. He felt sure of her now, and, anyway, William Bagwell was a good workman, worthy of promotion. Telling Mrs. Bagwell that he would immediately "do her business, which was to write to my Lord Sandwich for her husband's advance into a better ship as there should be occasion," he bade her go home, get rid of Mr. Bagwell, and await his coming. Docilely she accepted his kiss and left him.[15]

He wrote his letter that afternoon, and in the winter dusk walked to the Custom House stairs and took a boat down to Deptford. It was after dark when he landed. No one saw him hurrying through the frosty streets to Bagwell's house, where warmth and fearful love waited for him. But again, perhaps because he was in too much of a hurry, he had "a great deal of difficulty" with his modest mistress. At last he had his will of her as usual. Afterward, although he was sated with pleasure and tired by his struggle, he walked all the way home through the night, and so to bed. The next morning he woke with a "mighty pain" in the forefinger of his left hand, "from a strain," he said, "that it received last night in struggling avec la femme que je mentioned yesterday."

The finger had plenty of time to heal. Soon after this episode Mrs. Bagwell disappeared, not to return to Deptford until midsummer. Apparently Pepys' letter to Lord Sandwich was immediately effective, and Mr. Bagwell was appointed carpenter of the old *Providence* (a 4th rate warship of 358 tons, 30 guns, and 140 men), a position which he held for the next two years. In February and March, 1665, the *Providence* was one of the twenty-five ships in Lord Sandwich's winter guard, based at Deal. In April it sailed with Lord Sandwich's Blue Squadron against the Dutch, was sent to Hosely Bay to be made into a fireship after the Battle of

Lowestoft, was back with the Fleet in July, and then was sent to wet dock in Deptford for repairs. In times of war it was the duty of a sailor's wife to follow her husband to his port of embarkation and to await his return in a sea-side boarding-house, at Harwich, Deal, Portsmouth, or elsewhere. Ironically, by paying his debt to Mrs. Bagwell, Pepys managed to lose her for five long months. He had not counted on such wifely devotion.[16]

# VII

# Plague and Pleasures

# 1665

On February 23, 1665, Mr. Samuel Pepys was thirty-two years old, in good health except for occasional bouts with his old enemy, colic, and prospering mightily. Two weeks earlier his pensioner Thomas Barlow, the former Clerk of the Acts, had died. Pepys was as sorry, he said, as it was possible for anyone to be for "a stranger, by whose death he gets one hundred pounds per annum." February was notable also for two other important events. On the fifteenth, recommended by his friend Thomas Povey, virtuoso and epicure, Pepys was elected to membership in the Royal Society. On the twenty-fifth he took a bath—the first recorded in the five years so far covered by his journal. He felt no particular need to wash, but five days earlier Elizabeth and Mercer had gone to a hot-house—a bathing house with hot baths—to bathe, and Elizabeth had taken a resolution of being thereafter very clean. "How long it will hold," said Pepys cynically, "I can guess." But she kept her resolution to the extent of refusing to sleep with him until he cleansed himself with warm water.

Attendance at the meetings of the Royal Society—with learned lectures to hear and strange experiments to see—became a pleasurable habit. The bathing, unfortunately, did not, either for Elizabeth or Samuel. Of course no one else in their world bathed regularly; in fact, physicians warned their patients against baths, prescribing them for medical purposes only. Fortunately lavender, bergamot, orange-flower water, and musk were plentiful.

On March 1, true to a promise made a long time ago, Pepys gave Elizabeth twenty pounds to buy clothes for Easter. Very soon she blossomed out in a gown of flowered, ash-colored silk, with a fine lace whisk over her breasts and shoulders. She tried the effect of blonde artificial curls attached to one side of her own dark head—"light-coloured locks, quite white almost"—but Pepys, objecting to them as unnatural, would not let her wear them. A pity, too; they were fashionable and made her very pretty.[1]

On March 4 war with Holland was formally proclaimed at the Royal Exchange, one of the best examples of a purely commercial war in all history. Thereafter, as troubled spring gave way to tragic summer, Pepys was increasingly busy, often working from early morning until midnight or later, and well nigh falling asleep over his letters. He had little time for women. With Mrs. Bagwell absent he turned again to Betty Martin, safely delivered of a son on March 9, and recuperating in lazy state. He went to see her once or twice during her month of "lying-in," but had no pleasure with her. Her husband had gone off to France on a mysterious errand, and Betty had become "mighty reserved and resolved to keep herself so" until Mr. Martin's return. Pepys was amused at the notion of wanton Betty turning chaste, but she was a card too dog-eared to be worth playing at the moment.[2]

In March still more duties fell on Pepys' shoulders, and with them more rewards. Thomas Povey, a fine fellow but something of a fool and certainly no accountant, in despair turned over to Pepys his job as Treasurer of the Tangier Commission. Pepys got the three hundred pounds a year salary and three-sevenths of all "rewards and considerations" from contractors. All of this new work added to his duties for the Navy kept him in a constant bustle and stir, running back and forth from the Navy Office to the Royal Exchange, Westminster Hall, the Exchequer, and Whitehall. But the King himself took notice of him now, called him by name, and talked with him about Naval affairs, and the great Duke of Albemarle—old General George Monck, a quiet, thick-bodied, heavy-faced man—told him that he was "the right hand of the Navy," and that he did not know what could be done without Mr. Pepys. It was all very flattering, but best of all was the fact that his new work brought him increased profits, and his savings, in spite of heavy spending, mounted rapidly. At the end of April he was worth one thousand four hundred pounds.[3]

To do Mr. Pepys full justice, his work was good, even though the Navy Office was handicapped by incurable poverty. The great Fleet which sailed for Holland on April 21 under the Duke of York's command was a well-tempered weapon ready for war. For a month it cruised off the Dutch coast, daring the hated "butter-boxes" (Dutchmen) to come out and fight; but Holland's Fleet was not ready. With beef and beer running low, the Duke had to return to England for supplies.

On June 3 the enemy Fleets finally met in a pitched battle off Lowestoft. All day long anxious Londoners listened for the sound of guns, going to the parks, the river, or down to Greenwich to catch the little, far-off undulations of sound, "like the noise of distant thunder," said John Dryden, "or of swallows in a chimney." At nightfall the sounds died away. After five days of suspense came glorious news: the English had broken the Dutch line, completely routing the foe, and, but for the false orders given during the pursuit by a cowardly courtier, Henry Brouncker, might have utterly destroyed the Dutch Fleet. Still, it was a great victory. The English ships were battered but afloat, and the Fleet had lost only eight hundred officers and men. The Dutch lost twelve ships of the line and about five thousand men.[4]

But England's joy was dampened by domestic fear. All through the long dry spring, garbage, offal, and filth had collected in the streets and alleys of London, with no rain to wash it away. Black rats had grown fat and multiplied, and in their bodies bubonic plague was brewing its deadly poison, preparing to break out in epidemic force as it had so many times before.

With the coming of warm weather the dreaded plague, carried by fleas from rats to men, appeared in the slums where the poor lived in crowded squalor. On June 7 Pepys saw several houses in Drury Lane "with a red cross upon the doors and 'Lord have mercy upon us' writ there." The sight disturbed him so much that he felt compelled to buy "some roll-tobacco to smell to and chaw, which took away the apprehension." On June 20, appointed as a day of thanksgiving for the victory at sea, the London bills of mortality, understating the facts, recorded 168 deaths from plague in the preceding week. As the figures rose week by week, panic swept the city.

According to seventeenth-century science, bubonic plague came originally from poisonous miasmas and night air, and was spread by contagion. Under the leadership of the Lord Mayor, Sir John Lawrence, the London authorities did what little they could to stay the spread of pestilence. Following an ancient custom, they ordered all dogs and cats slain, at twopence a head to the killers. They closed the theatres, pro-

hibited public gatherings and entertainments, and even for-
bade formal funerals. Victims of the plague were either
carried to overflowing pest-houses or locked up in their
homes for forty days—or until the plague had slain one by
one every member of a family. The only aid for an infected
family came from dirty old hags who served as nurses, and
food and drink were brought by the watchmen who stood
guard with halberds at the doors. "Searchers of the dead,"
ignorant old women paid by the parishes, examined corpses
for the "tokens" of the plague—round, scarlet spots on the
skin—and "bearers," with bells and dead-carts, went through
the streets by night, crying "bring out your dead!"[5]

Confronted by hideous death, lower-class citizens too poor
to leave London stayed on in their rat-ridden tenements,
bought charms from mountebanks and anti-pestilence pills
from quacks, drank plague-water (brandy flavored with
herbs), chewed or smoked tobacco, soaked their heads in vine-
gar, prayed—and died raving in agony. The upper classes
sought safety in flight. As the weekly death rate mounted in
June and July, a trickling exodus from London swelled to a
torrent. The King set the example, fleeing with his official
family up-river to Hampton Court, thence to Salisbury, and
finally to Oxford. The rich fled in coaches followed by wagon-
loads of their goods and valuables; lesser folk went by horse
or afoot, with bundles on their backs. Officials, clergymen,
and even many physicians and apothecaries ran from the
stricken city. Pepys, frightened to the marrow, stayed on. The
Dutch were wounded but by no means defeated. The English
Fleet had to be repaired and provisioned in a hurry, and
only he could do the work.

For one reason or another he got very little help from his
colleagues. Sir William Penn had returned to sea, acting as
second in command of the Fleet under the Duke of York,

and later as vice admiral under the Earl of Sandwich. Commissioner William Coventry, the Duke's secretary, followed his master at sea and on land. Sir William Batten and Sir John Minnes avoided London as much as possible and were not to be relied on. Sir Thomas Harvey, appointed an Extra Commissioner in January, 1665, fled from London and stayed away all through the plague year. The other new Extra Commissioner, William, Lord Brouncker, was willing enough and no coward—he stayed with his mistress, Mrs. Williams, at his house in Covent Garden until mid-August—but he was completely without experience. At this time of crisis Samuel Pepys was the head and heart of the entire vast Naval establishment.

Early in July he sent Elizabeth and two of her maids, Mercer and Mary the Third, to stay at Mr. William Sheldon's house in Woolwich, a safe ten miles down-river from London. Thereafter, for the rest of the year, he saw his wife only occasionally, dropping in from time to time for an hour or two or to spend the night, admiring the painting which she had taken up as an avocation in the spring, and which he found "very curious," or listening absently to her complaints about her maids. He was depressed to find that, contrary to the adage, "absence makes us a little strange instead of more fond." He kept his own headquarters in Seething Lane, retaining his boy, Tom Edwards, and two maids, Alce and Susan. In his wife's absence he fell into the morning habit of having Susan comb his head to rid it of lice. He enjoyed the scratching of the comb, but he took even more pleasure in playing with Susan's breasts while her hands were busy. After a while he decided that he had better leave off such pleasant titillation lest it cause him some "major inconvenience." Even in the midst of plague and war, Pepys had to have some sensual pleasure, if only as a relief from the grinding routine of official life.[6]

His vows against plays had expired on May 15, and he saw no reason for renewing them. Anyway, on June 5 the theatres were closed for the duration of the plague. Mrs. Bagwell was still at the seaside, and late in June, when Betty Martin's husband returned, the Martins joined the mass exodus of the footloose and fearful, not to return until the following February. Lacking both his mistresses, Pepys was forced into continence. He was not without desires: the sight of loose women standing in their doorways in Drury Lane could still put evil thoughts into his head; but Cocky of Fleet Alley had taught him to beware of professionals, and there was no amateur doxy at hand. Once when a young wife came to his office to beg that her husband, a pressed man, should not be sent to sea, Pepys, with the well-developed sensitivity of the libertine, suspected that he could have done anything he wished with her, but he hesitated and the opportunity passed. However he was not entirely without erotic amusement. Hampered though he was by his many duties, by his dread of the plague, and by his fear of being seen on an outing at a time when he was supposed to be at work, Pepys still managed to rake up a couple of likely girls with whom he had a little fun.[7]

Both were barmaids. One of them, Sarah, a young kinswoman of the Herberts, who kept the Swan Tavern near Westminster Hall, Pepys had known since early January. She was a merry, free-hearted wench, and very good company. Pepys had fallen into the habit of dropping in at the Swan whenever he could for dinner, a drink, and a little kissing and toying when he found Sarah alone. The other maid, Mary, at the Harp and Ball near Charing Cross, was a later acquaintance. She was a modest, very pretty girl ("formosa!"

said Pepys), who had lost a sweetheart in Wales and had come to London to get a husband. Pepys divided his attentions between the two maids, sometimes visiting both in the same day, always sure of a few kisses and caresses. They were coarse and ignorant, but his love of beauty endowed them with erotic glamour. He called them his "flowers," and enjoyed stroking their petals. They allowed him all sorts of liberties, but he was careful not to pluck them. Maids were dangerous.

One June day, taking care not to be seen and recognized, he took Sarah of the Swan, "the fairest flower," by coach to Tothill Fields, the open country between Westminster and the village of Chelsea. At a convenient country tavern they alighted and, said Pepys, "in with the fairest flower to eat a cake, and there did do as much as was safe with my flower, and that was enough on my part." Afterward he drove back to Westminster and delivered the "rose" where it belonged. Six weeks later he persuaded the other blossom, Mary of the Harp and Ball, to go on an outing with him. He met her at the New Exchange in the Strand, and took her by coach north to Highgate and thence to the village of Hampstead. "Much pleased with her company," he said, "pretty and innocent, and had what pleasure almost I would with her." At night, "weary and sweaty," he drove back to town and deposited this flower in St. Martin's Lane. He was content to cultivate his bed of roses; he was afraid to lie in it.[8]

These were only rare moments of pleasure in the early summer; in the main Pepys' days and night were devoted to ships and supplies. On July 5 the Fleet set sail again, this time under Lord Sandwich's command. During the rest of the summer it scoured the Channel and the North Sea, vainly seeking the enemy, making an abortive attack on Bergen in Norway, where the Dutch East India Fleet had taken refuge, and capturing homeward bound Dutch merchantmen.

With his heaviest work done, Pepys turned a part of his time and tremendous energy to arranging a marriage, eventually solemnized on July 31, between his cousin Jemimah, daughter of the Earl of Sandwich, and Philip, son of Sir George Carteret, Treasurer of the Navy. His share in the business gave him a great deal of pleasure. Besides, it afforded him an excuse to get away now and then from hot, dry London, where the church bells tolled without end, and the carts rumbling through the streets at night bore the heaped-up dead to swollen churchyards or to trenches in the fields.

While Elizabeth stayed on at Woolwich, Pepys was lavishly entertained by the Carterets at their Deptford mansion and by his kinfolk, the Mountagus, at Dagnams, a manor house near Romford, twelve miles east of London. In general he had grown cynical about marriage; as he said on another occasion, "Strange to see what delight we married people have to see these poor fools decoyed into our condition." But the Carteret-Mountagu marriage was no trivial love match; it was a matrimonial alliance, a merger between two rich and powerful families, and Pepys was the broker, the go-between who carried the terms of the marriage—conditions, dowries, and settlements—back and forth to a happy conclusion. In addition, he introduced the two young people to each other, soothed and coaxed them into accepting the union with good grace, and, as an experienced amorist, gave young Philip instructions on how to make love.

On the wedding night there was none of the ribaldry usual at seventeenth-century marriages—heavy drinking, coarse jesting, undressing the bride and groom, and flinging the stocking as a signal to fall to. Everything was done with perfect decorum, and Pepys was delighted. At the proper time he led the shy groom to the canopied bridal bed, kissed the bride, already shivering between the sheets, and then drew the curtains, "with the greatest gravity that could be, and so good night." Although he had spent most of July constantly on the go, for Pepys it was a month passed "with abundance of joy, and honour, and pleasant journeys, and brave entertainments, and without cost of money."[9]

He even found time that month for an orgiastic interlude. One day he saw Mrs. Bagwell waiting in his outer office, but he was in haste and could not stay to talk. Probably no words were needed, a look was enough. Pepys must have known that Bagwell's ship, the *Providence*, was in wet dock at Deptford for repairs. Mrs. Bagwell's appearance at his office was all the hint he needed: she was at home again, and the way to her bed was open. Now he was all on fire to visit her.

Four days later he was invited to spend the night at the Carterets' mansion in Déptford, where he had to talk (endlessly, it seemed to him) about the marriage plans. It was long after supper before he could make an excuse and slip away into the warm night, but he had "a design pour aller à la femme de Bagwell," and not even the amenities could stop him. As he hurried through the misty streets he doffed the personality of Mr. Pepys the wise counsellor, the man of business, the kinsman and faithful servant, and became Pepys the eager amorist. Bagwell's house on the outskirts of Deptford had a light in the window. The carpenter was away; there was no hindrance to pleasure, and no hurry. Pepys stayed until midnight and came away satiated and "all in a violent sweat" because of the heat, but with his fingers unstrained. Mrs. Bagwell's modesty had lost its muscle.

For the rest of the summer and fall the course of true lust ran as smoothly as time, business, the plague, and the rare presence of a wittol husband allowed. The *Providence* was an old ship in very poor condition; it remained in wet dock for months while the shipwrights and architects debated how to make it fit for sea. Presumably the carpenter stayed aboard most of the time; at least he was hardly ever home to hamper lechery.[10]

On the first of August Pepys returned again to London where, according to the weekly bills, in the past week 3,014 had died, and of these 2,010 of plague. But, to avoid quarantine, so many householders had attributed plague deaths to other causes that the true bill of plague victims was probably much higher. In Pepys' own parish of St. Olave's, Hart Street, forty had died of plague in one night, and St. Olave's bell rang incessantly. Under the hot sun the city lay supine with the silence of death. Everyone kept indoors as much as possible, with doors and windows tightly closed against infection, and sometimes, in the hottest weather, with coal fires burning to disinfect the air. The streets were "mighty thin of people," and all Pepys' old haunts—St. James's Park, Vauxhall, the Exchange, and Westminster Hall—were empty, while in echoing Whitehall only the Duke of Albemarle, alone among the great officers of state, continued stolidly in business.

There were plans afoot to move the Navy office to Greenwich; meanwhile Pepys had to continue shuttling back and forth from his office to Deptford, Greenwich, Woolwich, and sometimes still farther downriver to great warships anchored at the mouth of the Thames. There was no pleasure in this kind of a life. Pepys was a family man, fond of his home, his wife, and even his servants. In August he managed to spend only six nights with Elizabeth at Woolwich, usually arriving late, going to bed "sleepy and weary," and rising betimes. Only once does he speak of going to bed with his wife "with great pleasure."[11]

As much as possible he kept away from the slums of the city, where the plague continued to mount to its fearful

September climax. When business took him through a stricken area he went with the resignation of a stoic. He had made his will, all his papers were in order, and he was prepared in body and soul "should it please the Lord to call me away." Once he wrote to Commissioner Coventry (now Sir William), "The sickness in general thickens upon us, and particularly upon our neighborhood. You, sir, took your turn at the sword; I must not therefore grudge to take mine at the pestilence." In any situation involving physical conflict, Samuel Pepys was a rabbit; yet he walked the dreadful streets of London like a man.[12]

One night his subconscious mind brought his fears and yearnings to a happy resolution in a dream, "which was," he said, "that I had my Lady Castlemayne in my armes and was admitted to use all the dalliance I desired with her, and then dreamt that this could not be awake, but that it was only a dream; but that since it was a dream, and that I took so much real pleasure in it, what a happy thing it would be if when we are in our graves (as Shakespeere resembles it) we could dream, and dream but such dreams as this, that then we should not need to be so fearful of death, as we are this plague time."[13]

Since his little life could not be rounded by a sleep, he turned to Mrs. Bagwell. One afternoon in August she came to his Seething Lane office for an hour of tousing and tumbling. On another day, as he was walking from Greenwich to Deptford, he overtook "old Bagwell," the carpenter's father, who tagged along with him into town and insisted that Pepys visit his daughter-in-law, although the canny shipwright must have known that his son was at work. Not at all loath, Pepys went along, finding Mrs. Bagwell home alone. After the usual greetings and commonplaces, Sir Pandarus of Troy went his way, leaving the happy pair together so that

Pepys could have his will of his mistress. Again, on an afternoon ten days later, Pepys met Mrs. Bagwell and her mother
in a Deptford street, and upon invitation, "went in to the
daughter's house with the mother." After he had done what
he had "a mind to" with the daughter, he sat awhile, drinking and talking, and by and by went away. We are not told
how the complaisant mother occupied herself while Pepys
was doing as he wished with her daughter. Perhaps she held
the door, to cough and cry "Hem!" if anybody came.[14]

On August 26 the Navy Office was moved to Greenwich,
and shortly afterward Pepys moved his own headquarters
down-river. It was becoming increasingly difficult, as well as
more dangerous, for him to return to London every night.
He hated to leave Seething Lane—all his plate was stored
there, plus more than one thousand eight hundred pounds
in an iron chest—but he decided to take a chance, hoping no
one would think him fool enough to leave his treasure in an
unguarded house. The pestilence was approaching its peak
and spreading to towns all over southern England. In the
week ending on August 27, 6,102 Londoners, almost a thousand a day, died of the plague—"but it is feared," said Pepys,
"that the true number of the dead this week is near 10,000."

On September 1, he sent Susan and Tom Edwards down
to Woolwich, leaving his other maid, Alce, alone at Seething
Lane to take her chances. Then he too took up his residence
at Woolwich and spent the rest of the plague year either at
Mr. Sheldon's house or in lodgings at Greenwich. Occasionally he had to make a hurried trip back to London, where,
on September 5, as a last desperate measure, fires were built
in the streets before every sixth house throughout the City
and its suburbs. For three days their flames made the nights
hideous and their smoke added to the stench of death and
decay rising from the desolate city. Nothing helped; in the

week ending on September 19, the recorded mortality reached the total of 8,257, of which 7,165 deaths were attributed to the plague. After that date, with the coming of rains and cooler weather, the totals declined week by week.[15]

Pepys was very glad to get out of London. On the day after his move he was at Deptford (just a stone's throw from Greenwich), and took the opportunity to celebrate by going surreptitiously to the house of the carpenter's wife ("a la casa de la guniaca de ma minusier"), where he did what he always seemed to have a mind to do. This was his last bout with Mrs. Bagwell for more than a month. He never allowed his appetite to interfere with his profits, and September brought him a chance too good to be missed.

On September 3 Lord Sandwich captured four Dutch warships, several smaller vessels, thirteen hundred prisoners, and two big Dutch East Indiamen with cargoes valued at four hundred thousand pounds. A week later, when the news reached the Navy Office at Greenwich, there was frantic joy. At last after all the year's expense in blood and treasure there would be some return from prizes to relieve the Navy's money famine. Unfortunately, Lord Sandwich made the mistake of "breaking bulk"; that is, before turning over his prizes to the proper authorities, he permitted his officers and men to take out their shares in valuable goods which they promptly sold to enterprising merchants. The procedure was improper but not clearly illegal; moreover Sandwich claimed to have the Duke of York's permission. The net result was waste, spoilage, petty thievery, and a national scandal.

Always eager to make a fast farthing, Pepys, in partnership with a merchant friend, Captain George Cocke, bought up five thousand pounds' worth of silk, cinnamon, nutmeg, and indigo. Since their only title to the commodities was a bill of sale from Lord Sandwich, the partners had many anxious

moments and some battles with Customs Officers, the Commissioners for Prizes, and the Duke of Albemarle's men (who
had to be bribed) before they got their precious goods safely
warehoused in London. Eventually Pepys netted a profit of
five hundred pounds. Lord Sandwich, who gained little from
his prizes, was to pay dearly for his rash action in breaking
bulk: that winter his enemies in Parliament forced his re-
moval from command of the Fleet, and to save him from
possible impeachment the King had to send him off as Ambassador Extraordinary to Spain.[16]

Even though by October the plague was in all the river
towns and particularly bad in Deptford, Pepys, who had been
continent too long, had to see Mrs. Bagwell. Because he was
well known in Deptford, he was obliged to make his visits
secretly, preferably after dark. On October 5 he went to
Whitehall to see the Duke of Albemarle on Navy business.
"Lord," he said, "what a sad time it is to see no boats upon
the River; and grass grows all up and down White Hall
court, and nobody but poor wretches in the streets!" After
his work was done he dallied a while with "the fairest flower"
—Sarah of the Swan Tavern, still bravely in business in the
Palace Yard. Toward dusk he took a boat down to Deptford,
where he was lucky enough to find his mistress at home.
"Round about [Mrs. Bagwell's house] and next door on every
side is the plague," he said, "but I did not value it, but there
did what I would con elle, and so away."[17]

For the rest of the autumn, partly because of the plague
raging in Deptford, but more because he had other sources
of pleasure, Pepys sought out Mrs. Bagwell only rarely. With
his usual luck he had found other ladies to amuse him. What
he wanted from women was not so much consummation
(although he never turned down a well-made bed) as it was
companionship, erotic play, and merriment. With men he

talked shop or politics, deplored the woeful mishandling of the Dutch War, or discussed the sad condition of England under a careless King who wasted all his time with courtesans, "feeling and kissing them naked." With women Pepys could dally, jest, and imitate his master, forgetting for a while broken ships, mangled bodies, mutinous workmen, "the horrible crowd and lamentable moan of the poor seamen" who lay starving in the streets for lack of money to pay them, the everlasting play of political intrigue, and the horrors of the plague. What he wanted most in his few hours of ease was to be "mighty merry." Sometimes he found merriment in mixed company, with singing and dancing. Sometimes he found it in kissing and caressing a pretty girl. He liked all women and played with many; he lay with only a few.[18]

In October, finding that he wasted too much time walking the three miles from Woolwich to his office, he rented lodgings for himself in Greenwich, leaving Elizabeth and her maids still at Mr. Sheldon's house. With his new landlady, Mrs. Clerke, lived two handsome young women: her daughter, Mrs. Daniell, wife of John Daniell, a seaman with the Fleet, and John's sister, Sarah. Mrs. Daniell was "a pretty conceited woman big with child," and free enough with her kisses. One night Thomas, Lord Rutherford, a very wanton gentleman, supped with Pepys, made merry with Mrs. Daniell who served them, and "would be handling her breasts, which she coyly refused." She was not coy with Pepys. Rutherford was a lord, but Mr. Pepys was the Clerk of the Acts, a powerful official whose favor could mean quick promotion for her sailor-husband. On another night when Pepys returned late to his lodgings he found shy Mrs. Daniell waiting up for him to beg a lieutenancy for her husband. He had the pleasure of caressing her and "kissing her again and again." The next night he supped with Mrs. Daniell on a mess of little birds killed by her husband, "and after supper," he said, "were alone a great while, and I had the pleasure of her lips, she being a pretty woman, and one whom a great belly becomes as well as ever I saw." The Daniell family campaign for promotion was well launched.[19]

Next door to Pepys' lodgings lived little Frances Tooker, a pretty young wanton just budding into womanhood. Pepys admired her, kissed her as often as he could, and sometimes dallied with her freely, doing what he wished with his hands in her bosom and under her petticoats while she combed his head. He was careful of her maidenhood, but some other amorist was less scrupulous; a year later Pepys was shocked to learn that "little Mrs. Tooker hath got a clap as young as she is, being brought up loosely by her mother," who had set a very bad example. It did not occur to him that he might have contributed to her downfall.[20]

Greenwich provided even more innocent amusements than kissing and dallying. The little town was crowded with Naval officials and refugees from the plague, among them Edward Coleman, a singer and composer (very good company when he was sober); his wife, famous for having sung the role of Ianthe in Davenant's *The Siege of Rhodes* nearly a decade ago; madcap Mary Knep, an actress and singer at the Theatre Royal; Nicholas Lanier, a singer and composer; Thomas Hill, the musical merchant; Captain Edward Rolt, an excellent singer; gay Lord Brouncker and his painted mistress, Madam Williams; Captain Cocke, a very merry man; and Pepys' old friend "La Belle" Pierce, the surgeon's wife, no mean singer herself. Sometimes Elizabeth came over from Woolwich with Mercer, Tom Edwards, and Barbara Sheldon, her landlord's handsome daughter; and Pepys hired a fiddler for an evening of dancing and song.

One October night he came home to his lodgings (three

rooms and a dining room) to find a jolly crew dancing. After a while they all fell to singing, and Mrs. Coleman delivered some of her parts from the old opera with great spirit. Outside the autumn rains fell, a cold wind blew, and a few miles up-river the spotted death still stalked the streets of London, but the little knot of refugees reveled on in the warm, candle-lit dining room until well past midnight. "Thus we end the month merrily," Pepys reported, "and the more for that, after some fears that the plague would have increased this week, I do hear for certain that there is above 400 [less], the whole number [of deaths] being 1,388, and of them of the plague, 1,031."[21]

On November 8 Pepys hoped it might be safe to visit Mrs. Bagwell again. In the late afternoon he went to Deptford by water, and finding himself too early walked about in the fields outside of town until dark. Again he was so lucky as to find his mistress alone. He did what he would with her to his full content. But he was mistaken about the plague: "about eight at night," he said, "did take water, being glad I was out of the town, for the plague, it seems, rages there more than ever."

Surely Mrs. Bagwell was happy to see him for his own sake, but she still had a commercial motive for her harlotry. The Bagwells were prospering—they even had a maid now—but the carpenter was ambitious. We may take it that she pleaded with Pepys to find a still better post for her husband, and that he agreed to do what he could. Some time later, on the chance that a place might be open in the *Swiftsure*, a 3rd rate, he wrote to Sir William Coventry recommending Bagwell for the job. Luckily he did not get it; in the following summer the *Swiftsure* was captured by the Dutch, while Bagwell was still carpenter of the fireship *Providence*.[22]

With the hard frosts of late November, the plague death

rate fell off rapidly, and the refugees began streaming back to London from every corner of the kingdom. When the weekly toll fell to 333, Pepys judged it safe for Elizabeth, Mercer, and Susan to return to Seething Lane (Mary the Third had left for good earlier in the month). Pepys stayed in Greenwich to be near his office and to enjoy his freedom and his gay companions. He had great hopes of another new friend, Mistress Judith Penington, "a very fine witty lady, indifferent handsome," who lodged with Mr. Benjamin Glanville at Greenwich. Another refugee from the plague, she was unmarried, about twenty-four years old, and socially far superior to Pepys' other loves. Her background was formidable: her father, Alderman Penington, had been a famous Puritan: one of her brothers, Isaac, was a well-known Quaker, and the other, Arthur, became a Roman Catholic priest. When Pepys first met her he had no thoughts of dalliance. Yet, after a long day at his office or in the wind and rain on the river, he found peace and pleasure in merely sitting by her fireside of an evening and talking, so witty and sensible she seemed. She was just such a "discreet, understanding" woman as Elizabeth should have been.

He was to find that she had other attractions too. One night Pepys and his friend Captain Cocke found her sitting "undrest [without her gown] in her smocke and petticoats by the fireside." They sat with her, talking, drinking, and feasting their eyes on the charms disclosed by her loose attire. Greatly daring, Pepys moved closer to her, rested an arm about her shoulders, and at last slipped his wanton hand down under the lace-edged bosom of her chemise. To his surprise and delight she made no objection; his hand was allowed to remain where it was in cosy comfort.

Now that the ice was broken, whenever Pepys called on Mrs. Penington he was free to enjoy his favorite indoor sport, to play "avec ses mamilles," and to plunge even deeper. With such encouragement he grew bolder. One cold December night he had supper with the lady at her lodgings and was mighty merry and very free with her. At last, very late, he begged her to undress herself into her nightgown [dressing gown]," pretending that he thought of having her picture drawn in negligée. He would walk about in the street until she was ready. She agreed easily enough. "So I did walk forth," said Pepys, "and whether I made too many turns or no in the darke cold frosty night between the two walls up to the Parke gate I know not, but she was gone to bed when I come again to the house." He never saw her again.[23]

In a way he was lucky: a maiden from an upper class family was not to be taken lightly. Anyway, it was time for Pepys to get back to his old routines. For months, because of his disorganized life, he had been unable to make up his Tangier records and balance his private accounts. He had even neglected his beloved diary for long stretches; once he was thirteen days behind in his entries.

As for his savings, he knew that he had long ago passed his goal of two thousand pounds. Now, if he wished, he could be a knight and keep his coach, or he could retire to Brampton, buy more land and set up as a country squire. But no man ever has enough money; enough is always a little more than he has. What with his full salary as Clerk of the Acts, his gratuities from merchants, the profits from his venture in prize goods, his dealings with the Tangier victualers, and his salary and share in the profits as Treasurer of Tangier, Pepys had been making money hand over fist. Never satisfied, he had even dreamed up a new job, contriving to get himself appointed as Surveyor-General of Victualing for the Fleet at a salary of three hundred pounds a year plus very sizable perquisites. Once he got five hundred pounds at a stroke from Denis Gauden, the victualer.

At the end of the year, with the Fleet safely stowed in winter quarters and the seamen paid off by ticket—bills calling for payment at some date in the distant future—he finally took the time to work out his tangled accounts. To his great joy he discovered that he was worth four thousand four hundred pounds (nearly $90,000), "for which the Lord be praised!" In one year he had increased his estate by two thousand seven hundred pounds, in spite of many extra expenses. "I have never lived so merrily," he wrote, "(besides that I never got so much) as I have done this plague time, by my Lord Bruncker's and Captain Cocke's good company, and the acquaintance of Mrs. Knipp, Coleman and her husband, and Mr. Laneare, and great store of dancings we have had at my cost (which I was willing to indulge myself and wife) at my lodgings." The ill winds of war had brought Mr. Pepys nothing but good.

# VIII

# London in Joy and Tears

# 1666

W HAT WITH Mrs. Tooker's comb, Mrs. Daniell's pneumatic bosom, and Mrs. Knep's sweet voice, Pepys found the
company at Greenwich so delightful that he lingered on
over the Christmas season and into the new year. At last
Elizabeth, who was becoming jealously aware of his weakness
for beauty, came down to fetch him home. She put her finger
on the real cause for his delay. "She is in the right," he confessed, "that I would have a little more of Mrs. Knipp's
company before I go away." He was half in love with the
pretty little actress—"my dear Mrs. Knipp"—and had been
since he first met her a month ago at Mrs. Pierce's lodgings.

For over a year Mary Knep had been a member of the
King's Company of Comedians and privileged to wear the
royal livery. Overshadowed by such experienced actresses as
Anne Marshall and Elizabeth Weaver, and too young for
anything but minor roles, she was still highly valued as a
singer. Her husband, "an ill, melancholy, jealous-looking
fellow," had something to do with horses at the Smithfield
markets, as "a kind of jockey." Mary was an "excellent, mad-
humored thing," witty, full of fun, and like most actresses
of the age free with her kisses and caresses. It was very easy

for Pepys to get her on his knee in a crowded coach and play with her breasts while she sang. Of all her songs, his favorite was a little Scotch ballad called "Barbary Allen." She wrote him notes, signing them by that name, and he replied, signing his letters with the name of another popular song, "Dapper Dickey." It was all very pleasant trifling and completely innocent. He hated to leave her and the other gay refugees at Greenwich, but most of them would soon be going back to London too.[1]

Pepys enjoyed life in all its infinite variety. It was good to get back to town, renew old friendships, find out who had died and who had survived the plague, reorganize his house and the Navy Office, now re-established in Seething Lane, meet with the virtuosos of the Royal Society, browse among his beloved books and papers, and settle back into the pleasant rut of normal life. The western suburbs where the gentry lived were still "infinitely naked" of people, but the City, in spite of at least seventy thousand plague deaths (about one out of every six citizens), was almost as full as ever. The King had ventured as near London as Hampton Court, and one day Pepys had the delicious pleasure of hearing his Majesty say, "Mr. Pepys, I do give you thanks for your good service all this year, and I assure you I am very sensible of it."

It was delightful, too, to go jaunting abroad to shops and pleasure gardens in a coach again, and when all the refugees were back in town it was great fun to go to somebody's house of an evening for music and dancing. One night Lord Brouncker and Madam Williams, Captain Cocke, Mrs. Knep, Pepys, Elizabeth, and Mary Mercer gathered at the Pierces' fine new house in Covent Garden, were "mighty merry," and sang and danced with great pleasure. Even Pepys danced, the first time in his life, he said, in company.[2]

Everyone in Pepys' circle of friends was gay that winter,

with the joy of relief after danger. There was little other
reason for merriment. There were dead friends to mourn;
the war with Holland, stalemated by winter, was due to break
out again in the spring; and the Dutch, now supported by
France and Denmark, were preparing a mighty Fleet. The
challenge had to be met, but England's trade had been
ruined by war and plague, and there was very little money
to be had. Parliament, looking for a scapegoat for the nation's
ills, threatened to call the Navy Office to account and mean-
time starved the service on which everything depended. No
matter. Pepys and his friends were alive and full of high
spirits. Death had passed them by; the luxury shops in the
Strand were opening one by one; the King and his Court
would soon be back at Whitehall; and there was even talk
of opening the theatres. The plague toll in January decreased
to fifty or fewer a week, and the first time Pepys went to
church snow had covered the fresh graves in the churchyard.
It was easy to forget the hideous past, ignore the future, and
dwell in the peaceful present.

Most of Pepys' friends and kinsfolk had come through the
plague unscathed, although there were sad gaps in St. Olave's
parish, and his clerks, Will Hewer and Tom Edwards, had
both lost their fathers. Pepys had lost only his old friend
Peter Luellin (with whom he had once visited a bawdy-
house), his aunt Edith Bell, and a few miscellaneous cousins.
All was well with his family at Brampton except for the fact
that Paulina, "a pretty good-bodied woman, and not over
thicke, but full of freckles and not handsome in face," was
still single. To encourage possible suitors Pepys offered to
give her a dowry of four hundred and fifty pounds from his
own pocket.[3]

Elizabeth's family, too, had survived the plague. In September Pepys had heard that her father was very ill and "like

to die." He sent the family twenty shillings, and the sick man recovered. The senior St. Michels, proud in their poverty, never visited their daughter at Seething Lane, and, although they liked him well enough, never asked their son-in-law to visit them in any of the hovels they inhabited. Six or eight times a year, Elizabeth would go to see her parents (once taking them "some apples, neat's tongues, and wine"), and Pepys would drop her off at or near their miserable lodgings. Once the old couple were living in "so ill-looked a place, among all the whore houses" in Longacre Street, that Pepys was troubled to have Elizabeth visit them. Balthazar St. Michel, who had married beneath him and had lost his pride, was frequently at Seething Lane with his wife. Pepys tried to help him, got him admitted into the Duke of Albemarle's Guards, and later found him a post in the Navy as a muster-master (personnel officer) of a squadron.[4]

The Sieur de St. Michel was too proud to beg, and, although Pepys was sorry for the old couple and often troubled by their condition, it was not easy for him to offer charity unasked. Yet in 1667, when they went to Paris to live, he sent them three gold jacobuses (worth about twenty-four shillings each) and hoped they would remain abroad. He could have made them an allowance, but he was helping Balty—the Navy post was worth one hundred pounds a year —and it was a son's business to take care of his parents. Pepys had his own family to worry about.

Yet he had money to spend on pleasure, on his house, and even on Elizabeth. He commissioned the painter John Hales to do a portrait of her as St. Catherine, a popular pose. The sittings were fresh occasions for gaiety: Pepys, Mrs. Knep, Mrs. Pierce, and Mary Mercer were regular visitors at the studio, chatting or singing while the painter worked. During his exile at Greenwich Pepys had set to music a song from the second part of *The Siege of Rhodes*, beginning,

> *Beauty retire; thou dost my pity move,*
> *Believe my pity, and then trust my love.*

He taught the song to Mrs. Knep, who sang so well at their gatherings that he thought it a very fine song indeed.

The portrait was very fine, too; it cost fourteen pounds, but it was well worth the money. Alas, two hundred years later a dour Scots nurse, offended by the depth of Elizabeth's painted decolletage, slashed the canvas to ribbons. Hollyer's engraving after Hales shows Elizabeth half-length in draperies which disclose her shoulders and much of her plump bosom. Her right hand holds a tired palm branch. The face is a smooth oval crowned with dark hair in ringlets interlaced with pearls. The mouth is small, the upper lip an impossible cupid's-bow, and the facial expression vaguely vapid.[5]

Music and dancing were not quite enough to satisfy Pepys' appetite for pleasure. He wanted the excitements of sex, the stimulus to the senses which Elizabeth could no longer give him. His pleasure came not merely from being wanton, but from being wanted. Most of the women in his private life were (or pretended to be) as eager for pleasure, as quickly stimulated, as he. They were mercenary only incidentally as they sought places or promotions for husbands. They ran from Pepys coyly, heads turned to smile, and when caught they responded with abandon. Pepys wanted to sport with Mrs. Bagwell in the shade, or with the tangles of Betty Martin's hair.

Unfortunately, Betty Martin had gone off with her husband, God knew where, and Mrs. Bagwell, her understudy, had followed her husband to Portsmouth, where the *Provi-*

*dence*, now repaired and ready for war, was berthed. Of Pepys' newer prospects, Judith Penington and Mary of the Harp and Ball had disappeared, Mary Knep was still untried, Frances Tooker was too young, and Mrs. Daniell, a likely wench, was hibernating at Greenwich, awaiting the fruit of the womb. (Her son John was christened on May 20, 1666.) From time to time Pepys visited Sarah of the Swan for a little dalliance, but he was afraid to do anything more with "the fairest flower." Constrained to virtue, he was becoming intolerant of sinners. He was shocked to hear that his friend John Creed had tried to rape a woman at Oxford when the Court was staying there, "and her crying out saved her." The report of Creed's wickedness, said Pepys, "do a little make me hate him." At times even Mr. Pepys had been forced to use his strength to gain his end, but his women had never cried for help.[6]

On February 20, three days before his thirty-third birthday, Pepys was in Westminster Hall on business. Hearing that Betty Martin had returned to town without her husband, he threw his affairs aside, waited until she came to her booth, and then carried her away to her lodgings, where he did what he had "a mind" to do with all the gusto of a sailor ashore after a long voyage. (Ten months later, a month after Betty had given birth to a daughter, she suggested to her lover that he was probably the child's father; it had "come la meme jour that it ought to" if it had been conceived at this meeting.)[7]

Now life was richer with Betty in town, even though she had "come to be very bad, and offers anything, that it is dangerous to have to do with her." Pepys braved her dangers as often as his affairs permitted, and sported with her whenever he found her without her husband, who returned to London in March and seemed to have nothing to do but sit around and spoil sport. Once, to get rid of Mr. Martin, Pepys

sent him out for wine, taking wicked advantage of his absence. Perhaps it would be best, after all, to get him a job
at sea. "The poor man I do think would take pains," said
Pepys, salving his conscience, "if I can get him a purser's
place, which I will endeavour."

Two months later one Samuel Martin, no doubt Betty's
husband, was purser of a merchant ship, the *East India
London*, which the Naval Commissioners had hired as an
auxiliary. Curiously, Pepys does not describe his efforts in
Martin's behalf at this time. Later he was to regret his kindness. One day he saw the vain fellow strutting through Westminster Hall while everybody "did fleer and laugh upon
him, crying, 'There is plenty grown upon a sudden.'" Pepys
was troubled because, he said, "methought the people do
gaze upon me as the man that had raised him, and as if they
guessed whence my kindness to him springs." Still it was a
small price to pay for the freedom of Betty Martin's bed.[8]

Pepys was far from idle during the winter and spring of
1666, but, as usual, his indulgence in pleasure kept him from
devoting his full energy to business. Yet he made his daily
rounds, wrote his letters, kept his accounts, mended his
fences with friends and patrons—the Carterets, the Mountagus, Sir William Coventry, and the Duke of Albemarle—
and learned that Lord Sandwich's fall from favor had not
affected his own prestige. He went on steadily with his work
of preparing the Fleet, and on March 1 returned to his former disciplinary vows, adding some that were even more
severe.

A week later he slipped back into his old ways. He was
at Sir William Batten's house, "and there Mrs. Knipp coming
we did spend the evening together very merry, she and I
singing, and, God forgive me! I do see that my nature is not
to be conquered, but will esteem pleasure above all things,

though yet in the middle of it, it has reluctances after my business, which is neglected by my following my pleasure. However, musique and women I cannot but give way to, whatever my business is." The next day he invited Mrs. Knep and Mrs. Pierce to dinner and spent a merry afternoon with them and Elizabeth, going out to the New Exchange to buy gloves and stockings, to Hales' to see Elizabeth's portrait, and to the Cakehouse hard by for cakes. "The truth is," he said, rationalizing, "I do indulge myself a little the more in pleasure, knowing that this is the proper age of my life to do it; and out of my observation that most men that do thrive in the world, do forget to take pleasure during the time that they are getting their estate; but reserve that till they have got one, and then it is too late for them to enjoy it with any pleasure." His own estate continued to grow by sheer momentum; by the end of March he was worth five thousand pounds.[9]

For two more months pleasure continued in the ascendant. When Elizabeth's portrait was done, Pepys decided to have his own likeness painted with the music of "Beauty Retire" in one hand. Hales posed him so that he almost broke his neck looking over one shoulder. Now it was his turn to be still while the ladies, Pierce, Knep, Elizabeth, and Mercer, formed a cheerful gallery—"and the picture goes all the better for it." The face of the portrait (now in the National Portrait Gallery in London) reflects no merriment, only the strain of a twisted neck.[10]

Pepys' woman-hunger grew with indulgence. One day he took "two or three wanton turns about the idle places and lanes about Drury Lane, but to no satisfaction, but a great fear of the plague among them." He was happy to learn that pretty Betty Howlett, the haberdasher's daughter—"she I call wife, and one I love mightily"—had married William

Michell, son of Mrs. Michell, a bookseller in Westminster Hall, and was coming to live in Thames Street, not far from Seething Lane. Thereafter he sought out the young Michells often, trying to get little Betty in a corner for a kiss or two, or to sit beside him in a coach for a variety of pleasures. He still pleased himself with Sarah of the Swan, and was lucky enough to be alone with her for a good while on Easter Sunday. To add to his collection he found a new maid, kissable, comely, "blɛck" (i.e., brunette) Nan, servant to an old woman, a paper ruler, in Pannier Alley. It was surprising how much paper the Navy Office had to have ruled.[11]

On the afternoon of April 18, as Pepys was driving from Westminster Hall to King Street, he saw his former love, Jane Welsh, once maid to his barber, Jervas. Always cautious, he drove on a little farther, dismissed his coach and walked back, catching up with her as she was about to take a boat at Westminster Stairs. She told him that she was going across the river to Lambeth. Pepys followed in another boat, and met her at an alehouse where they drank and talked. He does not say that she was seedy and down-at-heels; one can only guess at her condition from the care he took to avoid being seen with her.

She told her story briefly; as Pepys already knew, her "servant," the poor fiddler Harbing, had turned out to be already married. She denied that she had lain with Harbing several times in the barber's house, as Jervas had asserted more than a year ago. Pepys merely recorded the burden of their talk without comment, but obviously he no longer believed her tales. The old magic, her innocence, was gone; she was only a foolish girl, no longer even pretty. Since Elizabeth had gone off for a brief visit at Brampton, he could have reveled as he chose, but he was not tempted. He left her without trying to assay her tarnished virtue. Taking a boat to the City, he met Mrs. Pierce and Mrs. Knep by chance in Cornhill and carried them to Fish Street for a gay supper of prawns and lobsters.

Throughout the winter and early spring Pepys' relations with his wife were friendly, if not often amorous. He had learned, whenever they fell out, "to practise more temper, and to give her her way" whenever he could without loss of authority. On the day after her return from Brampton he reported "an houre or two's talk with my poor wife, who gives me more and more content every day than other." But "content" was not "pleasure." Immediately after this chat, Pepys took a coach to Westminster, met Betty Martin, and took her across the river to their old trysting place, the King's Head Tavern, "and there spent an hour or two with pleasure with her."

So long as Elizabeth obeyed him, lived thriftily and discreetly, and attended to her wifely duties, Pepys was content; he made few other demands upon her. In return Elizabeth seemed to be content so long as nothing crossed her and she had her share of outings and parties, a new petticoat or gown now and then, plus caps, scarves, gloves, and laces. Her mind rarely rose above the purely material. In April, fulfilling a long-standing promise, Pepys was content to spend eighty pounds for a pearl necklace which added briefly to Elizabeth's content.[12]

When she was not content everyone suffered, including her domestics, who came and went in an endless stream. On March 29, Alce, the cook-maid, quit, and Pepys persuaded Jane Birch to come back and serve as cook until a new maid could be found. In April two nameless women came in succession, stayed a day each, and departed. It was May before a new cook, Mary the Fourth, relieved Jane of her pots and pans and let her take up her superior work as a chambermaid.

But Mary stayed only two months. Her replacement, Luce, was an ugly girl but a good servant who stayed for nearly a year.[13]

In the winter Elizabeth got along very well with her husband's two women friends, Mrs. Knep and Mrs. Pierce, usually taking one on their outings with Pepys, gossiping with them, entertaining them in her home, and joining in the gallery at Hales' when Mrs. Pierce, in her turn, began to sit for her portrait. But gradually she grew jealous of the two ladies, either because both were pregnant, a happiness denied her, or more probably because her husband so obviously preferred their company to hers. Neither a wit nor a singer, she began to feel left out when the jolly trio jested and sang.

To re-establish herself she turned to her painting again, and quarreled violently with Samuel when he refused to let her master, Browne, come to dinner daily. "Very angry we were," said Pepys, "and I resolved all into having my will done, without disputing, be the reason what it will; and so I will have it." Frustrated in one direction, Elizabeth tried to shine in company by repeating long stories out of her favorite reading, *Le Grand Cyrus*, "which she would tell, though nothing to the purpose, nor in any good manner." The other ladies listened in polite, bored silence until Pepys, exasperated, bade her be still. "This she took unkindly," he said, "and I think I was to blame indeed; but she do find with reason, that in the company of Pierce, Knipp, or other women that I love, I do not value her, or mind [pay attention to] her as I ought." The fury of a woman scorned is nothing to that of a wife ignored.[14]

One day when Pepys met Mrs. Knep at Mrs. Pierce's house, took both ladies gadding for a merry hour or two, and then brought them home with him, he found Elizabeth "in mighty pain and mightily vexed" at his being abroad with them.

When the two ladies had left she blazed out in a fury, calling them "whores and I know not what," he said indignantly, "which vexed me, having been so innocent with them." That night when Pepys went sullenly to bed alone, Elizabeth came up later in great pain with a fit of colic, called to him for help, and begged his forgiveness. When her pain subsided the two went "very kindly to sleepe and good friends in the morning." But Elizabeth's jealousy remained, a cause for brooding and bitterness.[15]

With the approach of warm weather, Pepys' bureaucratic conscience nagged him incessantly, appearing like a spectre to warn him from his pleasures. He was no longer spurred by the need to grow rich, although he continued to live frugally and to gloat monthly over his swelling heaps of gold. But by now his work had become his life. He lived by the sense of achievement; having tasted the wine of success he thirsted for more. He had to give his best to the Navy for the joy of a job well done, and for the praise of his masters. But to do so he had to conquer again his love of pleasure.

On May 4, weary of his "late idle courses," he bound himself by strict vows to stay closely to his business until Whitsunday (June 3 in 1666). But two weeks later, being in Deptford on business, and knowing that Mrs. Bagwell had returned, he had to go in search of her. "Lord," he said that night, "to see with what itching desire I did endeavour to see Bagwell's wife, but failed, for which I am glad, only I observe the folly of my mind that cannot refrain from pleasure at a season above all others in my life requisite for me to show my utmost care in." But on the following Sunday his itching desire drove him to Westminster. He went straight to Betty Martin's lodgings ("she staying at home all the day for me"), and did what he would with her. His love of pleasure would not be mastered.[16]

Pepys' self-reproaches must not be taken too literally. Even with time out for pleasure, he was handling an enormous load of public business. Much of his success as an administrator lay in his ability to turn quickly from one situation to another, concentrating on each in turn. His capacious and orderly mind kept his affairs all neatly docketed and labeled; occasionally his head was too full of business to find room for pleasure, but it was never so full of pleasure as to make him seriously neglect his public business.

It was not his fault that the first battle of the summer campaign resulted in a victory for the Dutch. The English Fleet was ready, armed, provisioned, and manned. But the King had appointed as joint-admirals his cousin, dashing, headlong Prince Rupert of Bavaria, and the obstinate, hard-headed Duke of Albemarle, who commanded a ship as if it were a troop of horse, crying "Wheel to the right," or "Wheel to the left." Late in May, as a calculated risk, Rupert was sent off into the Channel with thirty ships to meet the empty threat of a French attack. On June 1 Albemarle with fifty ships found himself facing eighty-five Dutch sails off the coast of France near Ostend. A sensible commander would have retreated, but Albemarle, always contemptuous of the Dutch, insisted that he would give them "their bellies full." He did, and was well-nigh digested. For three days the overwhelming Dutch array battered Albemarle's Fleet, forcing it to retreat and capturing or burning ship after ship. On the fourth day the English Fleet, now reinforced by Rupert's squadron but still heavily outnumbered, returned to the attack. Sheer mettle was no match for gun metal, but it helped save the English from a complete rout. The Four Days' Battle ended with both sides exhausted; however, the English lost twenty ships and about eight thousand men, while the Dutch lost four to seven ships and only two thousand men. Score one for Holland.

Momentarily dazed by the news of the disaster, Pepys and his colleagues quickly rallied and set to work again. The shattered Fleet had to be augmented by hired merchant vessels, refitted, supplied, and got ready for sea in a hurry before the combined Dutch and French forces could stage an invasion. The brunt of the work fell as usual on the Clerk of the Acts. After celebrating his release from his oaths by a satisfying visit to Betty Martin on Whitsunday, Pepys drew up a new set of rules to carry him over to Christmas, including a vow never, on penalty of forfeiting five shillings to the poor, to go abroad except on public business. But he left himself a neat little loophole: if for six consecutive days he had kept all his vows, he could dispense with any one of them on the seventh day.

According to this unholy sabbatarianism, on June 13 he was free to go again in search of Mrs. Bagwell. In the evening he went down to Deptford, waited around until it was quite dark, and then walked to her house, where he did what he would with his expectant mistress. His ardor was tempered by fear when he learned that her maid had died of the plague, and the quarantine had been lifted just the day before his visit. "So I parted thence," he said, "with a very good will."[17]

The next day he was hard at work, and the task of refitting the Fleet went on a-pace. In late June there were all sorts of panicky rumors afloat: that the French had taken the Leeward Islands, that the Dutch Fleet was out again, heading for the coast of France with one hundred and thirty ships, and that six thousand French soldiers were ready to embark, with twelve thousand more in reserve. The government alerted the militia forces of all the coastal counties, and Mr.

Pepys, preparing for flight, began quietly changing his silver
money into gold.[18]

On July 25 (St. James's Day) the two Fleets met again in
the Channel off the mouth of the Thames. This time the
English won a short but bloody battle, putting the Dutch to
flight and losing only one major ship and some five hundred
men. The Dutch lost twenty ships and seven thousand men
killed and wounded.

August 14 was appointed as a day of Thanksgiving for the
victory. That night the Pepyses and their friends were very
merry after supper at Mrs. Mercer's house in Crutched
Friars, laughing, shouting, flinging fireworks (serpents and
rockets), and smutting each other with candle grease and
soot until most of them were "like devils." Then the party
adjourned to Seething Lane for drinks and dancing. Relief
and joy carried them to absurd lengths: Pepys, Will Batelier
(a young wine merchant), and one Mr. Banister dressed like
women; Mary Mercer put on a suit belonging to Tom Edwards and danced a jig, and Elizabeth, Nan Wright, and Peg
Penn donned male periwigs. "Thus we spent till three or four
in the morning," said Pepys, "mighty merry." The next day
they heard the best news of all, that in a brilliant raid on
the Dutch islands of Vlieland and Ter Schelling Sir Robert
Holmes had destroyed two Dutch warships, one hundred and
fifty merchantmen, and immensely valuable stores on the
islands. As the summer drew towards its close, the English
Fleet held command of the narrow seas.[19]

Quite naturally Pepys' private life suffered during this
season of storm and stress. Sometimes all he could do was
to snatch a kiss from the willing lips of young Betty Michell
or Sarah of the Swan as he flew about his business. But the
nature of his work was such that he could usually arrange
for breathing spaces, particularly on a seventh day when he

was free to dispense with one of his vows. In July and August
he managed a few calls on Mrs. Martin (who was now grossly
"big with child"), and in the course of flying visits to Deptford he got to at least see and chat with Mrs. Bagwell.

Now he complained about his lack of pleasure, but he
seemed always able to find a pretty woman to dally with.
If no one else, there was always Elizabeth's personal maid,
Mary Mercer, who, while she was helping her master to dress
in the morning, permitted him to handle her breasts—"they
being the finest," he confessed, "that ever I saw in my life."
Then there was attractive Elizabeth Burrowes, widow of
Lieutenant Anthony Burrowes of the *Centurion*, a 4th rate
warship. Pepys had first met her a year earlier at her mother's
shop in Westminster, and thought her then "a very pretty
woman for the mother of so many children." After her husband's death in December, 1665, she came to the Clerk of
the Acts for help in getting some money due from his ship.
This was the beginning of an amorous friendship; Pepys
"had a kiss or two of her," and found her modestly agree-
able. Since Mrs. Burrowes was intimate with Mrs. Martin,
Pepys met her occasionally at the latter's lodgings. Twice in
the summer (once forfeiting five shillings to the poor) he
took her on outings by coach to Lisson Green near Padding-
ton, treating her to food and drink, and sporting with her
in his usual two-handed fashion—"but all honest."[20]

A new acquaintance of mid-summer was Doll Lane, Betty
Martin's younger sister, as vulgar and coarse as Betty but
not so handsome—"a bad face, but good bodied girle." Pepys
met her one afternoon (a seventh day) when he called on
Mrs. Martin and found Betty, Doll, and Mrs. Burrowes to-
gether. After a while two other women came to call, Mrs.
Eastwood, a pretty widow, and Mrs. Fenton, unmarried.
Surrounded by five buxom, jolly wenches, Pepys, the ladies'

man, was in his element, and "here merry," he said, "kissing and looking on their breasts, and all the innocent pleasure in the world." When Doll sang a jigg, and the recently widowed Mrs. Eastwood "seemed to be sick and fainted" because it had been her husband's favorite song, Pepys cheered her up. "By and by," he said, "I made her as merry as is possible, and touseled and tumbled her as I pleased." There can be no doubt that he had a way with women— maids, wives, or widows.[21]

During the summer Pepys saw very little of Mrs. Knep and Mrs. Pierce, no doubt because both ladies had fulfilled their biological functions in June, and therefore, according to custom, "lay in" for a month. Each gave birth to a boy, and both infants died within a few weeks. The two families gave no outward signs of grief; perhaps custom had staled their woe. In Restoration England thirty-six out of every one hundred children died in infancy.[22]

In August, only a week or so after Mrs. Pierce had buried her child, she and her husband, the surgeon, called on the Pepyses one afternoon and found the equally bereft Mrs. Knep already there. Nothing was said about the dead infants. It could have been a gay occasion, but Elizabeth had been nursing her grudge against the two ladies a long time. She was in a "chagrin humour" and spoiling for a fight, very "slighting" to her guests, and finally downright offensive. Taking occasion to mention a report about herself, that she "was grown a gallant [fashion-plate]," she made it clear that she thought Mrs. Pierce the malicious gossip who had started the rumor. If people only knew, said Elizabeth, with a spiteful glance at her husband, how few suits of clothes she had had these past two or three years! Mrs. Pierce replied tartly that such idle talk should not trouble Mrs. Pepys. She herself, she said, had been victimized by a report that she was

crooked in body, a canard (she hinted broadly) which had
come from Seething Lane. Elizabeth flushed, but (said Pepys)
had the wit not to admit that she was the author of the libel
—"though she has said it twenty times."

By now the atmosphere was frigid. Annoyed and shamed,
Pepys managed to change the subject and to get Knep to
sing with him, but the pleasure of the visit was spoiled. After
a while he took his guests out to a tavern (Elizabeth refused
to go along), treated them with his best civility, and excused
his wife's ill humor as well as he could. When he got home
he found Elizabeth still "mightily out of order, and reproaching Mrs. Pierce and Knipp as wenches, and I know not what."
But Pepys refused the challenge, quietly "let all pass," and
went to bed in silence.

Elizabeth's conduct had been inexcusable, but Pepys knew
that a scolding would do no good and might do harm by
stirring up her fiery temper. Yet she must be checked lest
she take the bit in her teeth and run wild. A week later when
Pepys audited her kitchen accounts, he deliberately "took
occasion to fall out with her for her buying a laced handkercher and pinner [cap] without my leave." He was concerned, he said, about the principle involved, not the trifling
cost of the items—"I would not permit her to begin to do so
lest worse should follow." At all costs he must be master.
Both went to bed that night angry, and rose the next day
neither friends nor enemies, cold and silent. But before the
day was over they were friends again. On the following day,
with the theatres still closed, Pepys tried to mend matters
by taking Elizabeth and Mercer to the Beargarden on the
Bankside, where a bull was to be baited by a pack of mastiffs.
They saw "some good sport of the bull's tossing of the dogs,"
said Pepys, "one into the very boxes. But it is a very rude
and nasty pleasure"—unseemly sport for ladies.[23]

August ended quietly, with the Fleet at sea again hunting
for the Dutch. The summer had been hot and dry, and on
Saturday, September 1, a strong wind came up out of the
east. That night the King's baker, whose shop was in Pudding
Lane near the foot of London Bridge, went to bed without
making sure that his fires were out. At two o'clock in the
morning his apprentice woke up choking, found the house
full of smoke, and roused the household. The baker, his wife,
his daughter, and his man all escaped by climbing through
a garret window to the roof of the house next door. His maidservant was left behind to become the first victim of the
Great Fire of London. An hour later, Samuel Pepys at Seething Lane, a quarter of a mile to the east of Pudding Lane, was
wakened by his maid Jane to see a fire in the City. Yawning,
Pepys went to his window, saw that the flames were some
distance away, and went back to bed, missing the prelude to
a great civic tragedy.[24]

When he got up Sunday morning Pepys learned that above
three hundred houses had burned during the night, and that
the fire was raging furiously all along Fish Street, north of
the Bridge. All his love of sight-seeing roused, he hurried
out and climbed to a high place on the nearby Tower. From
this vantage point he saw "an infinite great fire" to the west,
blazing at the north end of the Bridge and sweeping west
and north into the City under the pressure of the strong
east wind. The tightly packed houses in the old City, built
of timber and lath covered with plaster, were tinder-dry, and
the warehouses along the river were full of combustibles,
oil, coal, spirits, tar, and sulphur.

Taking a boat at Tower Stairs, Pepys was rowed up-river
through the Bridge toward the heart of the fire. Against a
background of roaring flames and billowing smoke, he saw
hundreds of people flinging their goods into lighters along

the bank, and running madly from stairs to stairs to save
their own lives. The sight was so appalling that for an hour
he could only sit in his boat and watch. Then, seeing that
no attempts were being made to fight the fire, Pepys went
on up to Whitehall, reported to the King, and suggested that
his Majesty order houses to be pulled down in the path of
the flames.

He was right; there was no other way to control a fire.
With nothing but buckets, barrels on wheels, and two-handed
squirts, only trifling amounts of water could be poured on
a burning building. But a gang of brawny men with chains
and grappling hooks could easily tumble the slightly built
houses to the ground, leaving gaps to stop the flames. Bearing
the King's orders to the Lord Mayor, Pepys took a coach to
St. Paul's, and thence hurried a-foot through the wild uproar,
confusion, and smoke of the City, dodging loaded carts,
streams of people with bundles on their backs, and the sick
carried in their beds. In Canning Street he found the hot,
distracted Lord Mayor with a handkerchief around his neck.
"Lord!" he cried, "What can I do? I am spent: people will
not obey me. I have been pulling down houses: but the fire
overtakes us faster than we can do it." In the universal panic
everyone thought only of saving himself and his goods, and
there were no fire companies.

After dinner Sunday Pepys spent the rest of the day with
Elizabeth and the friends who had been his dinner-guests,
going up and down the river, watching the wind-blown fire
grow and spread ever westward along the bank and up the
rising ground into the heart of the City. At dark, from a
little alehouse on the Bankside, they watched the fire grow;
"and as it grew darker," said Pepys, "churches and houses,
as far as we could see up the hill of the City, in a most horrid,
malicious bloody flame, not like the fine flame of an ordinary

fire. We staid till, it being darkish, we saw the fire as only one entire arch of fire from this to the other side of the bridge, and in a bow up the hill for an arch of above a mile long: it made me weep to see it. The churches, houses, and all on fire and flaming at once; and a horrid noise the flames made, and the cracking of houses at their ruin." Finally, "with a sad heart," Pepys took his wife home and started packing his goods and valuables.

No one in the Pepys' household slept that night. At four o'clock Monday morning Pepys loaded his chests of plate and silver money into a cart and took them to Sir William Rider's house at Bethnal Green, a safe two miles northeast of London. He spent the rest of the day at Seething Lane with his family, laboring to get his household goods over Tower Hill and into a lighter at the Iron Gate east of the Tower. He was much too busy saving his goods to pay attention to the fire.

The bellowing east wind blew all day. Elsewhere the sun shone in a clear hot sky, but over London it was a red ball seen dimly through a pall of smoke. One vast body of fire leaped up into the heart of the City, licking up Lombard Street, Cornhill, and the Royal Exchange; another body rolled along the river bank westward through Queenhithe, fattening on the rich food of wharves and stores. By Monday night the fire had devoured almost half of the City within its ancient walls. Nothing could stop it. When the fire-fighters made a clear space by pulling down houses or blowing them up with gunpowder, the fire leaped skyward across the gap and went its all-consuming way.

Monday night Pepys and his family snatched a little sleep, lying on quilts on the floor of the Navy Office. By daybreak they were all up and at work again, slightly handicapped by the loss of Mary Mercer. The girl had gone home to help her mother, and when she returned hot-tempered Elizabeth "bid her be gone again" for good. Against the force of the wind, now rising to gale strength, the fire burned very slowly eastward toward the Tower, but by Tuesday morning it was in Tower Street, creeping toward the foot of Seething Lane. Pepys, Penn, and Batten busied themselves digging pits in the Navy Office garden, burying official papers, wine, and Pepys' Parmesan cheese. Tuesday saw the destruction of Cheapside, the Guildhall, and all the City north to Cripplegate, while to the west the fire overwhelmed St. Paul's Cathedral in a gout of flame that melted the lead roof, and then roared on toward Newgate and Ludgate into the suburbs, flowing down Fleet Street toward the Strand. To an observer across the river London was a huge spreading cloud of smoke and flame.

Tuesday night the wind veered to the south and slowly died. The exhausted fire-fighters—citizens, soldiers, dockyard men, and seamen from the Fleet, all led by the tired King and his brother—redoubled their efforts. At two o'clock the next morning, Pepys, alarmed by reports that the fire was at the bottom of Seething Lane, took his family and two thousand three hundred and fifty pounds in gold down to Mr. Sheldon's house in Woolwich. By daybreak he was back in London, fully expecting to see the Navy Office in flames, but the blowing up of houses had stopped the fire's eastward progress. The great Fire was under control but not yet quenched. It burned all day Wednesday, but the wind had fallen to a flat calm, and by sunrise on Thursday the fire had died out. The ruins smoked for weeks, and from time to time small fires broke out in cellars and unconsumed wreckage.

The City within its walls was almost completely destroyed: 13,200 houses, 87 parish churches, and numerous public

buildings were burned to the ground, and more than a hundred thousand people were driven from their homes to rude
encampments in the fields. Strangely, only a half dozen or so
died in the flames, but hundreds of the sick and frail died
of exposure and hardship. The total cost of the Great Fire
has been estimated at nearly eleven million pounds, and, of
course, there was no such a thing as insurance. At least, by
purifying thousands of pest-ridden stink-holes, the fire helped
put an end to the plague.[25]

In the midst of calamity men are always true to their
natures: cowardly or brave, predatory, covetous, generous,
miserly, cruel, or lecherous. During the course of the fire
most men were cowards, but there were heroes too, notably
King Charles, who rode about unmindful of his safety with
a bag of guineas to reward the fire-fighters, and sometimes
dismounted to take a hand with spade or bucket. At the
same time there were thieves at work, pillaging deserted
houses all around the edge of the flames. There were profit-
eers who demanded and got as much as fifty pounds for the
rent of a cart, and there were good Samaritans who gave help
and refuge to the homeless. Yet one rich old miser, an alderman, gave only two shillings sixpence to be divided among
thirty seamen who had saved his house. Frantic mobs, convinced that the fire had been set by England's enemies,
attacked every foreigner in the street, and nearly dismem-
bered a Frenchman carrying a boxful of "fireballs," which,
too late, were found to be tennis balls.[26]

True to his nature, too, Samuel Pepys, the man of property, first made sure of all his goods and valuables. Then,
with the fire out and all his household safe at Woolwich
while he slept in a room at Sir William Penn's lodgings, he
was free (on his "seventh" day) to try a new experience, to
revel all night at Deptford in Mrs. Bagwell's arms. He sent

the carpenter off to join his ship, and laid his plans with Mrs. Bagwell. On the morning of September 12 he dallied away an hour or two at Westminster, doing what he would with Betty Martin. After dinner he went down-river, past the still smoking ruins of the City, to Deptford where his household goods were stored, and spent a long afternoon seeing to their loading on a yacht to be brought back home to Seething Lane. When it was quite dark he made his stealthy way to the carpenter's house.

In the secret night he found everything exactly as he had hoped: a warm welcome, a pair of loving arms, and a mistress loosely dressed to serve his riotous appetite. He did, he said, "do all that I desired." But he had not counted on the revulsion of satiety. Yesterday he had dreamed of spending a long night carousing on the couch of luxury. Now, after consummating once, his lust had turned to ashes. For the moment he hated both the woman and the deed, and could think only of getting away from both. Using as his excuse the groundless argument that the carpenter might return, he got up, said farewell, and went sadly back up-river to his borrowed bed.

# IX

# A Noise of Strumpets

# 1666
# ——
# 1667

By the end of September everything was normal again
at Pepys' house in Seething Lane: the beds and hangings
were in place, the chests of plate and money safely stowed,
and Pepys' beloved books all arranged in their neat, uniform
rows. His little section of East London was not even scorched,
but he had only to walk to the foot of Seething Lane and
three hundred yards west on Tower Street to reach a vast
waste of blackened rubble, gaunt towers, and skeleton steeples
where the City of London had stood in all its pride. Churches,
shops, factories, and houses were gone—and with them the
carts and horses, the crowds of shoppers, the cries of street
vendors, and the "What d'ye lack?" of bawling apprentices.
Dozens of Pepys' friends had lost everything they owned, and
two of his kinsmen, Tom Pepys, a turner, and Anthony Joyce,
a leather-seller, had been burned out.

Re-building had begun—in brick and stone this time—
almost before the ashes cooled, but ten years were to pass
before the new City would be complete. Now the ruins were
haunted by thieves and footpads. When Pepys had to go

through the desolate City by coach after dark, he carried his
naked sword across his knees. For weeks after the fire he was
haunted by "dreams of fire, and falling down of houses."[1]

At the office every day he did little but listen to the pleas
of merchants seeking payment for their bills. Almost daily
he went to Whitehall, or to nearby St. James's Palace where
the Duke of York lived, to complain about the Navy's debts
and needs. Called before a Committee of Parliament he
defended the conduct of his office; called before the King's
Council he urged the need for money to build up a powerful
Fleet. The Parliament which met in late September voted
the King one million eight hundred thousand pounds, a great
sum, but not enough even to pay his Majesty's debts. Moreover, although Parliament could vote taxes, the King could
not collect them; war, plague, and now fire had brought England to the edge of bankruptcy. When the Navy asked for a
mere fifty thousand pounds for current expenses, the King
could find only five thousand pounds. Ships had to be laid
up to rot at their wharves; workmen starved in the dock-
yards; the unpaid seamen clamored for their money and
rioted when they were paid off in tickets; and the long-
suffering merchants refused further credit.

At Court, on the 'Change (now meeting at Gresham
College), at the Navy Office, and in the surviving taverns,
sober men shook their heads, prophesied the destruction of
the nation, feared an invasion in the spring, and complained
about the government. If only the King and his brother
would pay attention to business (they said) instead of minding only their pleasure! But the King was still running after
pretty Frances Stuart, and the Duke of York was given up to
"bitchering" (as good Mr. Evelyn called it) with his newest
mistress, Lady Denham. In his moments of self-pity Pepys
thought seriously of retiring to Brampton with his little for-

tune. There he might live peacefully, and study, and pray for his King and country.[2]

But the life of an administrator, with all its troubles, was still rich and varied—and very well paid. In September Pepys, Penn, and Batten begged the loan of a Dutch prize, a 6th rate man-of-war renamed the *Flying Greyhound*. Equipping and manning it at their own expense, the partners sent it forth as a privateer to prey on Dutch and French shipping. They profited considerably from the prizes captured by their piratical commander, Captain Hogg, who made little distinction between friend and foe. By the end of 1666, "the year of publick wonder and mischief," Pepys was worth six thousand two hundred pounds. The safety of his money and plate was becoming a vexing problem. In November he had nearly two thousand eight hundred pounds in gold locked up in a chest in his study. He knew it was not safe there, but he had nowhere else to keep it, and he was wary of lending it to the goldsmiths, who were the bankers of the day.[3]

Although the Navy Office still had plenty of paper work to do, Pepys no longer had the incentives of war and ambition to keep him at his desk, especially after the King and his Council decided not to set out a Fleet and to try instead to make peace with Holland. He drifted contentedly enough through the wet, gloomy autumn and the coldest winter England had ever known, now active, now passive, as the winds of politics blew. Habit kept him going through the motions, but, especially when the Duke of York and Sir William Coventry were out of town, he often played truant, turning to domestic affairs and to all sorts of pleasures.

His family and his household took up some of his time. His younger brother, John, having taken his degree at Cambridge, had recently been ordained in the Church of England, and in October Pepys sent for him to come and stay in Lon-

don while he looked about for a pastoral post. Pepys had very
little hope for his melancholy brother's success as a clergyman. He had preached only twice; his voice was bad; and
he had no taste for scholarship—a sorry prospect for a church
which prized oratory and learning above piety. But he was a
sober, harmless young man, who caused no trouble and
busied himself in numbering and cataloguing Pepys' books.
When he returned to Brampton in February—still a shep-
herd without a flock—Elizabeth and Samuel were sad to see
him go.[4]

A month after the Great Fire, Pepys persuaded his wife
to let Mercer come back, only to find that the foolish girl
had had enough of service and wished to live at home. The
Pepyses and their neighbors, the Mercers (Mary, her mother,
and her sister Anne) continued on friendly terms and often
saw each other, but Pepys had to engage a new personal maid
for Elizabeth. He found a slattern named Barker, who never
achieved the dignity of a Christian name in the *Diary*. Something of a singer, and not bad looking when she was properly
dressed, Barker was a mean-spirited creature with the soul
of a charwoman. She had rather, she said, "be put to drudgery
and to wash the house than to live as she did like a gentlewoman." Elizabeth endured her for seven months before
turning her off as incompetent and a liar.[5]

In October, under compulsion, Elizabeth called on her
enemy Mrs. Pierce, sullenly patched up the quarrel she had
started, and even invited Mrs. Pierce and Mrs. Knep to
dinner two days later. Pepys was "infinitely merry" with his
friends at dinner, and afterward took all three ladies to the
New Exchange in the Strand and bought them perfumed
gloves. The friendship between the three families seemed to
be back on its old footing, but jealousy still gnawed at Elizabeth's vitals. Nonetheless, there were some very merry parties

that winter. One, given by the Pepyses late in January, was memorable. Mrs. Pierce, who had a wide acquaintance among theatrical people, had promised to bring some of the players for the evening. A number of other invited guests came early, among them Will Batelier, Mary and Anne Mercer, Captain Edward Rolt, Mrs. Anne Jones, and Elizabeth's former dancing master, Pembleton—a master stroke of Pepysian diplomacy. Anon, about seven or eight o'clock, in came Mrs. Pierce with Henry Harris, of the Duke's Company of Comedians, and Mary Knep, almost unrecognizable in the country dress and straw hat which she had worn that afternoon in a performance of Suckling's *The Goblins.* "A merry jade," said Pepys.

He had provided four fiddlers and quantities of food and drink. In the large outer office of the Navy Board, well swept, and garnished with candles for the occasion, the company danced and sang until midnight, stopped to eat supper, and then danced again "with extraordinary pleasure" until three o'clock. Toward morning Mrs. Knep fell ill, and Elizabeth took her to the Pepyses' house and put her to bed. After everybody else had left, Pepys and Mrs. Pierce went into the house and upstairs in the dark to waken Knep. "And there," said Pepys, "I handled her breasts and did baiser la, and sing a song, lying by her on the bed, and then left my wife to see Mrs. Pierce in bed to her, in our best chamber, and so to bed myself, my mind mightily satisfied with all this evening's work, and thinking it to be one of the merriest enjoyments I must look for in the world." But there was a fly in his cup of pleasure: his band of fiddlers insisted on getting thirty shillings for their night's work.[6]

Elizabeth was jealous of both Mrs. Pierce and Mrs. Knep, but she had reason to be jealous only of the actress. Curiously Pepys never tried to be intimate with pretty Mrs. Pierce, kissing her only by way of friendly salute, but with Mary Knep he was very free, sometimes even in his wife's presence. Of course Elizabeth had no notion how much more reason she had to be jealous of the other women in her husband's life—Mrs. Bagwell, Betty Martin, Elizabeth Burrowes, Mrs. Daniell, Doll Lane, Sarah of the Swan, and Betty Michell. Once or twice in the winter and spring of 1667 she came very near finding out.

With plenty of time for pleasure, Pepys paid little heed to his vows (except against plays), and let his amorous fancies and hands roam at will. Yet for much of the winter he was at least technically continent. One reason for his temperance was the fact that for three months after Betty Martin had given birth to a daughter in November, Pepys, disturbed by the thought that he might have fathered the infant, feared to meddle further with the mother.

It seems, too, that his moment of revulsion after his September orgy with Mrs. Bagwell had left him with a certain distaste for the carpenter's wife. At any rate, he neglected her, somewhat to her chagrin. Her husband's ship, the *Providence*, was still in service, but with so many ships-of-war being laid up the Bagwells' fortunes depended more than ever on Mr. Pepys' favor. One day in October when Pepys had been at Deptford on business and was walking homeward by a short-cut through the fields (without even calling on his mistress!), Mrs. Bagwell spied him from her window, climbed over the garden fence in her haste, and walked some little distance with him. Pepys does not report her conversation, but we can guess that it was a mixture of reproaches, invitations, and pleas for her husband.

In November Mrs. Bagwell, bent on luring Pepys back to her bed, made two trips upriver to the Navy Office. Pepys took her into his private office and did what he would with her (kissing and tousing), without, it seems, much enthusiasm. Patient Mrs. Bagwell bided her time. The storms and cold of mid-winter made travel between Deptford and London dangerous, but late in January she got word to Pepys of a propitious day for a visit. By this time he was sharp-set again; in addition he had hopes of a better post for the carpenter. After dinner on February 1—"a thick misty and rainy day"— he took a boat down to Redriffe and thence, to escape meeting anyone who might know him, walked across the fields to Deptford. The carpenter was conveniently absent, but his pliant wife was waiting, and Pepys found it easy to lead her upstairs to bed, where he reveled freely in her arms. Afterward they went downstairs again, and "by and by," said Pepys, "su marido [her husband] come in, and there, without any notice taken by him, we discoursed of our business of getting him the new ship building by Mr. Deane, which I shall do for him."

Five days later he sent Mr. Bagwell to Sir William Coventry with a note urging his employment on the carpentry of the *Resolution,* a 3rd rate warship under construction at Harwich. His recommendation was duly honored. On March 4 he made a surprise visit to Deptford, found his mistress washing, and "did hazer [do]" all that he wished with her. Afterward he sent for the carpenter to tell him the good news and warn him to leave that week for Harwich. His reward for all this kindness was only a sense of virtue; dutiful Mrs. Bagwell followed her husband to Harwich, and Pepys lost his chance to "hazer" anything with her for more than a year. He turned once again to Betty Martin.[7]

Pepys' temporary abstinence from Mrs. Martin and his subsequent loss of Mrs. Bagwell increased his interest in his other wenches, who were wanton but still technically undefiled. Success had made him bolder. Now he was no longer content merely to kiss and toy; his tousing and tumbling implied intimacies which would have outraged all but the most immodest. Generally his wenches fell in with his whims and cooperated. Sometimes they struggled, but he was not easily rebuffed. Unlike Elizabeth, they were not "ladies" to be treated with respect. They were Pepys' inferiors, the servants of his pleasure, his hand-maidens.

Now and then in the autumn of 1666, when he called on pregnant Betty Martin, he found Doll Lane or Elizabeth Burrowes present. One Sunday afternoon, meeting both ladies in Betty's lodgings, he "did tumble them all the afternoon" as he pleased, while Betty looked on with envy. Sometimes through the winter he met Mrs. Burrowes at his office or elsewhere and spent an hour kissing her, playing with her breasts, and coaxing her to try even bolder intimacies. He discovered that Doll Lane was as wanton as her sister and often took her out to such warm, cheerful taverns as the Dog, the Bell, or the Rose, for an hour of drinking, talking, and games under the table. He might, he said, given time and place, have done anything he wished with Doll. Usually he was content to handle her breasts and disarrange her petticoats.[8]

Then there was Mrs. Daniell, who came up from Greenwich one wintry day to beg for her husband's promotion. Pepys took her into his private office, kissed her, explored her bosom, and made some painless promises. His pretty barmaid, Sarah of the Swan, seemed lost to him when she left her tankards and bottles in November to marry a shoemaker. But Pepys kept in touch with her; now that she was married he began to have some hopes of getting into bed with her. She still visited the Swan, and one night, in the course of a convivial evening, Pepys "did lay the beginnings of a future amour con elle"—a bud that never flowered.

Sarah kindly provided a younger sister, Frank, as her successor at the Swan. Pepys, who loved to nibble at nubility, found her as coming as he could wish. Once he was a little chagrined when her uncle, Mr. Herbert, came into the bar while he was "tumbling of la little fille" and found her without her gorget and with her young breasts half disclosed. But Mr. Pepys passed the situation off with a laugh, and Mr. Herbert said nothing. The Clerk of the Acts was privileged—and to young women irresistible. There was Margaret Penn, for example, the fifteen-year-old daughter of Commissioner Penn and sister of the soon-to-be famous Quaker, William Penn. Pepys had known her as a homely child; now, suddenly, she was a woman and desirable. Even though she was betrothed to Anthony Lowther of Yorkshire, she permitted Mr. Pepys to kiss her in private and play with her breasts, and after her marriage in February she allowed him even more freedom. She came to Pepys' office one day, and there he handled her breasts and kissed them and her mouth—"which she took fort willingly."[9]

There was nothing abnormal about Pepys' interest in youth. He was a man of his time, a world which agreed that teen-age girls were women, ripe for seduction or marriage. Barbara Villiers was only fifteen and not at all precocious when she lost her virtue to the Earl of Chesterfield (twenty-six). Frances Stuart was barely sixteen when King Charles (thirty-three) fell in love with her and did his best to seduce her. Frances Brooke was eighteen when she married Sir John Denham, then in his fifties. A year later she became the mistress of the Duke of York (thirty-three). Nell Gwyn was fifteen when she succumbed to the actor Charles Hart (about thirty-five); she was seventeen in the summer of 1667 when she left the stage briefly as mistress to Charles, Lord Buckhurst (thirty-four) ; and she was eighteen when she became mistress to the King, whom she called her "Charles the Third." The favorite theme of Restoration comedy is the marriage of a rich old man to a youthful beauty who is promptly seduced by the nearest young gallant. Many an aging actress must have blushed under the paint to hear herself described on the stage as fresh, beautiful, blooming, and sixteen—the ideal age.

The fact is that seventeenth-century youth had a monopoly on beauty. What with bad diet, disease, frequent child-bearing, and medical malpractice, a beauty who reached maturity with her figure intact, with all her teeth and hair, and with her face unmarred by smallpox, was an exception to the rule. Elizabeth Pepys, married at nearly fifteen, had lost at least two irreplaceable teeth (one a front tooth) by the time she was twenty-one, and when she was twenty-seven her husband was troubled at her "hair coming out so much." Fortunately she escaped disease. When pretty Frances Stuart fell prey to smallpox everyone predicted that her beauty would be wholly spoiled, "which," said Pepys, 'is the greatest instance of the uncertainty of beauty that could be in this age." Five months later, when he saw her for the first time after her recovery, he agreed sadly that her face had lost much of its charm.[10]

Pepys' infatuation with young Betty Michell grew in part from his admiration for her beauty. At one time he thought her one of the prettiest women that he had ever seen in his life ("une de plus pretty mohers that ever I did voir in my vida"). But it is likely that something stronger moved him: the longing to experience again the ecstacy of his first love, an emotion which had been so intense as to leave him transported. He remembered it one day at the theatre as he listened to the wind music in a revival of Massinger's *The Virgin Martyr*, "which is so sweet," he said, "that it ravished me, and indeed, in a word, did wrap up my soul so that it made me really sick, just as I have formerly been when in love with my wife." Ever since he had known little Betty he had jestingly called her his "wife" because she made him think of his own Elizabeth in the first flush of womanhood. Now that Betty had grown up, perhaps he could recapture with her some of the lost enchantment of his youth. At some time in his middle years every man tries to turn back the clock. The hands move, but the striker still sounds the hour.[11]

Betty Michell, whose parents, the Howletts, were haberdashers in Westminster Hall, had been betrothed since childhood to the older son of the Michells, booksellers in the Hall. When the groom-to-be died of the plague, his brother William inherited the promised bride. Betty was well pleased; she had always preferred the younger brother, a little fellow but a man of mettle. The two were married on March 19, 1666, and the parents combined to set them up in a strongwater (brandy) shop in Old Swan Lane off Thames Street, west of London Bridge. It was a good location and they prospered. In September they were burned out by the Great Fire, but by the end of October the energetic young husband had built a flimsy booth on the old site and was back in business again. Later he added a pretty little house behind the booth.[12]

From the beginning of their married life, Pepys, making much of his old friendship with the Howletts and Michells, had taken the young couple under his wing. He invited them often to dinner (fortunately Elizabeth liked them), took them by boat or coach to Westminster of a Sunday to visit their families, dropped in at their shop frequently for his "morning draught," the usual alcoholic substitute for breakfast, and took every possible occasion to make love to Betty behind her husband's back.

He had always felt a strong affection for Betty, and now his romantic imagination persuaded him that he was in love with her, just as he had been in love with "innocent" Jane Welsh, the barber's maid. He spoke of her in words that he never used with Mrs. Martin, Mrs. Bagwell, or Doll Lane. "I do exceedingly love her," he said, or "I love her very much," or "I aimais her de toute my corazon." Her image was so often in his mind that once he mistook another woman for her, "taking her a clap on the breech, thinking verily it had been her." He was happy merely to be in her company, dining or talking, but platonic love was not enough; the flesh, too, must be satisfied. During the summer and autumn of 1666 he tried often to get her alone for the tousing and tumbling which were his usual preliminaries to seduction. The fact that she was pregnant bothered him not at all.[13]

What troubled Mr. Pepys was the fact that he could never get Betty Michell alone; she was always with her family or her husband, a jealous and alert young man. But the Clerk's ingenuity was not to be balked. On December 2, 1666, he borrowed Sir William Penn's coach and took Elizabeth and the Michells to Westminster to the christening of Betty Martin's daughter, born on November 24. What with wine and cakes and much good company, chiefly shopkeepers and their wives from the Hall, it was night before the party broke up. On the way home by moonlight Betty Michell sat beside Pepys, who got her hand into his lap and held it to him in a fashion so intimate that a truly modest young woman should have been distressed. Three weeks later, on the way to Westminster in a coach with the Michells, he tried to repeat the pleasure, "but she did in a manner withhold" her hand, perhaps because it was daylight. That night on the way home with the young couple, he had better luck, "she making many little endeavours para stir su main but yielded still." Again, in January, on the way down-river from Westminster in a boat, Pepys got Betty's hand to him under his cloak. By now she was well-educated; after all, she had grown up in a coarse and vulgar world. Ten days later when she again sat beside him in a coach, he took her hand "which," he said, "elle did give me very freely now." He did whatever he wished with it, to his great pleasure.[14]

It was time now to try for an assignation at a tavern. For the first time in his libertine career Pepys had to deceive a suspicious husband. On the morning of February 11 he called at the Michells' shop and, with a plausible reason, persuaded Michell to send his wife to meet both the Pepyses that afternoon at the New Exchange. (Of course he had not the slightest intention of bringing Elizabeth along.) About five o'clock, when Betty appeared at the New Exchange, she was surprised to find Pepys alone, but he had a good lie ready and without more ado carried his love across the river to a cabinet-maker's, where he spent twenty shillings on a dressing-box for her. He was glad to learn that it would take an hour or so to finish the box properly, "thinking to have got elle to entrer to a casa de biber [wine shop]." But Betty preferred visiting a sister who lived nearby, and Pepys was forced to waste an hour wearily walking the streets. When he met Betty at the cabinet-maker's the work was still not done, and the mistress of the shop invited them to wait in her kitchen. She took Betty for Pepys' wife—"which I owned," he said, "and her great belly, and there very merry, till my thing done, and then took coach and home. . . ." Although it had been a disappointing day, at least he had Betty amorously alone in a coach.

But by now it was long after dark. Pepys' pleasure was

spoiled by the thought that young Michell, worrying about his wife's absence, might go to Seething Lane to inquire, and finding Mrs. Pepys at home "would not only think himself, but give my femme occasion to think strange things." His simple deceit was growing into a tangled web. Betty appeared unconcerned, but without protest she got out of the coach at the turning nearest to her house and walked the rest of the way with him, as if coming from Seething Lane. Michell had indeed worried, and had just sent his maid to inquire at Seething Lane. As quickly as he dared, Pepys took leave and ran home, stopping at his doorway "in a sweat" to think what he could say to Elizabeth. "As God would have it," he said, "while I was in this case (the worst in reference à my femme that ever I was in in my life), a little woman comes stumbling to the entry steps in the dark." When Pepys challenged her she asked for his house, and he recognized her voice; Michell's maid had loitered on the way and he had beaten her by a hair. With his heart full of joy he told the woman that her mistress was safe at home; confidently, then, he entered his house and found his wife unsuspicious and everything as it should be.

But all was not well with Betty Michell. As Pepys was to learn, young William was a tough little fellow who would stand for no nonsense from his wife. (His mother-in-law complained that he abused Betty and made "a slave of her.") We do not know what he said to Betty the night she came home so late, but the next time Pepys was with her he found her changed. He was coming home by boat one night with the Michells, "it being fine moonlight," and tried to snuggle up to Betty as usual, but she shrank from him, keeping close to her husband and refusing to let Pepys take her hand. When they landed at the Old Swan Stairs, Pepys sent young Michell back to the boat on a fool's errand, hoping for a kiss from Betty, but she turned her head away. "Shall I not touch thee?" he asked, and she answered coldly, "I do not love touching." Pepys went home deeply troubled by her attitude. "But," he said virtuously, "I think I shall make good use of it and mind my business more."[15]

Although he did not realize it at the time, this was the ignominious end to his affair with Betty Michell. The two families remained on friendly terms; the Michells often came to dinner; and in April Mrs. Pepys helped deliver Betty's daughter and stood godmother when the child was christened. But Betty, fearful of her husband's anger, took care to avoid being alone with Mr. Pepys. For months Pepys nourished his hunger on the spare diet of visits and talks, but he had learned to be patient. He felt sure that eventually he would trap his shy bird. Once, half a year after his one fruitless assignation with Betty, he found her alone in her brandy-shop and kissed her heartily. She accepted his kiss, he said, "with a great deal of seeming regret, which did vex me. But however I do not doubt overcoming her as I did the moher [woman] of the monsieur at Deptford." Perhaps he might have if young Michell had been in the service of the Navy.[16]

Pepys' resolve to mind his business was an empty threat. Even though the Lord Chancellor was pleased to say that "no man in England was of more method, or made himself better understood" than he, Mr. Pepys was working at only half speed. Sometimes he was really busy and did the King good service, but with only flying squadrons at sea instead of a full-sized Fleet to be manned and victualed, he often had so little to do that he felt he was hardly earning his various salaries and perquisites. Yet his estate continued to grow. On his birthday, February 23, he thanked God for his health and his "condition of estate, much beyond whatever my

friends could expect of a child of their's, this day 34 years."
He was now worth six thousand eight hundred pounds.[17]

In the winter and spring of 1667 he was free to devote as
many hours as he wished to pleasure: plays, music, and, of
course, women. Even his mother's death on March 25 interrupted his pursuit of pleasure only briefly. He was deeply
touched and wept heartily when he read John's letter with
its account of her final hours and her last words, "God bless
my poor Sam," but then he reflected how fortunate it was
that she had not outlived his father—"she being helpless"—
and felt better. What a nuisance if he had been obliged to
keep her in his own house—a quarrelsome, troublesome old
woman! Pepys had as much filial piety as the next man, and
was sensible of the debt children owed their parents, but, like
most children, he was not eager to pay it. Nevertheless, concerned as always about appearances, he promptly put his
household in mourning. Three days later he went to the
theatre again.[18]

The public theatres had been open since late November,
1666, and Pepys saw his share of plays, sometimes breaking
the vows which he had re-written at the first of the year.
He saw five plays in December, four in January, three in
February, five in March, eight in April, and three in May.
He might have gone to the theatre even more often in April
had not Elizabeth warned him that his office staff was talking
about his minding his pleasure too much. Of course he followed with interest the fortunes of Mary Knep, who was
"coming on to be a great actor," and who introduced him to
the backstage life of the Theatre Royal. One day in January,
after the play was over, she took Pepys, Elizabeth, and Dr.
and Mrs. Pierce backstage to meet witty Nell Gwyn, "a most
pretty woman." Pepys kissed her with relish. Mrs. Knep insisted that they all stay in a side-box to watch a rehearsal of

the dancing for the next day's play. "And so away thence," said Pepys, "pleased with this sight also, and especially kissing of Nell."[19]

Spectacles, plays, puppet-shows, dances—"Polichinelli" in Moorfields, or a ball at Court with beautiful women in rich dresses, and "my Lady Castlemayne, without whom all is nothing"—delighted Pepys' eyes and charmed his ears. Even when one day he went to Hackney Church he looked for beauties while his ears trembled to the deep-toned notes of the organ. (He thought seriously of buying an organ for his own church, St. Olave's.) At Lord Brouncker's house he heard some fine Italian singers whom he thought not at all superior to Mary Knep. He took great delight in Mary's singing, was always gay in her company, and liked to make her little presents. Cunningly Elizabeth made him agree that whatever he spent on Knep he should spend as much on her. Pepys was willing; anything for a quiet life. Besides, Elizabeth, too, was a source of musical pleasure. Eager to please her husband, she had studied singing, the viol, and the flageolet all winter. With her, Barker, and Mercer, who often dropped in, Pepys whiled away many an evening piping and singing. As the weather grew warmer the quartette took to singing in the garden, to the pleasure of the neighbors. Pepys' liking for his wife's company seemed to increase with her musical proficiency. Once he wrote, "so home to supper and sing a little with my dear wife, and so to bed." In the *Diary*, "my dear wife" is a rare phrase.[20]

To some extent the innocent pleasures of plays and music drew Pepys away from the sullied delights of sex. True, he had returned to Betty Martin's bed (cursing himself for his folly), and now and then in the spring he dallied with Doll Lane, Mrs. Burrowes, Mrs. Daniell, little Frank of the Swan, or Peg Lowther—all strumpets in his intention if not yet in fact. But in the summer, although he rarely missed a chance to kiss and tumble beauty, his lechery seemed less frenetic. He had no new doxies in view, and he was content to touse his troop of trulls, turning, when his libido demanded it, to Betty Martin for consummation a-bed.

With complacency went carelessness. On an afternoon in May young Mrs. Daniell called at his house to plead for her husband's advancement. Greatly daring, Pepys took her out into the Navy Office garden, and there—Priapus in the shrubbery—kissed her, and smartly disarranged her clothing. In a little while, fearing his household might be spying, he sent her away, went briefly to his office, and then, still hot and red-faced, returned home. "There," he said, "was asked by my wife, I know not whether simply or with design, how I come to look as I did." Fearful that he had been seen, he blamed his heat of body and soul on the weather, and Elizabeth was satisfied. Mrs. Daniell continued her interesting visits (thereafter to Pepys' office where no one could see his "chaleur et de body and of animi") and late in September John Daniell was commissioned a lieutenant in the Navy.[21]

The spring and early summer of 1667 blended to form a halcyon season for Mr. Pepys, and if he had been content to let Elizabeth dress as she chose it could have been one of the most peaceful periods of their married life. There is no doubt that Elizabeth was careless about her clothes and had little taste, but he was irascible and intolerant. When she cut away "a lace handkercher sewed about her neck to her breasts almost," he fell out with her angrily. *His* wife would not appear on the streets so immodestly dressed. In November, 1666, when she wore a new set of the "fair locks" which had earlier annoyed him, he was vexed but silent. In May, 1667, when she wore them again he broke out in a passion, shaking his fist and swearing that "by God!" he would not endure them.

The day after his outburst he argued it out with Elizabeth. The debate began calmly enough, Elizabeth offering to refrain from wearing white locks in her husband's sight if he would give her the money "to lace her gown for second mourning." But Pepys ("like a severe fool," he said later) insisted on doing away with the locks for good. Reason gave way to passion on both sides, Pepys shouting at his wife, Elizabeth accusing him of "keeping company" with Mrs. Knep, her *bête noir*, and offering to give up the locks if he would give up the woman—"of whom [she said] she hath more reason to suspect than I had heretofore of Pembleton." The battle ended in a compromise, Elizabeth getting the money for her dress and agreeing to give up artificial hair while her husband lived.

A fortnight later Pepys lost his temper again. Elizabeth had dressed to go with him to a party at the Pierces'. But she appeared at last, said Pepys, "with her black moyre waist-coat, and short petticoat, laced with silver lace so basely that I could not endure to see her, and with laced lining, which is too soon [for second mourning], so that I was horrid angry." He flung away to his office in a pet, and missed the party. But the next day they were uneasy friends again, and at night sang in the garden with great pleasure.

Reasonably enough, Elizabeth felt ill-used, and wanted to debate the subject at length. One evening, after a pleasant hour of piping and singing, "she fell all of a sudden to discourse about her clothes and my humours in not suffering her to wear them as she pleased." After some high words on both sides, Pepys went to his chamber, picked up "Boyle's Hydrostatiques," and began reading aloud, "and let her talk till she was tired and vexed that I would not hear her, and so become friends, and to bed together the first night after 4 or 5 that she hath lain from me by reason of a great cold she had got."²²

Elizabeth had another cause for discontent this spring and summer. Although, like a good Christian husband, Pepys still slept with his wife every night except when sickness separated them, he had not "lain with her" as a husband since early February. Probably she felt no deprivation—she was not sexually passionate—but she was bound to feel herself neglected and ill-used. Yet she herself was partly to blame for her husband's indifference. A good wife is both mate and mistress, and she was neither; she was a player in her housewifery and a housewife in her bed.

Pepys felt himself to blame, too. He had been a failure as a husband, evading his responsibilities and taking his pleasure in other beds. Yet in a sense he was not really to blame. He had been married for twelve years, and now he was thirty-four—middle-aged by Restoration standards. At that period in any man's life the old ardor changes, yielding place to new. Pepys had merely followed his amorous, beauty-loving bent, and given himself up to the temptations of a morally untrussed world.

In his younger days, after he had been stimulated by dallying with a wench (or merely thinking of my Lady Castlemaine), he had turned naturally to Elizabeth. In effect, she had profited from his first timid adventures in sex. But as the years went by and the rift of incompatibility widened to an abyss, he grew bolder with women and more a gallant of the times. Now he was parcelling out his passion in small lots to new customers and had none left for the old trade. When he wanted gaiety, merriment, and physical excitement, he sought—according to his needs—one of his gamesome ladies: Mary Knep for wit and music, Doll Lane for tavern work, or

Elizabeth Burrowes for jaunts a-field. When he wanted consummation he visited Betty Martin—irregularly, but on an
average of twice a month, usually on a Sunday afternoon.
Betty had learned long ago that the way to a man's heart
was through his loins. She was always ready for a bout, always
eager to please, and scented with the spice of danger to add
gusto to sex. Pepys' life had fallen into a pattern in which
Elizabeth had her place only as his regular housekeeper and
occasional companion.[23]

In June the Dutch Fleet broke the pattern temporarily.
Early in the month everything was quiet in London. Pepys
had cast up his accounts at the end of May to find that he was
worth six thousand nine hundred pounds; he was seriously
thinking of keeping a coach. His father, who had come to
town in pain with a hernia of long standing, was getting
comfort from a new steel truss. The household was quiet.
Elizabeth had dismissed Barker for lying and Luce for
drunkenness. Nell Payne, who at some earlier date had replaced Susan, became the Pepyses' cook-maid, and a new girl,
Mary the Fifth, was hired to help her. Jane Birch, a trusted
servant, remained as chambermaid. Except for the fact that
Pepys' eyes were suffering from strain, all was well at Seething Lane. Public matters were well enough, too. Of course
the Dutch Fleet was in the Channel, and the militia of the
coastal counties had been alerted, but, with negotiations for
peace going on at Breda, no one seriously expected an attack.
On Sunday, June 9, Pepys slipped away after church for an
unholy hour with Betty Martin.[24]

On Monday came the news that the Dutch were in the
Thames estuary. With the greater part of its Fleet laid up at
Chatham on the river Medway, all the Navy Office could do
was to send hastily improvised fire-ships down the Thames.
On Tuesday the Dutch bombarded Sheerness, where the

Medway empties into the Thames estuary. On Wednesday a powerful squadron came up the Medway with the tide. Scorning the feeble opposition of forts and militia, the Dutch broke the great chain fastened across the Medway at Upnor Castle, launched a small-boat and fire-ship attack against the English warships moored at Chatham docks, burned three great ships and captured two. Six men in a small boat towed the English flagship, the *Royal Charles*, out to sea. The attack on Vlie and Ter Schelling was amply revenged.[25]

Fully expecting that the Dutch would next sail up the Thames and attack London, the King summoned the City trainbands (militia) and ordered ships sunk to block the river below the City. The well-to-do packed up their goods and got ready to flee. Infected by the general panic, Pepys, at two hours' notice, sent his wife and his father off by coach to Brampton with one thousand three hundred pounds in gold, all that they could handle. A few hours later he sent after them a clerk on horseback with one thousand pounds in gold and silver. To provide against emergencies, he contrived a money-belt for himself, a kind of "girdle" stuffed with three hundred pounds in gold—an unwieldy mass bulking about his middle. Then he made his will and went back to work.

But the Dutch were content with their revenge. While London shook with wild alarms, and all England, crying out against the King's ministers, called for a Parliament, the invaders bore their prizes in triumph home to Holland, leaving their Fleet in the Channel to menace the English shores. Alone at Seething Lane, Mr. Pepys worked steadily, collected his papers for defense against the Parliamentary storm which he knew was sure to come, and for amusement dallied with his pretty cook-maid, Nell Payne, "playing with her breasts." On June 19 Elizabeth came home alone. When Pepys heard that she and his father had buried all his money in the garden at Brampton in open daylight, "where, for aught they knew, many eyes might see them," he was stark mad, fell out with his wife, and went to bed without speaking to her again that night.[26]

July was as troublesome as June. Pepys went on building up his paper defences. Sir George Carteret, Treasurer of the Navy, traded jobs with Lord Anglesey, Deputy Treasurer of Ireland, smartly avoiding the wrath to come. Parliament met in a quarrelsome mood and was promptly prorogued to October. The Dutch Fleet made so many feints at invasion at different spots along the coast that Sir William Batten cried, "By God, I think the Devil shits Dutchmen"; and the King and his Court gave themselves up to "swearing, whoring, and drinking, and the most abominable vices that ever were in the world."

Mr. Pepys had his private vexations too. On July 3, when he sought diversion with Mrs. Martin after nearly a month of abstinence, he found her "all in trouble, and what was it for but that I have got her with child . . . and is in exceeding grief, and swears that the child is mine, which I do not believe." Still, as far as Pepys knew, he was Betty's only lover, and Purser Martin had been at sea for months. Perhaps it would be wise to get him home in a hurry.

Three days later Pepys learned with joy that it was a false alarm: Betty was not "con child." In his happiness he sent for a bottle of wine and treated Betty, Doll, and their buxom landlady, Mrs. Cragg. But the fright was enough to make him cautious thereafter. The purser's ship was not due home until early in the autumn, and, although Betty, once her fright was over, was eager to have Pepys return to his wonted ways, he sternly avoided her bed until mid-September.[27]

Deprived of both his mistresses, Pepys was ready to turn to his wife again, but he was out of practice. His long neglect had dulled the edge of his desire, and between them lay a gulf of strained relations. They were friendly enough on the surface, but Pepys was edgy, and Elizabeth, feeling herself ignored and neglected, was spoiling for a fight. One afternoon Pepys came back from Lord Sandwich's house to find Elizabeth "in a dogged humour" because he had not come home to dine with her at noon. She said something sharp; he lost his temper, pulled her by the nose, and berated her for her impudence. After that, said Pepys, "we fell extraordinarily out, insomuch that I going to the office to avoid further anger, she followed me in a devilish manner thither"—scolding like a fishwife—"and with much ado I got her into the garden out of hearing, to prevent shame, and so home, and by degrees I find it necessary to calm her, and did." They made peace that night, warily, with weapons ready—and fell out again the next morning.

Pepys tried to give Elizabeth more attention. Avoiding his private pleasures, he took her on little outings, by water up to Barn Elms, by coach to Islington and Marylebone, and once for a long, lazy Sunday at Epsom. She remained "mighty musty," nursing her grievances. On August 1, after a play at the Theatre Royal, Pepys insisted that they take Mrs. Knep on an outing to a pleasure resort in Chelsea, and Elizabeth was "out of humour, as she always is when this woman is by." In bed the next morning Elizabeth taxed her husband with his over-kindness to the actress, "leading her, and sitting in the coach hand in hand, and my arm about her middle." Refusing the challenge, Pepys got up and dressed, while Elizabeth talked on, raking up old scores. When he was ready he went off to his work without a word. Uneasily conscious that he was much to blame for Elizabeth's moods, he wrote that night, "I do not do well to let these beginnings of discontent take root between us." He increased his kindness and attentions.

Ten days later, on a Sunday (when he would have gone ordinarily to visit Betty Martin), he took Elizabeth and their jolly, gossipy neighbor, Mrs. John Turner, for a jaunt to the Wells at Barnett and thence to Hatfield. It was a satisfying day, with good company, good food, an excellent sermon in the Hatfield Church, a pleasant walk in the park, and many fine sights. The Pepyses went to bed that night "with exceeding great content." The next morning Elizabeth woke up very early to call her maids to their washing. Samuel rolled over, hugged his wife to him, "it being cold now in the mornings . . . ," and at long last bridged the gap between them.[28]

# X

# The Tamer Tamed

## 1667
---
## 1668

Bored with its bootless skirmishing, the Dutch Fleet sailed home to its harbors. Peace, signed at Breda on July 31, was finally proclaimed in London on August 24, 1667; it brought a sense of relief but little rejoicing, and only a few bonfires in the streets. England lost a million or so square miles in Africa and gained only the trivial little colonies of New York and New Jersey in America. In spite of the cost in blood and treasure, the war had settled nothing. Within a few years it would have to be fought all over again.

But in England the bill was still unpaid: the national disgrace demanded scapegoats. Chancellor Clarendon, who had never been in favor of the war, had to take most of the blame for England's frustration and defeat. On August 30 the crusty old lawyer gave up his seals of office, and three months later, to escape a charge of high treason, he fled to the continent, where he ended his days.

There were moments in the autumn and winter of 1667 when the Clerk of the Acts was ready to flee too, especially after his good friend Sir William Coventry resigned his posts as Commissioner of the Navy and secretary to the Duke of York. Fortunately Pepys had all of August and September to prepare the defense of his office, and, because of lack of money for ships and men, very little else to do. The nation was so impoverished that the King, owing his linen-draper five thousand pounds, still had no handkerchiefs and only three bands for his neck.

Pepys had so little to do that he spent half his time trying to forget his worries. In August he went thirteen times to the theatre, twice visited the booths and puppet shows of Bartholomew Fair, and spent part of a Sunday at church trying to get his hands on a pretty maid who stood by him. He desisted only when she took pins from her pocket and prepared to prick him if he touched her again. In September he went nine times to the theatre and once to the Beargarden to watch a sword fight, took Elizabeth to Bartholomew Fair, drank and played with Doll Lane, teased the barmaid at the Swan, and resumed his regular visits to Betty Martin.[1]

The usual changes took place in the Pepys household. Tom Edwards and Jane Birch (perhaps because they were falling in love) continued their faithful service. Mary the Fifth, who deserted in July because she wanted time to play, was replaced by a new girl named Bridget. Pretty Nell Payne was discharged in August for gossiping, and in September Nell the Second, "an old tall maid," took her place as cook.

Toward the end of September the arrival of Elizabeth's new personal maid, Deb Willett—a replacement for the spiritless Barker—marked the beginning of a change in Mr. Pepys' private life. Introduced by the wine merchant, Will Batelier, Deb was a grave, pretty little girl just budding into womanhood. For the last seven or eight years she had been in a school at Bow, a village three miles east of London, where she had learned the graces and accomplishments of a gentlewoman. "A little too good for my family," Pepys mused, "and so well carriaged as I hardly ever saw. I wish my wife may use her well." He was delighted with her and yet, knowing his weakness for beauty, apprehensive—"lest I may be found too much minding her, to the discontent of my wife."[2]

His fears were justified; two weeks later he reported that Elizabeth was "already a little jealous" of his attentions to Deb. "But," he concluded, "I will avoid giving her any cause to continue in that mind." His journal for this period gives no information to explain Elizabeth's jealousy. Indeed, Pepys, who tells us everything about his earlier loves, is strangely reticent about Deb at this time.

He recorded his public life in full. October was notable for the convening of a troublesome Parliament which promptly appointed a committee on accounts and a committee to search out miscarriages in the conduct of the war. It was notable, too, for the sudden death of old Sir William Batten, and the appointment of a new Surveyor, Colonel Thomas Middleton. Early in the month Pepys took his family on a trip to Brampton, stopping overnight on the way at the Reindeer Inn in Bishops Stortford, kept by his old acquaintance Betty Aynsworth, the former Cambridge bawd. At Brampton, working by night with the help of Will Hewer, Pepys dug up his buried money and, although the bags had rotted, and he had to run half the garden through a sieve, he was so happy as to recover all but twenty or thirty pieces. When he got back to London he was made still happier by the King's outright gift of a little, narrow-built, shallow-draft Dutch prize, the *Maybolt* galiot, easily worth four or five hundred pounds.

His headlong addiction to pleasure continued. In October he took Elizabeth and Deb to the theatre nine times. Once again Mrs. Knep took them up into the tiring rooms, where Nell Gwyn, in her smock and petticoats, was dressing, "and is very pretty," said Mr. Pepys, "prettier than I thought." It was a pleasure merely to look at her and Mrs. Knep, although his gorge rose to see how both were painted. His home too was more attractive with pretty Deb to look at, and hers was the pure blush of youth and innocence. But Pepys was by no means a reformed character. In October he sought out Betty Martin three times, and twice, when her husband was absent, sported with her to his full content.[3]

From November to March Mr. Pepys' private life languished. Although once in a great while when he went to bed he had "much discourse and pleasure" with his wife, most of the time he neglected her, as, during this period, he tended to neglect all his women. In four months he took no trips with Mrs. Burrowes or Mrs. Daniell, dallied only twice with the barmaid of the Swan, only once took Doll Lane to the Dog Tavern, where he kissed her, with feeling, and consummated only once with Betty Martin.

To some extent his virtue was the result of his interest in Deb, whose charms delighted his eyes and won his heart. He was very circumspect in his behavior toward her. For the first three months of her employment he let her alone. On December 22, unable to hold off any longer, he kissed her for the first time—"she being a very pretty humoured girle, and so one that I do love mightily." Very early in their friendship he fell into the habit of sitting late at night by the fireside to have his head combed by the little maid, whom he loved to have fiddling about him, but he kept his hands to himself, perhaps because she was so young (her breasts were just beginning to swell), perhaps because he feared a rebuff.[4]

But to Parliament goes most of the credit for Pepys' sober conduct this winter. In session from October 10 to December

19, 1667, and again from February 6 to May 9, 1668, the furious House of Commons used its new-found investigative power to make bloody work with the bureaucrats. The duty of defending the Navy Board fell on Pepys, its most innocent member. He had to appear before the Committee on Miscarriages on October 22 and 25 to answer for the shame of the Medway disaster, and again on October 30 to explain why seamen had been paid off with tickets—negotiable warrants— instead of cash. In November the House of Commons turned for a while to bigger game, drawing up articles of impeachment against Chancellor Clarendon and quarreling with the House of Lords, which refused to join in the chase. On December 3 the old fox slipped across the Channel to France.

The Navy officers, too, lay under the threat of impeachment. Through the winter Pepys worked feverishly to get all his records and accounts in order, straining his tired eyes to their painful limits, and even having his clerks dine with him so that he could talk business at meals. Plays (he saw seven in November, four in December and five in January), dinners, excursions, dances, and innocent games of cards gave him some relief from eyestrain and took his mind off his fears of the politicians at Westminster. Yet, what with "dreams of our defense to the Parliament and giving an account of our doings," he rarely enjoyed a good night's sleep. In February, when he heard that a courtier, William Fanshaw, was seeking his post in the Navy, he cried, "I wish he had it, so I were well and quietly rid of it; for I am weary of this kind of trouble, having, I think, enough whereon to support myself." Since he had not cast up his personal accounts for eight months, he could only guess at the worth of his estate.[5]

But this was a moment of self-pity. For the most part

Pepys' optimism secured him against the devils of despair and let him continue his ordinary life as if there were no axe poised over his neck. In December, for example, he began negotiating a match between his sister Paulina and a Huntingdonshire grazier, William Jackson, "a plain young man, handsome enough for Pall, one of no education nor discourse, but of few words." Pepys had no great love for Paulina, but she was his sister and must be provided for. There was no joy in dealing with such family matters, but one afternoon he played truant and took pleasure in the company of Mrs. Knep and Mrs. Pierce (when Elizabeth heard about it she was "mad as a devil"). And on the last day of the year, after nearly two months of continence, he "did hazer con" Betty Martin to his full satisfaction.

Pepys' family, near and far, was often troublesome. In January, Elizabeth, fearing that after Pall's marriage old John Pepys might want to come and live with his son, declared passionately that if he did so she would leave, and would shame her husband "all over the City and Court." While she was in this rancorous fit, she took occasion to complain again about her lack of money and liberty, and for a while the Pepyses had "very hot work." This argument ended in kindness, but trouble of another kind came later in the month when Pepys' cousin, Anthony Joyce, the leather-seller, who had never recovered from his losses in the Great Fire, tried to drown himself in a handy pond. He was fished out alive, and a few days later succeeded in dying of pneumonia. Since his death was doubtful, and the estate of a suicide was forfeited to the Crown, Pepys had to work hard to secure Joyce's small property for his widow and children. He breathed easier when a coroner's jury brought in a verdict of death by fever, without specifying the cause of the fever. On the whole, January was a dreary, unpleasant month, with only one evening of pleasure; a dance at the Pepyses' house, with good company, possets and cakes, and the Duke of Buckingham's musicians, "the best in towne."[6]

February was at least a little livelier. Pepys saw ten plays; spent a gamesome hour with Doll Lane at the Dog; and one night coming home with a coach full of ladies, laughing and singing, managed to get a lecherous hand on Mary Mercer's thigh under her petticoats. Mary was used to Mr. Pepys' little games and, without missing a note, she pushed his hand away, so that there was "no hurt done." A few days later, his libido on the boil, he bought, in a plain binding, an "idle, roguish book," Helot's *L'Escolle des Filles*. This fine piece of pornography he read avidly, but in the spirit of true scientific enquiry. "A mighty lewd book," he said, "but yet not amiss for a sober man once to read over to inform himself in the villainy of the world." When he had finished it, he burned it, so that it would not stand among his other books to his shame.

Turning to more serious matters, on February 12 he sealed articles with young Jackson, promising six hundred pounds as Paulina's dowry. Two weeks later Paulina was quietly married at Brampton, and months afterward John Pepys went to live with the Jacksons at their home in Ellington, near Huntingdon. Elizabeth never realized that her father-in-law hated her as much as she hated him.[7]

Early in February the Committee on Accounts summoned Pepys to explain his purchase of prize goods from Lord Sandwich. He defended himself ably and suffered only in temper. "I do find so poor a spirit within me," he said, "that it makes me almost out of my wits, and puts me to so much pain, that I cannot think of anything, nor do anything but vex and fret." Pepys was a fighting man only when he knew himself in the right, and the business of the prize goods had always haunted him. The Committee on Accounts was not done with him; all through the spring he was either appearing to answer charges or to supply it with information from his files.

The Committee on Miscarriages was after him too, again about the business of paying seamen by ticket. In spite of Pepys' arguments that the Navy Commissioners, lacking cash, had been forced to pay by ticket, the Committee reported the practice as a miscarriage to be censured, "which makes me mad," said Pepys, "to see them bite at the stone, and not at the hand that flings it." Passionate members of the House of Commons demanded the immediate dismissal of the Navy Board; cooler heads insisted on a hearing, and the House summoned the Navy officers to speak in their defense on March 5.[8]

The role of spokesman fell to Pepys. With Batten dead and Coventry and Carteret safely out of office, he had left among his colleagues who had served through the war only doddering Sir John Minnes, ineffectual Sir Thomas Harvey, Lord Brouncker, who thought only of saving himself, and Vice-Admiral Penn, who stood in grave danger of impeachment for neglect of duty at sea. Vexed and weary, Pepys accepted the task, and, the better to prepare himself, paid an unexpected Sunday afternoon visit to Betty Martin, whose lodgings he found full of company. But Betty, whose husband was out of a job, was always complaisant, and Pepys "did get an opportunity to hazer what I would con her"—in stealthy haste, with the murmur of voices coming through a closed door.[9]

In the next three days, hampered by his fearful colleagues, working until late every night, and sleeping little, he prepared his defense. He woke very early on the morning of March 5 and lay in bed fretting his heart out. At last he woke Elizabeth, who comforted him as well as she could, agreeing with him that it would be best to quit his office and live free from trouble in the country.

At nine o'clock he set out by boat for Westminster and arrived with time to drink half a pint of mulled sack at the Dog Tavern and a glass of brandy at a booth in Westminster Hall. Thus fortified, he marched bravely into little St. Stephen's Chapel and stood at the bar of the House opposite the Speaker. It was a familiar scene: the mellow carved oak and red velvet, the pomp of mace and staff, and the hostile-faced Members crowded together on either side, sitting on four tiers of benches. After the usual preliminaries, he launched into his speech. He talked without interruption for nearly four hours, from eleven-thirty to well after three. Complete master of his subject, he had all his facts and figures marshalled in glittering files. Moreover, once he was well under way, his fear vanished; he found himself as much at ease as if he were talking at his own table. The charm and eloquence which made him so dangerous to women won over all but the Navy's bitterest enemies—and those members who went out to dine and wandered back half drunk. When he had finished, and his fellow officers, rejoicing, told him that it was the best speech they had ever heard in their lives, he knew he had won the victory.

The next day applause and congratulations poured in upon him. Even the King said graciously, "Mr. Pepys, I am very glad of your success yesterday." All day long Pepys strutted about in public places, smiling modestly and taking careful mental notes of everything his admirers said. At night he went home to his worshiping household and spent the evening with Elizabeth, Deb, and Will Hewer, "playing at cards a little," but chiefly recounting the glories of the day. After a light supper he went to bed and slept well.

For days after his great speech he found that "all the world almost" still rang with his fame. Everywhere he went, he commanded a new measure of respect. One day at the King's Council board, when there was some fear that a proposal to hire seamen before their ships were ready might be considered a "miscarriage" by Commons, the King said with a laugh, "Why it is then but Mr. Pepys making of another speech to them." Everyone looked at Mr. Pepys, the Cicero of the Navy. With his fears of Parliament gone, and with his hard-won golden opinions still in their newest gloss, Mr. Pepys was a very happy man.[10]

He turned to his pleasures again—plays, music, dinners, and dances—with renewed zest. A confirmed hedonist now, he looked upon pleasure as "the height of what we take pains for and can hope for in this world, and therefore to be enjoyed while we are young and capable of these joys." Still amorously very capable, he enjoyed his women too. He visited Betty Martin three times in March. One day he picked up Mrs. Daniell, dallied dangerously with her in his coach, and then set her down, buying her eight pairs of gloves as a reward for her complaisance. On another day he did what he would (at last!) with Doll Lane at the Dog Tavern, in a room with neither bed nor couch. Afterward he gave her twenty shillings as a belated Valentine present. At home, growing bolder, he began making little advances to Deb when she came to help him dress in the mornings. She repelled his tentative hands with such sweet modesty that he could not take offense. His latest lyric love was still all angel.[11]

On April 2 Elizabeth took her maids Deb Willet and Jane Birch to Brampton for a two months' stay, leaving her husband with Tom Edwards, Bridget, and Nell the Second to provide for his comfort. That night Pepys was not in the least lonesome for Elizabeth. He missed Deb, and regretted that he had not kissed her goodbye.

For two months he was free to revel as he wished, with parties, outings, music, plays (fifteen in April and the same number in May), and, of course, women. His excuse for spending most of his time in pleasure was the increasing eye-strain which kept him from much reading and writing. The theatre was kind to his eyes (although the lights sometimes hurt them), and for some of his little games no vision was needed. Most of his amusements were, in his terms, innocent enough. He deflowered no virgins and consummated only twice with Betty Martin. But it may be that he had no more chances with Betty; her husband was always idling about the house, and early in May her daughter (Pepys' god-daughter) died.[12]

With his jealous wife two days' journey away, Pepys returned to his old fancy, Mary Knep, taking her on outings when her afternoon's work at the theatre was done. Once he carried her to the Lodge (a tavern) in Hyde Park, and treated her with food and drink while she regaled him with theatrical gossip. He heard with regret that his dear Lady Castlemaine had taken handsome Charles Hart, leading actor of the King's Company, as her stallion, and was "mightily in love" with him. But Pepys had aspired to Lady Castlemaine only in dreams; she was meat for better men. He took the good the gods provided, overcame his aesthetic objection to theatrical paint, and kissed Mrs. Knep with enthusiasm.

On other occasions he took the little actress to Vauxhall, to a tavern in Kensington, or to Mrs. Pierce's house for supper. One night when he was taking her to her own house in Covent Garden, Pepys, always a handy man in a coach and ready to act on the principle that only the brave deserve the bare, was "bold" with her for the first time in their friendship, finding her warm-fleshed and willing. Two nights later, while drinking with her, he was free to kiss her and to caress her epidermis as much as he wished, but he was still afraid to venture too far. At the Pierces' house one night early in May, finding Mrs. Knep asleep "on a pallet in the dark," he woke her in a fashion which was outrageously intimate but no doubt very pleasant. The next evening, on the way home in a coach with her after a pleasant outing at Marylebone Gardens, he pushed his wooing too hard, and Mrs. Knep, no novice at the game, rebuffed him. For the next three weeks he was seriously worried because Knep seemed to be avoiding him. Perhaps she was really angry and—dreadful thought!— might tell others about his essay on her virtue. But at the end of May when he met her again at Mrs. Pierce's house, he found her as friendly and gay as ever. Perhaps she was a little disappointed in him.[13]

Of course there were other women to kiss and tumble— and even to lie with. One pleasant April day he took Mrs. Burrowes for a bout of kissing and dallying in a coach. When he set her down, flushed and panting, he gave her, decently wrapped in paper, twelve half-crowns as his Valentine gift for the year before. On his way home one night after playing with Mary Knep, he met his former maid, Nell Payne, whose breasts he had once loved to caress, got her into the dark garden entry to his house, and revived pleasant memories. A few nights later, after a walk in the rain with Mrs. Peg Lowther, he had the pleasure of changing her shoes, a chance for a frontal attack too good to be missed. She was a little shy but very loving, whispering that she would like to have him for a husband "if it were to be done." Perhaps reminded of his own wife, he took time for a flying trip to Brampton and spent a pleasurable morning with Elizabeth, lying long a-bed. A week after his return to London, he visited Betty Martin, did what he would with her, and afterward made a flank attack on her landlady, Mrs. Cragg, "a pleasant, jolly

woman," who rather liked having her thigh fondled. When
Mr. Pepys was not busy with his life's work, the Navy, he
could be lustful as a satyr.[14]

Toward the end of May, Mrs. Bagwell, long resident at
Harwich, returned to Deptford when her husband, his ship-
building done, went to sea as carpenter of the *Rupert,* a fine
3rd rate. Advised of her return, Pepys was eager to couple
with her again, the first time in more than a year. He made
an appointment with her for the night of June 2, and spent
the afternoon of that day very pleasantly, driving with Mary
Mercer and a pretty friend of hers, Mrs. Knightly, out to
the village of Old Ford, where they walked in the summery
fields and sang, stopped for a drink at a tavern on the way
back to town, and so home. Then Mr. Pepys, a gentleman
of leisure, sauntered to the shop of Finch, his mercer, re-
trieved a cloak he had left there, and kissed pretty Mrs.
Finch. "So by water," he said, "it being now about nine
o'clock, down to Deptford where I have not been many a
day, and there it being dark I did by agreement aller a la
house de Bagwell, and there after a little playing and bai-
sando [kissing] we did go up in the dark a su camera [to her
bedroom] . . . and so to my boat again, and against the tide
home"—well-fed and happy.[15]

His wonderful freedom came to an end on June 5, when
(also "by agreement") he journeyed to Brampton to fetch his
wife home. But before returning to London he decided to
take a little vacation trip; for the opinions of those who were
sure to complain about his absence from his office, he cared,
he said, "not a turd."

Pepys, Will Hewer, Elizabeth, Deb, and Betty Turner
(daughter of John Turner, of the Navy Office) traveled
southwest from Brampton to Oxford, where they explored
the grey stone halls of Academe; and thence to Salisbury,

where they marveled at prodigious Stonehenge and the Gothic beauty of the old cathedral. From there, following guides, they drove to Bath, where, with some misgivings ("methinks it cannot be clean to go so many bodies in the same water"), they soaked themselves thoroughly in the Cross Bath. Refreshed and purified, the little party went on to Bristol (Deb's birthplace), and then by way of Reading back to London, arriving on June 17. It was a pleasant journey, marred only by some of Elizabeth's moments of wilfulness. On the last day Pepys rode silently in the coach, "somewhat out of humour all day," he said, "reflecting on my wife's neglect of things and impertinent humour got by the liberty of being from me, which she is never to be trusted with; for she is a fool."

Wise or foolish, she had "something in her gizzard" which she spat up only two days after the return to London. Some meddling gossip had told her all about the gay life her husband had led in her absence. She reproached him with it tearfully, accused him of indulging himself in pleasure while denying her any enjoyment, begged his leave to go to France and live there free from trouble, and made, said Pepys, "a deal of do." But with mild words and caresses he got her quieted down. Within another two days he had her under his thumb again and reasonably content. The next Sunday he wrote, "up and to church, and home and dined with my wife and Deb alone, but merry and in good humour, which is, when all is done, the greatest felicity of all."[16]

Felicity continued throughout the summer. Parliament had adjourned in May, leaving the Navy Board undamaged save for an impeachment charge—never pressed home—against Sir William Penn. (Peter Pett, Commissioner at Chatham, lost his job and spent many months in the Tower.) Since the signing of the Triple Alliance between England,

Holland, and Sweden in January, peace had come to brood briefly over Europe. The English Fleet was reduced to a bare skeleton, and Pepys' work was limited to picking over old bones and laying bare the faults of his colleagues.

His only serious worry was the condition of his eyes. Probably he had always been astigmatic, and his years of reading and writing by candle-light, plus the normal tendency to far-sightedness that comes with a man's middle years, had produced a condition which purges and blood-lettings could not cure. Optical tubes of paper gave him temporary relief and allowed him to continue his journal. At his office his clerks read to him and wrote at his dictation. At home he fell into the habit of having Elizabeth read aloud at night while he sat by the fireside and Deb combed his head. In the little pool of yellow candle-light, her eyes intent upon her book, Elizabeth could not see Pepys' hand stealing under the maid's petticoats. And when Deb came to dress him in the morning or help him undress at night—with Elizabeth busy elsewhere—he could take even greater liberties. By now he had broken down Deb's resistance, acustomed her to his intimate caresses, and taught her certain little tricks which gave him a great deal of pleasure. He was playing a dangerous game.[17]

Absorbed in domestic pleasure and growing daily more in love with pretty Deb, Pepys lost interest in most of his sports a-field. For two months he abstained from tavern lechery and even from Betty Martin. When he wanted variety he took Elizabeth and Deb to the theatre, to Bartholomew Fair, or for an evening jaunt to a pleasure garden. It was a long, rather dull, but strangely pleasant summer.

Yet Pepys had lost neither his eye for new beauties nor his itch for lechery. For example, there was the pretty wife of his new bookseller, whose shop was at the sign of the Bible in Duck Lane. Pepys kissed the lady once or twice in the shadows of the bookshop, but, although he had "a mind to her," and often visited the shop simply to admire her beauty, he lacked the confidence to attempt her virtue. Once in the late summer, his pent-up lust broke loose. On September 1, Betty Martin came to dinner unexpectedly, and the sight of her put evil thoughts into his head. Late that afternoon he wandered off by himself to Bartholomew Fair, and there a well-trained mare picked him as "him of the company that most loved a pretty wench in a corner." Pepys gave the horse's master a shilling and kissed the prettiest girl in the company. That night on his way home, stimulated by the day's activities, he stopped hopefully for a visit with his bookseller's wife, finding her weeping over some private trouble and unwilling even to talk. As he left, feeling frustrated, he was "set on by a wench that was naught," who wanted him to go to her lodgings in Shoe Lane. Instead he took her into his coach, gave her a shilling, and employed her services in a fashion designed to minimize the danger of disease.[18]

In mid-September Elizabeth, Deb, Mary Mercer, and Will Hewer journeyed to Cambridge to visit Pepys' cousin, Roger Pepys, and see the famous Sturbridge Fair. Bereft of Deb, and with his garden of other beauties long uncultivated, Pepys was at loose ends for pleasure. But he had earlier tried the modesty of his chambermaid, Jane Birch, and now he turned to her again, playing with her breasts—"which elle did give way to more than usual heretofore." He saw Mrs. Knep once and gave her a dinner plus five guineas "as a fairing," but he had no chance to make love to her. Since he made no attempt to visit Betty Martin, we may assume that she was out of town. He tried once by signs to get Doll Lane to leave her sister's booth in Westminster Hall and join him at a tavern, but she failed, or refused, to understand him.

Pepys was reduced to playing in his garden at night with his neighbor's daughter, Betty Turner, "a fine lady as to carriage and discourse," and pleasantly responsive to his sub-petticoat probings.[19]

Near the end of September, in company with young Edward Mountagu (Lord Hinchingbrooke) and his brother Sidney, Pepys traveled down into Hampshire to meet Lord Sandwich, who was coming home at last after his long embassy in Spain. Probably Pepys returned to London with the Sandwich party, and went thence to Cambridge to bring his wife home. For twelve days he made no entries in the Diary, resuming on October 11, after his return to London again. Once more he settled happily into his pleasant domestic rut: hired a new maid to replace Nell the Second who had grown "lazy and proud"; engaged plasterers and painters to refurbish his beloved house; bought a suit of "Apostle" tapestries for his best chamber; shopped for a coach and horses; and played with little Deb morning and night. Life at Seething Lane was pleasant, but its peace was the flat calm that precedes a storm.[20]

For the most part, Sunday, October 25, was like any other sabbath. Pepys went to church, came home to dinner, and spent the afternon placidly resting while Elizabeth and Tom Edwards took turns reading to him. In the evening Will Batelier dropped in and stayed for supper. Later that night, with Elizabeth still downstairs, Pepys sat by the dining room fire while Deb combed his head as usual and his hands played under her petticoats. At last, still embracing the girl with one arm (the other hand was busy), he rose to go to bed. Engrossed in his game he failed to hear Elizabeth's step on the stair—"which occasioned the greatest sorrow to me that ever I knew in this world," he said, "for my wife, coming up suddenly, did find me embracing the girl. . . ."

It was a time for shrieks to Heaven and instant vengeance, but Elizabeth was "struck mute." Even Mr. Pepys was "at a wonderful loss." While Deb slipped quietly out of the room, he tried to pass the situation off as trivial, but at the sight of Elizabeth's stricken face his usual flow of words turned to an empty babble. Wisely he gave up and went to bed, and Elizabeth, saying very little, soon followed him—but not to sleep. For hours she tossed and turned, thinking, perhaps, what weapon in her armory would stab deepest. At two o'clock she woke her husband and told him as a great secret that she was a Roman Catholic and had received the Holy Sacrament. Appalled at the revelation, yet scarcely believing her, Pepys hid his chagrin while she alternately wept and stormed, reproaching him for his inconstancy "and preferring a sorry girl before her." Since he did not know how much she had seen at her sudden entrance, he discreetly said nothing about Deb, contenting himself with fair words and promises of future love and kind usage. Toward dawn she became more composed at last, and both got a little sleep.

Pepys knew his wife too well to hope that the matter would end thus. All the next day at work he was troubled for Deb and rightly fearful for himself. Elizabeth sat gloomily at home, refused to speak to Deb, and was sullen with her husband. Angry, hurt, and jealous, she was incapable of reason; at the moment all she could think of was revenge. That night she went to bed in bitter silence. At midnight she woke Pepys and ranted at him passionately, declaring that she had seen him hug and kiss Deb. He confessed the first and denied the second, insisting that while he had been a little indiscreet he had done nothing wrong. Somehow, as Elizabeth raked up old scores, Mrs. Pierce and Mrs. Knep got into her tirade, and for the sake of peace he promised to write and sign an oath never to have anything to do with those gay ladies again. Moreover, he promised Elizabeth all kindness and "particular demonstrations" of his love in the future. At last she settled down, and "very kind we were," said Pepys, "and so to sleep."

But Mrs. Pepys was just beginning to enjoy herself. Again the next night she lashed herself into a fury even before bedtime, and for most of the night she railed at her husband, opening old wounds, calling names, and threatening to publish his shame to the world. When, goaded beyond endurance, he tried to get up and leave her, she held him in bed while she called a maid to set a lighted candle nearby—the better, perhaps, to see the effect of her ranting. Crushed by his own sense of guilt, and fearful that the maids might hear, Pepys did his best to soothe Elizabeth with "good words and fair promises," which finally had their effect, bringing him a few hours of sleep.

Elizabeth had learned how to make her husband suffer, and how to get even with him for her years of enforced submission to his will. Common sense demanded that she herself dismiss Deb at once, but to do so would be to lose some of her new-found power. Aware now of Pepys' affection for the girl, she wanted him to undergo the pain of dismissing Deb. Meanwhile she had both maid and master in cruel subjection. As she brooded night and day over her wrongs, and remembered past suspicions of her husband's behavior with other women, her inflamed imagination pictured forth erotic scenes which in their turn aroused her long dormant libido. Several times in the next few weeks her tears and ranting led to sexual excitement, and Pepys had to give her "particular demonstrations" of his love. In a queerly twisted way Elizabeth was having the time of her life.

For the next week or so Pepys had at least the shadow of peace in his gloomy household, "with some little grudgings of trouble" from Elizabeth. The reality, as he knew well, could come only after Deb's dismissal, but he could not bring himself to discharge her. He was afraid that he had ruined Deb, but not as he would like to ruin her. Unregenerate sinner that he was, he had "a good mind to have the maidenhead of this girl," if he could ever get her alone. But Elizabeth had changed the household routine, guarded him day and night, helped him dress and undress, and even watched to see that his eyes did not stray at meals. Once at supper he caught poor Deb's eyes and found them full of tears—"which do make my heart relent at this minute that I am writing this with great trouble of mind," he said, "for she is indeed my sacrifice." Enjoying her power, Elizabeth continued to insist that he himself must formally discharge the little maid. The only way to deal with temptation, as she reminded him in a curtain lecture, was to put it out of sight. "I see it will be," said Pepys, "and it is but necessary, and therefore, though it cannot but grieve me, yet I must bring my mind to give way to it."[21]

By day he continued to transact business after a fashion, although he was sometimes so distraught that he found himself recording his diary entries under the wrong dates. Yet it was better to work long at his office than to come home to his rancorous wife, who made his bed burdensome with tears and "talk and complaints upon the old business." Another man might have fought back. A bricklayer could kick his wife into submission and open his door to his doxy. A duke could afford to laugh at his jealous wife and acknowledge his mistress openly. But Pepys, a timid man, was middle-class by birth and breeding. Reputation was his immortal part, and the mere threat to publish abroad the fact that he, Samuel Pepys, Esquire, Clerk of the Acts of the Navy, dictator to parliaments, had been caught shamefully making love to

his wife's maid, frightened him to the marrow. Moreover,
his own awareness of his folly disarmed him. Although he
had merely played with Deb and not deflowered her, he had
reason to be "sorry and ashamed" of his conduct. He was
too troubled to see the bitter irony in the situation. His
sins had long deserved the punishment now being meted out
for a misdemeanor.[22]

Still he continued to temporize, unwilling to part with
Deb, and vainly hoping that the storm would blow over.
Elizabeth took stronger measures. One morning while Pepys
was at work she turned on Deb in a fury and bullied her
into a full confession of all that had passed between maid and
master. In the afternoon, still raging, Elizabeth summed up
all the evidence in the case, reproached Pepys for his perjury,
and so defamed Deb's character that even Pepys began to see
her, unjustly, as "a cunning girle, if not a slut." After listing
at length all her old grievances against her husband, Elizabeth reminded him how many temptations she herself had
resisted out of wifely fidelity, and told him for the first time
that even Lord Sandwich and later his son Lord Hinchingbrooke had separately tried her virtue. Pepys wept, acknowledged his own wickedness and his wife's virtue, begged for
peace—"and at last pretty good friends again." But that night
he had barely gone to sleep when Elizabeth woke him by
crying wildly that "she should sleep no more." He tried to
quiet her, but once launched she was unstoppable and "kept
raving till past midnight." At last Pepys agreed that he would
bid the girl begone, and would show his dislike for her. Then
with "new vows" of future love he succeeded in appeasing
the red-eyed Fury and went to sleep.

The next day, regretting his promise, he made no move
to carry it out. Elizabeth waited grimly until bedtime, determined to have her will by fair means or foul. After lying
quietly in bed a while, she suddenly started up, "and with

expressions of afright and madness," said Pepys, "as one frantick, would rise, and I would not let her, but burst into tears myself, and so continued almost half the night, the moon shining so that it was light, and after much sorrow and reproaches and little ravings (though I am apt to think they were counterfeit from her), and my promise again to discharge the girle myself, all was quiet again, and so to sleep."[23]

The following afternoon, with tears in his eyes, Pepys called Deb and Elizabeth into his study and told Deb to leave as soon as she could, and never to see him or let him see her as long as she stayed in the house. It was a painful scene: Deb wept, Elizabeth gloated, and Pepys sounded the depths of humiliation. But that night he slept better.

On November 14 when Deb finally left to go to a new job, Pepys was not allowed even to hand her her wages; Elizabeth took care of everything. In the morning before he went off to his work, he made a last effort to see Deb in the kitchen, secretly wrapping forty shillings in paper to give her, but Elizabeth refused to let him go through the kitchen and insisted that he leave by the front entry. When he objected, she flew into another rage, calling him "dog" and "rogue," and crying that he had "a rotten heart." Cringing before her fury, he went out dumbly by the front door.

But at dinner that noon Pepys was merry again. Although his heart still yearned after the little maid, he was, he thought, free of trouble at last. "And so at night home to supper," he said, "and then did sleep with great content with my wife." Significantly he added, "I must here remember that I have lain with my moher [wife] more times [in the three weeks] since this falling out than in I believe twelve months before. And with more pleasure to her than I think in all the time of our marriage before." They had been married for thirteen years.[24]

# XI

# Journey's End

## 1668
## 1670

$W$ith deb's departure the Willett affair should have
ended, but Pepys still lusted for her, and Elizabeth was on
the alert, eager to catch him breaking his vows. Either fool-
ishly or by design (hoping he would give her further cause
for jealousy and excitement), Elizabeth had let drop the information that Deb was now employed by a certain Dr.
Allbon, who lived in Whetstone Park, a haunt of thieves and
whores. After a little quiet detective work, Pepys learned that
Allbon, a broken fellow hiding from his creditors, had recently moved to Lincolns Inn Fields.

On the morning of November 18 Elizabeth was reluctant
to let Pepys leave the house, declaring her fear, or premoni-
tion, that he might seek out Deb, "which I do deny," said
Pepys, "for which God forgive me." With the lie fresh on
his lips, he spent most of the day hunting for Deb. Toward
evening he found a porter who had helped move Dr. Allbon's
goods, sent a message to Deb by him, and after dark drove
by her house and picked her up. In the coach he clasped her
to him hungrily, slipped a hand under her petticoats, and

kissed her again and again in a frenzy of passion. Afterward he gave her good, fatherly advice, "to have a care of her honour, and to fear God," and to suffer no other man to do with her as he had done. He gave her twenty shillings, a last, lingering kiss, set her down near her house, and drove home to tell his wife a fair tale of how he had spent the day, "with which the poor wretch was satisfied, or at least seemed so."[1]

He was never more mistaken. Elizabeth brooded over the story, found it all too pat and circumstantial, and by the witchery of feminine intuition leaped to the truth. The next afternoon, when Pepys hurried happily home to dinner, he found a flashing-eyed Messalina who greeted him with "false, rotten-hearted rogue!" and accused him of seeing Deb on the previous night. At first, thinking it impossible that she could know the truth, he denied the charge, but under the heat of her passion he wilted, gave way, and finally confessed.

Upstairs in their communal bedroom he had to endure Elizabeth's threats, vows, and curses all the long afternoon. She declared her intention of leaving her husband that very night, and demanded three or four hundred pounds as the price of her silence. Otherwise she would tell the whole world of his shame. As for Deb, "she swore by all that was good that she would slit the nose of the girle"—a peculiarly feminine vengeance, usually done with a pair of scissors.

Hungry and sorrowful, Pepys sat in abject misery, while his wife, her handsome face distorted with passion, talked herself hoarse. At last, in desperation, he called Will Hewer upstairs, told him everything, and begged for his help. Honest Will, crying like a child to see his beloved master and mistress in such trouble, set about making peace, and finally got Elizabeth quiet enough to state her terms: that Pepys should write and sign an oath never to see or speak to Deb again as long as he lived, and that thenceforth, when-

ever he went abroad during the day, he would take someone
—Hewer, Tom Edwards, or her—along as his guarantee of
good conduct.

Abjectly Pepys agreed, wrote and signed the required oath,
and "so to supper, and pretty kind words, and to bed." There
the kindness continued. Stimulated by erotic imaginings,
Elizabeth crowned her day of victory by inviting her husband's caresses. Before he slept, said Pepys, "I did hazer con
elle [do with her] to her content."

Dimly he was beginning to realize that he had never truly
understood this strange, whimsical, passionate woman who
had been his wife for thirteen years. From Hewer, who had
been her confidant, he learned that she had indeed resisted
"many and great temptations" during those years, maintaining her fidelity while he had trod the primrose path of dalliance. He had undervalued and mistreated her, and now, in
his new penitential mood, Pepys resolved never again to give
her occasion for jealousy, "there being no curse in the world
so great as this of the differences between myself and her."
With all his heart he hoped that this time of trouble would
pass.

But even after the climactic events of the day of victory,
Elizabeth was still unsatisfied. For years she had complained
about her solitary life, railed, quarreled, and wept to get the
attention her nature craved; now she could command it. She
had to subjugate her husband completely, humiliate him,
make him suffer again and again—a process which in turn
excited her sexually. The next afternoon, when Pepys came
home with Will, "hoping for a further degree of peace and
quiet," he found Elizabeth "in a horrible rage afresh." She
had no new cause for anger; her passion was completely self-
generated, but none the less real. Again she railed at her
husband, called him all the evil names she could think of,

struck him, and pulled his hair. Patiently Pepys submitted, and by tears and pleadings finally got her quieted down long enough to eat her dinner. Afterward, upstairs in her bedroom, Elizabeth went into her rant again, screaming for revenge and vowing once more that she would slit Deb's nose.

Again Will Hewer came to Pepys' rescue, getting from her a new demand: "that if I would call Deb whore under my hand," said Pepys, "and write to her that I hated her, and would never see her more, she would believe me and trust in me." To this Pepys agreed, but, boggling at the word "whore," he left it out of his letter. Elizabeth read it and tore it up, again in a rage. Then Hewer winked at Pepys, who, realizing that his faithful servant would never deliver the letter, wrote it according to prescript. Elizabeth read it, gave it to Hewer to deliver together with a bitter message from her, and from that moment began to be kind, "and we to kiss and be friends."

They spent the evening with "very great joy," and the night—perhaps after another "demonstration"—with "good sleep and rest." Pepys could not help thinking of Deb, even in the depths of his misery, but, "by the grace of God," he said, "though I love the poor girl and wish her well, as having gone too far toward the undoing her, yet I will never enquire after or think of her more, my peace being certainly to do right to my wife."[2]

The next day, with the Willett affair surely finished (Pepys thought), and his mind free from trouble, he began picking up the colorful threads of his normal life—all, that is, but the scarlet thread of adultery. It will be, he said, "my own fault if I be catched loving any body but my wife again." Perhaps he used the vigorous "catched" only for emphasis, but there is also the impression that he realized he had loved, not wisely but too openly, and was determined never to repeat the mistake. The game was not worth the scandal.

Earlier in November he had ordered a neat little coach, or chariot, "very genteel and sober." The body, large enough for four people, was covered with leather and suspended fore and aft on heavy leather straps in lieu of springs. With two new servants, a "little boy" and a coachman, in new liveries of green lined with red, the equipage was smartly handsome. On November 30 Elizabeth drove forth alone "to take the maidenhead of her coach," making a round of calls on envious friends. Thereafter when the Pepyses went abroad they rode in state in their fine chariot. Pepys rejoiced at this new glory which made him appear mighty great in his world, "at least," he said, "greater than ever I could, or my friends for me, have once expected." Only the horses failed to please him, and he replaced them with a splendid pair of blacks at a cost of fifty pounds. Once in a while he worried about spending so much money. For a year and a half he had not cast up his personal accounts, but he had reached such a level of prosperity that he could afford to spend freely. No matter what happened, he had enough to live on, and he could always retire to Brampton.[3]

His extravagance this winter included a number of dinner parties at which he displayed all his fine linen and dazzled his guests with a complete service of silver. Symbolic of his rise in the world was a dinner for Lord Sandwich, when, besides his lordship, he had as guests Henry, Earl of Peterborough, Edward, Lord Hinchingbrooke, Sir Charles Harbord, Sir William Godolphin, and Mr. Sidney Mountagu, Sandwich's second son. For these great men, seated according to rank at his table in all the glory of costly clothes and plumed hats, he had an elegant dinner of many dishes, not all on the table at one time but brought up, course after

course, by his maids. (Elizabeth stayed in her own chamber.)
After dinner the two earls sat down to cards, while Pepys
showed off his house and possessions to the other gentlemen.
It was a splendid entertainment, "the best of its kind," said
Pepys, "and the fullest of honour and content to me that
ever I had in my life." About seven o'clock, when his guests
had gone, he went to Elizabeth's chamber to sup with her
and get her to cut his hair and inspect his shirt. On his head
and body she found some twenty lice, "little and great." Pepys
wondered at their number, "being more," he said, "than I
have had I believe these twenty years."[4]

To the public world the household in Seething Lane
seemed prosperous and content. Privately Pepys was doing
all he could to keep his wife happy, even overlooking her
moments of slovenly housekeeping. For the first time in their
married life he arranged to give her an allowance of thirty
pounds a year for clothes (roughly $600), and merrily wrote
and signed an agreement to that effect. His haunting fear
that Elizabeth might really be a Catholic was partially relieved early in December when, of her own motion, she
went to St. Olave's Church with him. Still unsure about
her faith, he decided not to press the question. "I see she
is not so strictly so a Catholique as not to go to church with
me," he mused, "which pleases me mightily." At the theatre
Pepys tried to keep his eyes strictly on the stage, foregoing
the pleasure of looking about for pretty faces in the audience.
He was deathly afraid of stirring up Elizabeth's jealousy
again. When he found her uneasy at the King's Theatre
because Mrs. Knep, onstage, was trying to catch his eye, he
decided to try and avoid that house thereafter. He was not
very successful; in the first two months of 1669 he saw six
plays at the King's Theatre and eight at the Duke's.[5]

Guarded by Will Hewer or Tom Edwards whenever he

left the house, Pepys conducted himself with strict decorum. He was making a valiant effort to forget Deb. Ever since the November dénouement, he had prayed every night on his knees in his chamber, believing it, he said, "much the best for my soul and body to live pleasing to God with my poor wife." Thriftily he added, "and will ease me of much care as well as much expense." But in spite of his piety and church-going, Pepys was only a bread-and-butter Christian; his words flew up to Heaven, but his thoughts remained below.

To his distress, Elizabeth's jealousy still smoldered, ready to flame up with the first breath of suspicion. She was always finding new causes for jealousy, ripping up old wounds, and, incidentally, keeping Pepys reminded of Deb. Early in December she taxed him with dreaming about the girl, insisting that now and then he started in his sleep and cried out "Huzzy!" Although Pepys admitted to himself that he often thought of Deb in the daytime, he refused to accept responsibility for his dreams, and denied having any evil intent. If only he could forget her and never see her again! The merest glimpse of her in the street one day as he was driving along in his coach with Elizabeth, "did put me," he said, "into some new thoughts of her, and for her, but durst not show them, and I think my wife did not see her." He could not help his amorous nature, and Deb was still his lyric love, doomed to remain unstrummed.[6]

In mid-December he had to fend off Elizabeth's fury again, simply because she had heard, she said, that Deb was going about "mighty fine," and had a protector who gave her money. Pepys denied everything, and, lacking proof, Elizabeth had to be satisfied. One morning, three weeks later, when unexpected business called him away from his office for an hour or two, he forgot to take Hewer along. At noon Elizabeth, who always seemed to know what he had done or left undone, gave him some "hard words" for his fault, and plainly showed her distrust and jealousy. Gloomily Pepys carried on the usual routines of the afternoon and evening, and at night went to bed alone.

Waking out of a sound slumber about midnight, he saw his wife in her nightclothes huddled over the bedroom fireplace, adding fresh wood to the fire. Her only answer to his repeated questions and pleas that she come to bed was to cry that he was "a rogue and false to her." Pressed for details, she insisted that he had been seen about some roguery with Deb in a hackney coach, with the windows closed for warmth. She paid no heed to Pepys' denials and protests. At last he gave up and began to doze while she brooded sullenly, poking at the fire with the tongs.

Did the story of St. Dunstan, the blacksmith of Glastonbury, come to her mind as she sat there? It was a popular fable and widely known in the seventeenth century. As the story goes, Dunstan was working one day at the forge in his cell when the Devil came up to his latticed window, passed the time of day, and lingered to gossip. The saint replied in friendly fashion, meanwhile blowing up his fire until his tongs were red-hot. Then he picked them up, turned quickly, and caught the Evil One by the nose.

Elizabeth had a fire and a pair of tongs—and there in bed lay her wicked husband, placidly dozing. She was never one to let sleeping devils lie; at least she could rouse this one up and make him pay her the attention she so badly wanted. But let Mr. Pepys tell the story of what followed. "At last," he said, "about one o'clock, she came to my side of the bed, and drew my curtain open, and with the tongs red hot at the ends, made as if she did design to pinch me with them, at which, in dismay, I rose up, and with a few words she laid them down; and did by little and little, very sillily, let all the discourse fall; and about two, but with much seeming difficulty, come to bed and there lay well all night, and long in bed talking together, with much pleasure."

He found it hard to endure and even harder to understand her wild outbursts. Perhaps, he thought, she could not forget about his innocent little affair with Deb Willet, "but now and then hath her passionate remembrance of it as often as prompted to it by any occasion." But she needed no occasion. It may be less charitable but more accurate to suggest that she thoroughly enjoyed tantrums and tyranny, especially because fits of passion usually ended in love-making. She had found a new way to make her husband woo her.[7]

She seized upon any small excuse to make a scene; when Pepys' eyes wandered at the playhouse; when Mrs. Knep smiled at him once from the stage and he smiled back; and even when, by certain obvious signs, she knew that he was having an erotic dream. When his careful conduct left her with no cause for complaint, she fell back on invention. Thus in February she declared, in a torrent of tears, that Pepys was false to her with the chambermaid, Jane Birch; that he had gone into the girl's chamber while she was dressing, and there had been "naught with her." If Pepys had understood Elizabeth better he would have made love to her at once and saved himself trouble. Instead he laughed at the silly notion—he had only played with the girl's breasts a few times on the sly—but it took much argument and a great deal of patience to convince Elizabeth that he was innocent. At last, he said, "we were mighty good friends, and went to bed betimes . . . " for another "demonstration" of love. But the very next day Elizabeth (enjoying the results of the game) again pretended to be certain that her husband was "base with" Jane. This time Pepys settled the argument very simply: since Jane was to marry Tom Edwards near the end of March, he gave her notice to be gone by Easter. Balked, Elizabeth had to be content.[8]

She had one more fit in March. She had just about decided to hire as a replacement for Jane Birch a new chambermaid, a girl so handsome that, as she said repeatedly, she was concerned about the danger she herself ran in hiring her. (Was she trying to tempt her husband to further roguery?) Pepys came home one day to find his wife "in her closet [chamber], alone, in the dark, in a hot fit of railing." She had heard another tale, she said, this time that Deb was "living very fine, and with black [beauty] spots, and speaking ill words of her [former] mistress." Pepys was vexed. If the story was true, "the baggage is to blame," he said, "but, God knows, I know nothing of her, nor what she do, nor what becomes of her, though God knows that my devil that is within me do wish that I could." He was still more vexed when Elizabeth told him in her passion that she had decided to hire an ugly maid instead of the girl whose beauty she had praised and feared. Wearily he soothed and petted her into a better mood. "So down to supper, and she to read to me, and then with all possible kindness to bed." A week later, her fustian forgotten, Elizabeth hired the handsome maid, a girl named Matt, "a proper and very comely maid," who put some very improper thoughts into her new master's mind. But, except in imagination, Pepys wanted no more to do with his wife's maids.[9]

The Navy gained even more than Elizabeth from Pepys' reformation. With only his office as an outlet for his energies, the Clerk of the Acts found all kinds of extra work to do, collecting materials for a history of the Navy, proposing plans for financing and maintaining the establishment, chiding his colleagues for their slackness, and generally making himself a

nuisance to all easy-going bureaucrats. With the fall of
Chancellor Clarendon, the reins of state had shifted into the
erratic hands of the Duke of Buckingham and his faction of
followers, who eyed with longing the well-padded seats at
the Navy Board. Pepys' old patrons, the Mountagus and
Carterets, were out of favor; Sir William Coventry, sent to
the Tower in March for challenging Buckingham to a duel,
was helpless; and even the Duke of York could do little in
defense of his servants. But the Clerk of the Acts was now a
power in himself, too valuable a man to be replaced, too
strongly in favor to be displaced. At the end of March, when
Sir William Penn finally gave up his post as Commissioner,
Mr. Pepys, the last of the original Board of 1660, ruled
supreme at the Navy Office. He was thinking seriously of
standing for election to Parliament.

Privately the ruler himself was ruled, and growing restive
under petticoat tyranny. Despite his pious vows and prayers,
the devil within him was still his master. Yet with jailers
always at his heels he had no chance of seeing Deb, or of
spending an hour or two sporting with any of his fancy ladies.
Mrs. Bagwell was now established at Deptford again, and
early in March, when Pepys was in Deptford on business, he
escaped his guard and slunk away to her house. "There saw
her, and her mother, and our late maid Nell [Payne]," he
said, "who cried for joy to see me, but I had no time for
pleasure then nor could stay, but after drinking I back to the
yard, having a month's mind para have had a bout with
Nell, which I believe I could have had, and may another
time." Three weeks later, when Pepys went to Greenwich
to a funeral, he slipped away in the middle of the sermon
and walked to Deptford just to see Mrs. Bagwell. He had
time only for a tantalizing talk with her at her door.

His other ladies, in Westminster, were even harder to see,

and perhaps it was just as well. On March 17, when Pepys heard that Doll Lane had been brought to bed of a child at her sister's lodgings, he was glad that he had not dallied with her recently. Calling herself Mrs. Powell, she insisted that she had been married to one Rowland Powell, drowned at sea, but no one believed her story.[10]

With his erotic itch crying to be scratched, Pepys took advantage of his post by appointing himself and Colonel Middleton to go to Chatham on March 23 for a "pay." His real purpose was, he admitted, to "be at a little liberty myself for a day or two, to find a little pleasure, and give my eyes a little ease." He hoped to find the little pleasure with wanton Frances Tooker or one of her sisters at Chatham. Because Tom Edwards was marrying Jane Birch on the 26th, and Will Hewer was to be a groomsman, Elizabeth let him go to Chatham by himself. Deb, she knew, was in London, and so was her other *bête noire*, Mrs. Knep; she had no notion of the extent of her husband's philandering.

Frances Tooker was not at Chatham, but lucky Pepys found someone even better: pretty Rebecca Allen with whom he had been so deeply in love eight years ago. Now wife to Lieutenant Henry Jowles, she was "a very fine, proper lady," and so free in her conduct that, Pepys told himself, "elle is a whore, that is certain, but a very brave and comely one." One night at her father's house he got her into a corner out of sight of the company, "and there toker su breasts and baiser her without any force [i.e., she did not resist], and credo that I might have had all else, but it was not time nor place."[11]

He hated to return to London after only five days of freedom, but with Tom and Jane Edwards out of the house (the Pepyses gave them eighty pounds to start life together), and only complaisant Will Hewer or Jack, the "little boy," to guard him, Pepys found his bonds gradually relaxing. By this time, too, the fires of Elizabeth's abnormal passion, with no new fuel to feed them, were burning low, and she was reverting to her normal sexual lethargy. Moreover, she had found a new source of entertainment, a mild flirtation with Mr. Henry Sheres, an unattached young poet and engineer who had been with Lord Sandwich in Spain. Elizabeth quietly annexed him as her gallant, insisted that he be included in outings and parties, and often had him to dinner. At moments Pepys was slightly jealous, but so long as Elizabeth was busy and happy, he was free to do pretty much what he wished abroad. Except for comely Matt there was no one to tempt him to domestic sin. A new "middle-mayd" was nondescript and nameless, and the new cook-maid, Doll, who replaced Bridget in April, was a blackamoor.[12]

On April 9, greatly daring, Pepys eluded Will Hewer in Westminster Hall, and slipped away to spend an orgiastic hour with Betty Martin, the first in nearly a year. He was ready to fall back into his old courses. Four days later he spied Deb Willett in Whitehall courtyard, and his passion for her came flooding back. Sending Will Hewer off on an errand, he ran after Deb and caught up with her in the lobby of Whitehall Chapel. Their talk was brief. Pepys learned her new address—in Jewen Street—and charged her to tell no one that he had seen her—"and so with my head full of surprize and disorder, I away." That night, torn between love and honor, he confided to his journal, "my great pain is lest God Almighty shall suffer me to find out this girl, whom indeed I love, and with a bad amour, but I pray God to give me grace to forbear it."

On April 15 Mrs. Bagwell came to his office and slipped a note into his hand. Following instructions, he met her that afternoon in Moorfields, their old trysting place, but all the

taverns were so full that they parted, "leaving further discourse and doing to another time." Taking a coach back into
the City, Pepys passed through Jewen Street—"but stopped
not"—and met Deb on foot going up Holborn Hill. Unable
to resist temptation he stopped his coach, bade the coachman
wait, and caught up with Deb. In a little blind alehouse
nearby, Pepys kissed the girl, played with her breasts, and
explored her petticoats, finding her "mighty coy, and I hope
modest . . ." He gave her twenty shillings and arranged to
meet her next Monday in Westminster Hall. Then he went
back to his office and so home. Disordered in mind and body,
he spent the rest of the day fearful of discovery, but Elizabeth
was too busy with her own little games to notice.

A kindly God—or a girl's whim—saved him from further
dangerous intrigue; although on Monday he walked for two
hours in busy Westminster Hall, Deb did not come. With
his mind tuned to the erotic pitch, he went home for dinner
and then returned to the Hall, beckoned to Doll Lane (Betty
Martin was at Portsmouth with her husband), and took her
to her sister's lodgings for an hour of drinking, kissing, and
hand-play. A week later he saw Deb in the street again, and
exchanged a sly wink and a smile with her. Early in May,
grown desperate, he sought her out in Jewen Street and
learned that she was now in the service of a Greenwich tanner. He was tempted to go down to Greenwich at once, but
the days passed without opportunity for the trip, and finally
he prayed seriously to his pragmatic God, making a solemn
vow to let the girl alone. Perhaps he kept it.[13]

May, 1669, is the last month recorded in the *Diary*. Pepys
had his little chariot gilded and varnished, and on May Day
he and Elizabeth, in their best clothes, made a brave show
in Hyde Park, "with our new liveries of serge, and the horses'
manes and tails tied with red ribbons, and the standards there

gilt with varnish, and all clean, and green reins, that people did mightily look upon us." On May 12 Pepys found Betty Martin just returned from Portsmouth and "did hazer her," and that night his brother John came to town for a few days' visit. On the 18th Elizabeth had another tooth pulled, and two days later fell out with Matt the chambermaid and discharged her. And on the 31st, amorous to the last, Pepys found Betty Michell without her husband and kissed her, adding, "but had not opportunity para hazer some with her as I would have offered if je had had it." That night he closed his *Diary* forever.

"And thus," he wrote, "ends all that I doubt I shall ever be able to do with my own eyes in the keeping of my Journal, I being not able to do it any longer, having done now so long as to undo my eyes almost every time that I take a pen in my hand; and therefore, whatever comes of it, I must forbear; and, therefore, resolve, from this time forward, to have it kept by my people in long hand, and must therefore be contented to set down no more than is fit for them and all the world to know; or, if there be anything, which cannot be much, now my amours to Deb are past, and my eyes hindering me in almost all other pleasures, I must endeavour to keep a margin in my book open, to add, here and there, a note in short-hand with my own hand.

"And so I betake myself to that course, which is almost as much as to see myself go into my grave: for which, and all the discomforts that will accompany my being blind, the good God prepare me!"

He did not go blind, although for the rest of his long life he was heavily dependent on his clerks for most of his reading and writing. Earlier he had petitioned the King and the Duke of York for leave to spend three or four months of the summer abroad, giving as his excuse "the relieving of [his] eyes by such a respite from their present labor." The petition was granted with expressions of kindness and sympathy. However he had a deal of Navy business to finish up, and late in June, when the member of Parliament from Aldeburgh in Suffolk, Sir Robert Brooke, died, the Duke of York urged Pepys to become a candidate for the seat. But in spite of letters from the Duke and other great men, the wilful burgesses refused to elect a stranger, especially one scandalously rumored by his opponent to be a Catholic![14]

Late in August, provided with explicit instructions and letters of introduction from John Evelyn, Pepys set out for the continent with his wife. For nearly two months, to the great benefit of Pepys' eyes, they wandered through Holland and France, spending most of their time in Paris. It was a tour that remained always in Pepys' memory. Many years later he wrote to Evelyn that the journey had given him "a degree of satisfaction and solid usefulness that has stuck by me through the whole course of my life and business since."

On October 6 the Pepyses started their return journey, arriving in London on or about October 23. Almost immediately Elizabeth was stricken with fever—probably typhoid contracted in France. She grew steadily worse, and on November 10, when the physicians saw that there was no hope, she and Pepys took the Sacrament according to Protestant rites from the hands of Dr. Daniel Milles, rector of St. Olave's Church. A few hours later Elizabeth died. She was just twenty-nine years old.[15]

There can be no doubt about Pepys' sorrow and distraction. However troublesome Elizabeth may have been at times, however many his complaints against her, she had been his beloved wife and a part of him. He had loved her in his fashion, and death wipes out unhappy memories. In his grief

he remembered only the happy days: the ecstacy of first
love; the early years of poverty and striving when she had
worked loyally at his side; and all his jaunts and journeys
with Elizabeth the good companion. But life must go on.
Pepys buried the sad remains in St. Olave's Church, erected
to Elizabeth's memory a tablet with a noble Latin inscription
setting forth her virtues, and went back to his lonely house
and his work.

# XII

# Mary Skinner

## 1670
---
## 1703


W<small>ITH THE CLOSING</small> of the Diary our best source of information about Mr. Pepys' private life comes to an end. On May 31, 1669, the curtain came down without so much as a bow from the players. Deb Willett, Doll Lane, Betty Michell, Mrs. Burrowes, Mrs. Daniell, little Mrs. Tooker, Peg Lowther, and most of the barmaids and housemaids—the Janes and Marys and Nells so fondly immortalized by the dramatist —vanished without a trace. Some of the major players appeared from time to time for a few more years in the cloudy pages of official records. Mary Knep, for example, remained a member of the King's Company until 1678, when she too disappeared, probably into a grave. Betty Martin and her huband suffered a sea-change. Samuel Martin, purser, is the Samuel Martin who was consul (business agent) at Algiers from 1674 to 1679. Consul Martin, whose first act after he arrived at Algiers was to send Mr. Pepys a tame lion as a present, failed to make his fortune as a trader and died in debt about 1679. In July, 1680, the King granted a pension of one hundred pounds a year, "during pleasure and without account," to Elizabeth Martin, "relict of Samuel Martyn, esq, deceased, late consul at Algiers." Perhaps it was kindly Mr. Pepys who got Martin appointed to the post and who persuaded the King to give the widow a pension. Certainly he continued to befriend the Bagwells, and eventually Bagwell became a Master Carpenter on *The Prince*, a 1st rate man of war. But Mrs. Bagwell, never content, continued to plead for her husband's promotion. In 1689 one of Pepys' last acts before resigning as Secretary to the Admiralty was to recommend Bagwell for a post as assistant shipwright at Chatham.[1]

There is no reason to believe that Pepys' private life itself ended with the Diary, or with Elizabeth's death. In the autumn of 1669 Pepys was thirty-six years old, still vigorous, gregarious, and fond of amorous pleasure. We may be sure that, after a decent period of mourning (he was always careful to observe the amenities), he sought once more the company of his wenches and again idled away his spare hours in "discourse and doing" with them.

Pepys was never meant to live alone. Properly, in tune with the times, he should have married again, this time a woman of wealth and position. He was an excellent catch, and could have had his pick of candidates. But there is no hint in any of his or his friends' letters that he even contemplated marriage. Sentimentalists like to think that he was faithful to Elizabeth's memory. On the other hand, perhaps the reverse of Oscar Wilde's quip is true: "When a man marries again, it is because he adored his first wife." It may be that fifteen years of marriage with all its tensions and quarrels had taught Pepys to beware of falling into the trap again. He could take his pleasure where he found it, and he could always hire housekeepers, cooks, and maids. Many a Restoration gentleman, ignoring the stern admonition, "It is better to marry than to burn," chose to keep a mistress and burn.

Consciously or subconsciously, Mr. Pepys decided to "keep." Some time in 1670 a certain Mary Skinner joined his household, perhaps as a superior maid. She was the daughter of Daniel Skinner, merchant, of Mark Lane in St. Olave's parish. Once the Skinner family had been wealthy and important. It was still well connected; Mary's mother, Mrs. Frances Skinner, was a gentlewoman, whose sister had married Sir Francis Butler of Wood Hall, Hatfield. Formerly a successful importer, Daniel Skinner had suffered serious losses in the Civil War and never quite recovered. He was now so nearly destitute that he was casting about for a government job. In 1675 (perhaps through Pepys' influence) he became a "jerquer"—an examiner of ships' papers—in the Custom House, at a salary of one hundred pounds a year. He had a large family to provide for: Daniel, his eldest son; Mary; and seven children younger than she. No doubt Mary Skinner had beauty, or Pepys would not have looked at her twice, but it seems too that she was educated and refined—no simple, ignorant housemaid but a gentlewoman with a taste for books, art, and music.[2]

Beauty in his own house was an irresistible temptation to Mr. Pepys. Perhaps he followed his well-tested routine—sitting by the fireside of an evening while Mary combed his head, and his hands roved in delightful sub-petticoat exploration. Now there was no jealous wife to burst in and surprise him in the dallying and kissing which eventually brought him to the girl's bed.

That he seduced her as, given the chance, he would have seduced Deb Willett, there can be no doubt. Six years after the event, Mary's older brother Daniel (once John Milton's amanuensis) in a letter to Pepys spoke of his parents as complaining "that it was no small damage and loss that in the course of the relations that took place between you, you violated my sister." Yet the Skinners seem to have made no attempt to punish Pepys or to force him to marry their daughter. Perhaps they might have done so had she proved to be with child, or had he simply violated her and cast her out instead of taking her as his mistress on a long-term basis. There may have been a period of shocked anger when the liaison was discovered, but beggars could not be choosers, and in the Restoration, with so many notable examples in high society, there was very little shame attached to the epithet "mistress." Probably the Skinners were content to have Mary kept by a discreet gentleman of wealth and influence, and certainly the younger members of the tribe were ready enough to call upon Pepys for help and cash.[3]

We have to assume that Mary truly loved her keeper and worried very little about the immorality of the liaison. She was a woman of wit, charm, and character, and in the course of time she was accepted by all Pepys' friends, even by staid John Evelyn and his gentle wife. Pepys, who needed to love and be loved, found in Mary all that he could wish: sex, companionship, tenderness, and wisdom. The chances are she filled his private life so completely that he had no further need for gamesome wenches and other men's wives. Mary may not have been the long-sought lyric love of his springtime, but she was at least a peaceful song for his Indian summer. She became Pepys' wife in effect, if not in fact; yet, however much he loved her, he refused to put his unhoused free condition into the confines of matrimony.

Throughout the last thirty-three years of Pepys' life, the shadowy figure of Mary Skinner appears always in the background. While he was Clerk of the Acts and Secretary of the Admiralty (1670-1679), she does not seem to have lived with

him, either at Seething Lane or at Derby House in Cannon
Row, whither he moved some time after the Navy buildings
in Seething Lane were destroyed by fire on January 29, 1673.
During those years his household usually consisted of a housekeeper, a butler, a cook, one or two maids, some young clerks,
and, for a few years, an Italian singer, Cesare Morelli. Probably he kept Mary in private lodgings, reluctant to wake the
tongues of scandal. Two letters addressed to "Mrs. Skinner"
during the Popish Plot Terror of 1679-80, while Pepys was
under indictment, accused by Whig conspirators of "Popery,
Felony, Piracy, and Treachery," may have been written to
Mary at her aunt's home in Hatfield. They are cheerfully non-
committal notes, exactly what one would expect the cautious
Mr. Pepys to write to his mistress.[4]

Although he came unscathed through the net of Whig
plots, Pepys was out of office from 1679 to 1684, serving the
King only on a special mission with the fleet sent in 1683 to
evacuate Tangier. He was still high in favor with King
Charles and the Duke of York, and from 1684 to 1689 he
was Secretary for the Affairs of the Admiralty of England,
with a salary of two thousand pounds a year. In February,
1689, after the Whigs had brought William of Orange to
power and King James the Second had fled to France, Pepys
resigned his office and retired to private life, living with his
friend, Will Hewer, at York Buildings in the Strand. There
he busied himself with his avocations: collecting books and
prints, and materials for a projected history of the Navy;
overseeing various charitable organizations; corresponding
with other men of learning; and inquiring, as usual, after
anything new and strange. He grew old gracefully: he was
heavier now, with something of a jowl and a double chin.
His face had settled into the stern look that comes with years
of command.

At some time during his second secretaryship Mary Skinner seems to have become a permanent member of Pepys' household. No doubt all his intimates had long known of the relationship, and had been as guarded in their references to Mary as Pepys himself had been. (In a letter dated March 14, 1687, John Evelyn had slipped badly, calling her "Mrs. Pepys.") In his own letters, and probably in conversation, Pepys called her only "Mrs. Skinner" or "my lady." On Michaelmas Day, 1693, Pepys, his "lady," John Jackson (Paulina's younger son and Pepys' favorite nephew), and one or two other ladies were held up and robbed on their way to Chelsea in a coach. According to the reports of trials at the Old Bailey, "my lady Pepys [i.e., Mary Skinner] saved a bag of money that she had about her." It is possible that Pepys encouraged the popular delusion that Mary was his wife.[3]

The correspondence of Pepys' later years, especially after his retirement from public life in 1689, gives evidence of Mary Skinner's steadily increasing importance. When he discharged his irascible housekeeper, Mrs. Fane, it was Mary who persuaded him to give her another chance. At times she protected him from troublesome visitors. Once Balty St. Michel wrote to Pepys in a passion, complaining about the "female beast, which you keep" who "told me impudently and arrogantly you scorned to see me." Frequently, when Pepys was not well, she acted as his amanuensis; her writing was clear and firm, and her spelling much better than poor Elizabeth's. When Pepys sent John Jackson to the continent to make the Grand Tour, he commissioned the young man to buy some knick-knacks for Mary, and cautioned him always to send her greetings in his letters home. While Pepys lived in York Buildings with his faithful friend Will Hewer (who had become even richer than his former master), Mary had a personal maid and a room in the lodgings (a "Cabinet") of her own. Pepys had her portrait painted by Kneller.[4]

In 1700 Pepys took his family to Clapham, where (said Evelyn) he had "a very noble and wonderfully well-furnished house, especially with Indian and Chinese curiosities." The last years of his life were made painful by a recurrence of his old disease, the stone. In May, 1703, when he realized that his end was near, he added a codicil to his will, leaving an annuity of two hundred pounds to his mistress as a token of "esteem, respect, and gratitude to the excellent lady Mrs. Mary Skinner for the many important effects of her steady friendship and assistance during the whole course of my life within the last thirty-three years." The annuity was charged against the bulk of his estate—twelve thousand pounds— which he left to his nephew, John Jackson. In addition he directed that of twenty-eight thousand pounds due him from the Crown for loans and arrears of salary, five thousand pounds should go to Mary. The Crown never paid a farthing of the money.[5]

On May 25, assured that his uncle's death was imminent, John Jackson sent for Dean George Hickes to administer the last rites. In Pepys' bedroom, while Jackson, Will Hewer, and Mary Skinner awaited the clergyman's coming, the dying man beckoned Jackson and Mary to his bedside, took each by the hand and, speaking with difficulty, said, "Be good friends. I do desire it of you." Dr. Hickes came at last, per-formed the Office for the Sick, and gave Pepys absolution for all the sins of the flesh. "The service done," wrote Jack-son, "uncle said, 'God be gracious to me,' blessed the Dean and all of us, and prayed God to reward us all, and Mary Skinner then appearing, [he] said, 'and thee in particular, my dear child'; whereupon we all kissed him and retired."

He died early the next morning. Mary survived him by twelve years.[6]

On May 26, 1703, John Evelyn wrote, "This day died Mr. Samuel Pepys, a very worthy, industrious and curious person, none in England exceeding him in knowledge of the navy, in which he had passed through all the most considerable offices, Clerk of the Acts and Secretary of the Admiralty, all of which he performed with great integrity. . . . He was universally beloved, hospitable, generous, learned in many things, skilled in music, a very great cherisher of learned men of whom he had the conversation." Evelyn might have added that Mr. Pepys had been thrice elected to Parliament, that he had been Elder Brother and Master of Trinity House, Treasurer of Christ's Hospital, Master of the Clothworker's Company, and President of the Royal Society. No one would remember—if, indeed, anyone ever knew— that in his youth Mr. Pepys had loved nothing so much as a wench in a corner.

# Notes

I am deeply grateful to the Master and Fellows of Magdalene College, Cambridge, for permitting me to consult the Smith transcript of Pepys' Diary in the Pepysian Library, and to Dr. R. W. Ladborough and Mr. D. Pepys Whiteley for their kind assistance. In the following notes all date references are either to H. B. Wheatley's edition of the Diary or to the Smith transcript. Authorities frequently cited are referred to by abbreviations or by the author's name, as follows:

Bryant. Arthur Bryant, *Samuel Pepys, The Man in the Making,* 1933.

*Cat. Pepysian MS. Catalogue of the Pepysian Manuscripts,* ed. J. R. Tanner, 1903.

*CSPD. Catalogue of State Papers Domestic.*

Harris. F. R. Harris, *Life of Edward Mountagu, First Earl of Sandwich,* 2 vols., 1912.

Heath. *The Letters of Samuel Pepys and His Family Circle,* ed. H. T. Heath, 1955.

Howarth. *Letters and the Second Diary of Samuel Pepys,* ed. R. G. Howarth, 1933.

Ogg. David Ogg, *England in the Reign of Charles II,* 2 vols., 1934.

*Pepys Club. Occasional Papers of the Samuel Pepys Club,* 1917-1925.

*Pepysiana.* H. B. Wheatley, *Pepysiana,* 1899.

Smith ms., Transcription of the shorthand Diary by the Reverend John Smith, Pepysian Library, Cambridge.

Tanner. *Further Correspondence of Samuel Pepys,* ed. J. R. Tanner, 1929.

Wheatley. *The Diary of Samuel Pepys,* ed. Henry B. Wheatley, 1893-99.

Whitear. Walter W. Whitear, *More Pepysiana,* 1927.

## I. Mr. Pepys

1. *Pepys Club,* I, pp. 38-39.
2. Arthur Ponsonby, *Samuel Pepys,* 1928, p. 16.
3. Nov. 3, 1661; Nov. 20, 1668.
4. *Pepys Club,* I, 78, 86; C. MacLaurin, *Post Mortems, Mere Mortals,* 1953, pp. 174-76.

## II. BETTER TO MARRY

1. May 26, 1664; Whitear, pp. 33-42; Donald Dale, "The Early Life of Pepys," *Notes and Queries* 181 (November 1, 8, 1941), pp. 240-42, 256-59.
2. Nov. 1, 1660; Feb. 4, 1663; March 11, 1668.
3. Dale, p. 242.
4. Nov. 7, 11, 1660; Nov. 26, 1661; July 26, 1663; Jan. 30, 1664; Oct. 7, 1667; Whitear, p. 6.
5. March 29, 1667; Howarth, pp. 44-47; H. B. Wheatley, *Samuel Pepys and the World He Lived In*, 1895, pp. 241-50.
6. June 15, 1663; Nov. 10, 1668; Edwin Chappell, "Elizabeth Pepys," *Somerset Year Book*, 1933, No. 32, p. 33.
7. Oct. 19, 1661; April 5, 1663; Francis Osborn, *Advice to a Son*, 1656-59, pp. 51, 60, 66, 68.
8. Howarth, p. 44.
9. Jan. 31, July 5, 1663; Feb. 10, 1664; Edwin Chappell, "Pepys' Wedding Day," *N&Q*, 164 (July 1, 1933).
10. Feb. 25, 1667; Howarth, "Pepysiana," *Times Literary Supplement*, April 7, 1932; Dale, p. 257; Heath, p. 188.
11. Aug. 15, Dec. 22, 1661; Aug. 15, 1663; July 4, 1664; Bryant, p. 29.
12. Oct. 13, 1660; Jan. 11, 1661; May 2, 1663; Sept. 29, Oct. 7, 1664; May 14, 1666.
13. Nov. 14, 1668; William Gouge, *Of Domesticall Duties*, 1622, pp. 210, 222.
14. Aug. 6, Oct. 31, 1660; *Pepys Club*, I, 90. Smith ms., Oct. 24, 1663.
15. Oct. 7, 1664; Osborn, p. 49; Howarth, pp. 1-19.
16. March 26, May 1, 1660; Aug. 26, 1661.
17. Nov. 7, 1660; Harris, pp. 115-143; *Journal of the Earl of Sandwich*, ed. R. C. Anderson, 1929, pp. 33-4.
18. Jan. 24, 28, Feb. 24, 26, 27, 1660.
19. Feb. 21, March 6, 10, 17, May 2, 3, 1660.
20. May 17, 19, 20, 1660.
21. *The Diary of John Evelyn*.

## III. THE CLIMATE OF PLEASURE

1. *Acts and Ordinances of the Interregnum*, 1642-60, eds. C. H. Firth and R. S. Rait, 3 vols., 1911, II, pp. 387-89.
2. *Middlesex County Records*, ed. J. C. Jeaffreason, III, 1888, xvii, pp. 252, 291, 295.
3. Anon, *A Letter to a Member of Parliament*, 1675, in *The Harleian Miscellany*, 1810, VIII, pp. 68-69.
4. March 25, 1668; see also J. H. Wilson, *All the King's Ladies*, 1958.

5. April 26, 1667; A. I. Dasent, *The Private Life of Charles II*, 1927, pp. 16-74; J. H. Wilson, *The Rochester-Savile Letters*, 1941, p. 68.
6. Feb. 8, 1663; Dec. 8, 1666; Roger North, *Lives of the Norths*, 3 vols., 1826, II, p. 164.
7. May 30, 1668; J. H. Wilson, *The Court Wits of the Restoration*, 1948, pp. 24-46.
8. June 22, 23, 28, July 10, 17, Sept. 20, 1660.
9. Sept. 26, 1661; July 28, 29, 1663; Whitear, pp. 84, 103.
10. Aug. 29, Dec. 12, 1660; March 22, 25, Nov. 13, 1661; April 21, 1664.
11. July 18, Sept. 4, 29, Oct. 9, 19, Dec. 31, 1660; Jan. 18, 19, 25, 28, Dec. 25, 1661; Jan. 4, Feb. 14, 1662.
12. Sept. 4, 1660.
13. Sept. 10, Oct. 4, 13, 29, Nov. 2, 1660.
14. Aug. 12, Sept. 2, 4, 22, 1660.
15. April 2, 9, 11, 14, 1661.
16. Aug. 31, 1661.
17. March 26, 1662.
18. March 22, April 5, June 5, 1661.
19. July 6-21, Aug. 30, 1661; Whitear, pp. 41-50.
20. Aug. 27, 31, Sept. 8, 1661.
21. Sept. 29, Oct. 26, Nov. 1, 1661.
22. Dec. 31, 1661; March 1, 2, 1662.
23. May 20, 30, 31, June 2, 3, 1662.
24. June 3, 9, 23, 25, 28, July 4, 21, Aug. 17, 19, Dec. 31, 1662.
25. June 30, July 3, Aug. 1, 6, 1662.
26. Sept. 7, 27, 30, 1662.
27. Jan. 23, Nov. 2, 1662.
28. May 12, Sept. 2, 1661; Feb. 3, 1665.
29. Nov. 3, 1662.
30. Philip W. Sergeant, *My Lady Castlemaine*, 1911, pp. 13-21, 24, 32.
31. July 13, 1660; April 20, Oct. 14, 1661.
32. July 23, 26, Sept. 7, 1661.
33. May 14, 21, July 16, Aug. 23, Sept. 21, Oct. 20, Dec. 15, 1662; Jan. 21, May 8, 1667.

## IV. An Apprentice Libertine

1. Oct. 5, 26, 1662.
2. Oct. 31, Nov. 12, 13, 14, 1662.
3. Nov. 21, Dec. 2, 1662; Jan. 6, 12, 31, 1663.
4. Dec. 5, 9, 10, 26, 1662; May 28, 1663; see J. H. Wilson, *All the King's Ladies*, 1958, pp. 145-6.
5. Dec. 22, 26, 1662; Jan. 6, 8, 1663.
6. Jan. 9, 1663.
7. Dec. 6, 1661; Jan. 14, 17, 22, Feb. 12, 1663.

8. Feb. 4, June 24, Aug. 19, Oct. 21, 1662; Jan. 26, Feb. 6, March 6, 10, 1663.

9. Feb. 14, 21, 23, May 4, 1663.

10. March 12, 14, 16, 18, April 1, 24, 25, May 15, 1663.

11. July 6, 1662; April 26, May 1, 1663; March 30, 1667.

12. May 2, 3, 1663.

13. Dec. 22, 1661; May 4, 12, 15, 16, 1663.

14. May 16, 19, 20, 21, 24, 1663.

15. Feb. 4, 1664; see C. W. & P. Cunningham, *The History of Underclothes*, 1951, pp. 62-6.

16. May 26, 1663.

17. May 28, 29, 1663.

18. May 31, June 3, 4, 1663.

19. May 31, June 7, 14, 15, 1663.

20. May 15, June 24, 29, 1663.

21. Aug. 12, 1660; Hilary Saunders, *Westminster Hall*, 1951, pp. 23, 207-17; Tom Brown, *Amusements Serious and Comical*, ed. A. L. Hayward, 1927, pp. 36-8.

22. June 23, 30, July 1, 7, 1663.

23. July 9, 17, Aug. 7, 1663.

24. July 13, 1663.

25. July 18, 24, 1663; Bryant, p. 207.

26. July 25-27, Aug. 4, 1663.

27. July 1, Aug. 4, 11, 1663.

28. Aug. 12, 14, 15, 1663.

29. Aug. 16, 19, 30, 1663; Bryant, p. 209.

30. Aug. 17, 20, 25, 27, 29, 1663.

31. Sept. 15-21, 1663.

32. Sept. 4, 7, 9, 23, 24, 1663.

## V. WIVES AND MAIDS

1. Oct. 27, 31, Nov. 3, 6, 9, 29, 1663.

2. July 28, Oct. 3, 5, 31, 1663; Whitear, p. 81.

3. Oct. 21, 24, Dec. 6, 1663.

4. Nov. 2, 1663.

5. Nov. 12, 15, 16, 17, Dec. 28, 1663.

6. Aug. 10, Nov. 17, Dec. 14, 31, 1663.

7. Nov. 6, Dec. 22, 1663; George Etherege, *The Man of Mode*, 1671, I, p. 1.

8. Nov. 13, 1663; Jan. 16, 1664. See Edwin Chappell, *The Secrecy of the Diary*, 1933.

9. Feb. 1, 1664.

10. Jan. 9, Feb. 8, 9, 29, 1664.

11. April 3, 20, 1664.

12. Feb. 3, 1664.
13. Jan. 2, Feb. 2, 23, 29, March 31, 1664.
14. March 15, 18, April 6, 1664.
15. Aug. 25, 1664; *Deuteronomy* 23:2; Hannah Woolley, *The Gentle-woman's Companion*, 1675, p. 214.
16. March 4, 27, April 2, 4, 24, 30, May 31, June 27, 1664.
17. Jan. 11, 18, 28, April 17, 1664.
18. May 11, 1664; Heath, p. 29, n. 5.
19. March 14, 26, April 5, 1664.
20. March 20, April 5, May 15, June 5, 13, 1664.
21. June 12, 1664.
22. July 4, 1664.
23. July 14, 16, 20, 1664.
24. July 20, 21, 23, 1664.
25. July 25, 28, 29, 1664.
26. Aug. 27, Sept. 8, 9, 1664; Whitear, p. 87.
27. Aug. 15, 1664.
28. Aug. 18, 19, Sept. 3, 6, 1664.
29. Sept. 11, 1664.
30. Sept. 20, 22, 27, 30, 1664.
31. Nov. 7, Dec. 9, 1664; Jan. 8, 13, 22, 1665.
32. Jan. 20, 27, April 6, 1665.

## VI. THE CARPENTER'S WIFE

1. Anthony Hamilton, *The Memoirs of Count Grammont*, ed. Gordon Goodwin, 2 vols., 1903, I, pp. 170-71; A. I. Dasent, *The Private Life of Charles II*, 1927, pp. 88, 92; J. H. Wilson, *The Court Wits of the Restoration*, 1948, pp. 11, 33, 53.
2. *CSPD 1661-62*, November (?), 1661; *Cat. Pepysian MS*, I, pp. 274-75, 141; *Diary*, Nov. 1, 1665.
3. Aug. 12, 22, 1665.
4. May 3, Aug. 3, 1664; Aug. 14, 1665; May 8, 1666; May 21, 1667.
5. Aug. 15, Oct. 2, 21, 1664; Nov. 29, 1665.
6. Jan. 23, Feb. 14, 1665.
7. Nov. 25, Dec. 6, 1665.
8. Oct. 7, 31, 1664; Feb. 28, 1665.
9. Dec. 20, 1664.
10. Nov. 27, Dec. 4, 11, 1664; Feb. 2, 4, 28, March 6, 29, 1665.
11. Francis Osborn, *Advice to a Son*, 1656-9 p. 60.
12. Jan. 8, 13, 20, 22, 1665.
13. Jan. 23, Feb. 3, 1665.
14. Jan. 27, April 6, 1665.
15. Feb. 14, 20, 1665.

16. Feb. 18, Aug. 12, 1665; *CSPD 1665*, March 26; *Journal of the Earl of Sandwich*, ed. R. C. Anderson, 1929, pp. 177, 195, 233, 245.

## VII. PLAGUE AND PLEASURES

1. Feb. 15, 21, 22, 25, March 1, 9, 12, 13, 1665.
2. March 9, 13, 23, 27, 30, 1665.
3. March 17, 20, April 17, 24, 30; Ogg, I, p. 114.
4. Dryden, "Essay of Dramatic Poesy," 1668; Ogg, I, pp. 286-88.
5. W. G. Bell, *The Great Plague in London in 1665*, 1924, pp. 52, 92, 102, 108, 127.
6. July 5, 13, 26, Aug. 6, 1665.
7. March 21, April 24, June 28, Aug. 12, 1665.
8. Jan. 2, May 15, June 1, July 3, 11, 1665.
9. July 16, 31, Dec. 25, 1665.
10. July 15, 19, 1665; *CSPD 1664-65*, July 6, Dec. 5, 16, 1665.
11. July 5, 12, 16, 22, 26, 29, Aug. 4, 6, 12, 14, 21, 28, 31, 1665.
12. Aug. 13, 1665; Tanner, p. 53.
13. Aug. 15, 1665.
14. Aug. 8, 12, 22, 1665.
15. Aug. 28, 31, Sept. 6, 1665; Bell, *Great Plague*, pp. 124, 237.
16. Sept. 2, 25, Oct. 7, Nov. 13, 1665; Jan. 1, 1666; Harris, II, p. 341; *Pepys Club*, II, pp. 158-64.
17. Sept. 20, Oct. 5, 1665.
18. Oct. 7, 16, 1665.
19. Oct. 23, Dec. 20, 21, 1665.
20. Nov. 23, 1665; Feb. 24, 1667.
21. Oct. 11, 26, 31, Dec. 6, 1665; Whitear, p. 91.
22. Tanner, p. 91; *Cat. Pepys MS*, I, pp. 268-69.
23. Oct. 8, Nov. 7, 13, 15, Dec. 17, 20, 1665. Chester's *London Marriage Licenses*, 1887, col. 953.
24. Oct. 27, 31, Nov. 8, 10, 24, 30, Dec. 2, 30, 31, 1665.

## VIII. LONDON IN JOY AND TEARS

1. Dec. 6, 8, 11, 1665; Jan. 2, 6, 7, 1666.
2. Jan. 5, 9, 12, 18, 19, 28, 1666.
3. Nov. 20, 30, Dec. 31, 1665; Jan. 14, May 31, 1666.
4. Feb. 17, 1664; Jan. 9, Sept. 12, Dec. 4, 1665; April 28, 1666.
5. Dec. 6, 1665; Feb. 4, 14, 15, 23, March 15, 1666; Whitear, Preface.
6. Feb. 18, 1666.
7. Feb. 20, Nov. 24, Dec. 18, 1666.
8. Feb. 28, March 18, 1666; March 8, 1667; *CSPD 1666*, May 7; *CSPD 1666-67*, Nov. 2, 1666.
9. March 1, 9, 10, April 3, 1666.

10. March 17, 28, 1666.
11. March 14, 23, April 2, 13, 15, 16, 25, May 2, 1666; Whitear, p. 127.
12. April 20, 28, 30, 1666.
13. April 23, 25, May 10, June 26, 1666.
14. May 3, 4, 12, 1666.
15. May 9, 1666.
16. April 11, May 4, 16, 20, 1666.
17. June 3, 6, 13, 1666.
18. June 18, 29, July 6, 1666.
19. Aug. 15, 1666; Ogg, I, pp. 298-303.
20. July 20, Dec. 21, 1665; May 20, June 13, July 2, 12, 18, Aug. 8, 1666.
21. Aug. 1, Oct. 26, 1666.
22. July 6, 26, 1666; Ogg, I, p. 295.
23. July 26, Aug. 6, 12, 13, 14, 1666.
24. Sept. 2, 1666; W. G. Bell, *The Great Fire of London*, 1920, pp. 21-23.
25. Bell, pp. 174-77, 224.
26. Sept. 8, 1666; Bell, pp. 75, 113, 117.

## IX. A NOISE OF STRUMPETS

1. Sept. 14, 15, 22, 25, 1666; Feb. 13, 1667.
2. Sept. 26, Oct. 3, 7, 13, 14, 19, 26, 1666.
3. Sept. 26, Oct. 3, 9, 23, Nov. 12, 1666; Jan. 7, 21, March 14, 1667; *Cat. Pepysian MS*, I, p. 278; Edwin Chappell, *Shorthand Letters of Samuel Pepys*, 1933, pp. 85-6.
4. Oct. 3, 17, Dec. 31, 1666; Jan. 8, Feb. 8, 1667.
5. Oct. 1, 8, 1666; May 12, 13, 1667.
6. Oct. 25, 27, 1666; Jan. 22, 23, 24, 1667.
7. Oct. 23, Nov. 1, 22, 1666; Tanner, p. 157; *CSPD 1667*, July 19, Aug. 7, 1667; Smith ms., Feb. 11, 1667.
8. Oct. 21, 26, 28, Nov. 7, 26, 30, Dec. 3, 1666; Smith ms., Jan. 2, 1667.
9. Nov. 5, 28, 30, Dec. 14, 1666; April 13, 24, 25, May 20, 1667; Chester's *London Marriage Licenses*, 1887, col. 865.
10. May 8, 1661; Dec. 28, 1663; Sept. 17, 1666; March 21, Aug. 30, 1668.
11. July 24, 1663; April 9, 1667; Feb. 27, 1668.
12. Jan. 9, 1664; March 23, June 9, Oct. 24, 1666; March 19, 1667.
13. Oct. 1, 1666; March 3, 20, 1667.
14. Dec. 2, 23, 1666; Jan. 27, Feb. 5, 1667; Bryant, p. 317.
15. Feb. 17, Oct. 14, 1667.
16. April 23, May 5, 1667.
17. Dec. 25, 1666; Feb. 14, 23, 28, 1667.
18. March 27, 30, 1667.
19. Dec. 7, 1666; Jan. 15, 23, Feb. 5, April 19, 1667.

20. Nov. 16, 1666; Feb. 12, 15, March 6, April 8, 12, 21, May 8, 1667.
21. May 23, 1667; *CSPD 1667*, Sept. 26.
22. Oct. 29, Nov. 22, 1666; May 11, 12, 29, June 4, 1667.
23. March 20, 31, April 14, 23, May 20, 26, June 9, July 3, Aug. 2, 1667.
24. May 13, 18, 21, 31, 1667.
25. June 10-15, 1667; Ogg, I, p. 312.
26. June 13, 17, 19, 1667.
27. June 26, 27, July 3, 6, 20, 24, 27, Aug. 21, 1667; Smith ms., Sept. 17, 1667.
28. July 12, 14, 18, 21, 24, 31, Aug. 1, 2, 11, 12, 1667.

## X. THE TAMER TAMED

1. Aug. 18, Sept. 2, 6, 9, 30, Oct. 4, 1667.
2. July 10, Sept. 2, 27, 30, 1667.
3. Oct. 5, 7, 12, 13, 23, 1667.
4. Nov. 3, Dec. 7, 1667; Jan. 11, Aug. 10, 1668.
5. Nov. 20, 1667; Feb. 23, 1668.
6. Oct. 11, Dec. 21, 30, 31, 1667; Jan. 6, 12, 21, Feb. 7, 18, 1668.
7. Feb. 6, 7, 8, 9, 12, 18, March 2, Aug. 29, 1668.
8. Feb. 5, 11, 22, 28, 1668.
9. March 1, 1668.
10. March 8, 18, 1668.
11. March 15, 18, 21, 25, 27, April 1, 1668; Bryant, p. 341; Smith ms., March 31, April 1, 1668.
12. April 16, 19, May 5, 21, 29, 1668.
13. April 7, 17, 21, 23, May 6, 7, 30, 1668.
14. March 24, 1667; April 9, May 6, 10, June 1, 1668.
15. *CSPD 1667-68*, May 21, 1668.
16. June 18, 19, 21, 1668.
17. Aug. 10, 18, 1668; Bryant, p. 365; Smith ms., Aug. 6, 1668.
18. Jan. 10, April 10, 20, July 13, Sept. 1, 1668.
19. Aug. 18, Sept. 15, 16, 20, 22, 26, 1668; Whitear, p. 130.
20. Oct. 13, 16, 20, 23, 1668; Whitear, p. 133.
21. Oct. 31, Nov. 3, 6, 13, 1668.
22. Nov. 5, 6, 1668.
23. Nov. 10, 11, 12, 1668.
24. Nov. 12, 14, 1668.

## XI. JOURNEY'S END

1. Nov. 16, 17, 18, 1668.
2. Nov. 19, 20, 21, 1668.
3. Nov. 5, 22, 28, Dec. 3, 5, 11, 1668.
4. Jan. 3, 6, 17, 23, 1669.

5. Nov. 27, Dec. 6, 9, 1668; Jan. 1, 4, 1669.
6. Nov. 20, Dec. 5, 7, 1668.
7. Dec. 18, 1668; Jan. 12, 31, 1669.
8. Jan. 20, Feb. 2, 7, 8, 1669; Smith ms., Feb. 8, 1668.
9. March 11, 12, 18, 1669; Smith ms., March 29, 1669.
10. Feb. 19, March 4, 17, April 9, 1669.
11. March 22, 23, 24, 1669.
12. April 1, 5, 12, 19, 23, 1669.
13. April 19, 26, May 4, 7, 1669.
14. Tanner, pp. 237-9, 244-53, 256-61.
15. *Private Correspondence,* ed. Tanner, 1925, II, p. 242; Bryant, p. 390; Howarth, p. 37; Wheatley, Preface.

## XII. MARY SKINNER

1. *CSPD 1672-75*, Dec. 9, 1672; Dec. ? 1672; Jan. 4, 1673; *Calendar of Treasury Books, 1672-75*, April 25, 1674, et seq., *Calendar of Treasury Books, 1679-80*, July 22, 1680, et seq; *Cal Pepysian MS*, II, pp. 362, 380, 419-20; Arthur Bryant, *Pepys, the Years of Peril*, p. 373; and *Pepys, Saviour of the Navy*, pp. 166, 386.
2. James H. Hanford, "Pepys and the Skinner Family," *Review of English Studies*, VII (July, 1931), pp. 257-70; *CSPD 1661-62*, p. 225; *CSPD 1667-68*, p. 134; *CSPD 1673*, Oct. 2, 1673; *Calendar of Treasury Books, 1672-75*, Feb. 25, 1675, et seq.
3. Hanford, op. cit; Howarth, pp. 54, 203, 272, 348.
4. Bryant, *Pepys, the Years of Peril*, pp. 120, 140; Howarth, pp. 84, 89, 96. It is unlikely that these letters would have been addressed to Mary's mother. Had Pepys been writing to the Skinner family he would have addressed Daniel Skinner, who lived until January 21, 1685.
5. Clara Marburg, *Mr. Pepys and Mr. Evelyn*, 1935, p. 141; Howarth, pp. 272, 284; *Private Correspondence,* ed. J. R. Tanner, II, pp. 265, 313; *Pepysiana*, pp. 43, 44.
6. Howarth, pp. 180, 202, 272, 283; Heath, p. 223; Whitear, pp. 149-50.
7. Evelyn, *Diary*, Sept. 23, 1701; *Pepysiana*, p. 248; Marburg, *Mr. Pepys and Mr. Evelyn*, p. 143.
8. *Private Correspondence,* ed. Tanner, II, pp. 313-14.

# Index